THE BIRTH OF TRAGEDY

FRIEDRICH NIETZSCHE (1844–1900) was born in Röcken, Saxony, and educated at the universities of Bonn and Leipzig. After a precocious start to an academic career which saw him elected to a professorship at the University of Basle at the age of 25, he was forced to resign completely from his post in 1879 due to prolonged bouts of ill health. From then on he devoted himself entirely to thinking and writing. His early books and pamphlets (*The Birth of Tragedy*, *Untimely Meditations*) were heavily influenced by Wagner and Schopenhauer, but from *Human, All Too Human* (1878) on, his thought began to develop more independently, culminating in the prolific production of the late 1880s. In early 1889 Nietzsche suffered a mental breakdown from which he was never to recover. He died in Weimar in 1900. *The Birth of Tragedy* (1872), Nietzsche's first book, has proved to be the most influential of his early works, an impassioned investigation of Greek tragedy and its relationship to contemporary German culture which was to set the terms for much of the aesthetic debate of the twentieth century.

DOUGLAS SMITH is Lecturer in French at University College Dublin. He has written a study of the French reception of Nietzsche, *Transvaluations: Nietzsche in France 1872–1972* (1996), and translated Nietzsche's *On the Genealogy of Morals* for Oxford World's Classics.

OXFORD WORLD'S CLASSICS

For almost 100 years Oxford World's Classics have brought readers closer to the world's great literature. Now with over 700 titles—from the 4,000-year-old myths of Mesopotamia to the twentieth century's greatest novels—the series makes available lesser-known as well as celebrated writing.

The pocket-sized hardbacks of the early years contained introductions by Virginia Woolf, T. S. Eliot, Graham Greene, and other literary figures which enriched the experience of reading. Today the series is recognized for its fine scholarship and reliability in texts that span world literature, drama and poetry, religion, philosophy and politics. Each edition includes perceptive commentary and essential background information to meet the changing needs of readers.

OXFORD WORLD'S CLASSICS

═══

FRIEDRICH NIETZSCHE

The Birth of Tragedy

═══

Translated with an Introduction and Notes by
DOUGLAS SMITH

OXFORD
UNIVERSITY PRESS

OXFORD
UNIVERSITY PRESS

Great Clarendon Street, Oxford OX2 6DP

Oxford University Press is a department of the University of Oxford.
It furthers the University's objective of excellence in research, scholarship,
and education by publishing worldwide in

Oxford New York

Athens Auckland Bangkok Bogotá Buenos Aires Calcutta
Cape Town Chennai Dar es Salaam Delhi Florence Hong Kong Istanbul
Karachi Kuala Lumpur Madrid Melbourne Mexico City Mumbai
Nairobi Paris São Paulo Singapore Taipei Tokyo Toronto Warsaw

with associated companies in Berlin Ibadan

Oxford is a registered trade mark of Oxford University Press
in the UK and in certain other countries

Published in the United States
by Oxford University Press Inc., New York

British Library Cataloguing in Publication Data

Data available

Library of Congress Cataloging in Publication Data

Data available

ISBN 0–19–283292–1

3 5 7 9 10 8 6 4 2

Typeset by RefineCatch Limited, Bungay, Suffolk
Printed in Great Britain by
Cox & Wyman Ltd., Reading, Berkshire

CONTENTS

INTRODUCTION

The Birth of Tragedy is a book about beginnings and endings—
the beginning and end of Greek tragedy and the beginning and
end of the decadence of nineteenth-century German culture. It
also marks a beginning and end in Nietzsche's life—the beginning of his career as a freelance philosopher and the end of his
career as a professional academic. As befits a work so concerned
with origins, it is a book which in its present form begins not once
but twice, first with the preface to the second edition of 1886,
then with the original dedication to Richard Wagner of 1872.
This double beginning signals the difference between the early
and the late Nietzsche, but also foregrounds one of the major
themes of the book—the ambiguity of dual origins, particularly
with respect to the twin impulses of the Apollonian and the
Dionysian. This ambiguity points in turn to the ambiguity of
the book itself as both a historical study of the origin of Greek
tragedy and a manifesto for the regeneration of contemporary
German culture through music. This introduction will examine
these questions in the course of an exploration of *The Birth of
Tragedy* in terms of its intellectual and historical contexts, its
argument, and the subsequent development of Nietzsche's ideas
and their legacy to later generations of writers and thinkers.

Contexts

Nietzsche published *The Birth of Tragedy* in 1872 at the age of
28, three years after being appointed Extraordinary Professor of
Classical Philology at the University of Basle in Switzerland. It
was his first book and might have been expected to mark the first
major step in an academic career. In fact, it provoked a polemic
which was effectively to end his career as a professional classicist,
partly because of its manifest, and at times overriding, concern
with contemporary rather than ancient culture and philosophy.

This concern was to motivate and inform all of Nietzsche's subsequent work, although he would continue to refer to the examples of classical culture throughout his career. The close association between *The Birth of Tragedy* and contemporary political events is signalled at points in the book by allusions to the recent Franco-Prussian War of 1870, in which Nietzsche briefly served as medical orderly before contracting dysentery and being invalided out of the army. In fact, Nietzsche wrote most of the book while on convalescent leave from the University of Basle in 1871. For the young Nietzsche, the recent military triumph over France and the subsequent foundation of the German Empire under Wilhelm I represented an enormous opportunity for the cultural regeneration of the newly unified nation. For Nietzsche, as for many of his contemporaries, these hopes were invested in German music and in the work of the composer Richard Wagner in particular.

To sympathetic contemporary listeners, Wagner's operas appeared to offer both an innovative musical aesthetics and a revival of traditional mythical content, elements of progress and continuity which appealed to a nation and culture in transition. Both elements—the aesthetics of music and myth—play a crucial role in *The Birth of Tragedy*. Partly as a result of Wagner's theory and practice, the aesthetics of music occupied a central place in the European culture of the time. As a non-representational form of art, music appeared to offer an escape from the confines of mid-nineteenth-century realism and swiftly became the model art of the Symbolist movement, its status epitomized by Walter Pater's celebrated declaration of 1873 that 'all art aspires to the condition of music' (*Studies in the History of the Renaissance*). This music-based aesthetics in many ways marks the beginning of the 'art for art's sake' movement, with its insistence on the autonomy of art from outside forces and the primacy of aesthetic over moral criteria, a sentiment echoed in Nietzsche's repeated insistence in *The Birth of Tragedy* that existence can only be justified as an aesthetic phenomenon (§§ 5, 24). Furthermore, in more detailed formal terms, the tendency of contemporary music, and that of Wagner in particular, to move away from harmony through chromaticism towards dissonance offered to artists working in other media the example of an art freed from traditional notions of the beautiful and opened up the possibility of an aesthetics premised on jarring contrasts of style and content.

The exemplary status ascribed to music received philosophical justification in the work of Arthur Schopenhauer, together with Wagner the most important early influence on Nietzsche's work. For Schopenhauer, music possessed an ontological significance— unlike other more superficial arts, it revealed truths about the nature of being itself. The key to Schopenhauer's interpretation of music lies in his elaboration of two notions inherited from Immanuel Kant—the phenomenon (*Erscheinung*) and the thing in itself (*Ding an sich*). In the *Critique of Pure Reason* (1781), Kant argues that the empirical world available to our senses is merely a world of phenomena, while the true essence of things, the things in themselves, remains beyond our perception. In *The World as Will and Representation* (1818/1844), Schopenhauer retains this distinction, translating it into his own terms—thus Kant's phenomenon becomes Schopenhauer's representation (*Vorstellung*) while Kant's thing in itself is identified by Schopenhauer as will (*Wille*). So the world as we experience it is a world of representations, one step removed from the world of the will, which is the essence of being. If we now relate this to the discussion of art, it is clear that representational art can only imitate the world we perceive and so provide representations of representations, which are then so to speak two steps removed from the ultimate reality of the will. Music, however, since it is a non-representational art, completely bypasses the world of representation and offers us direct unmediated access to the will. In philosophical terms, it is thus by far the most important of the arts. This view of the philosophical significance of music relative to the other arts informs the writings of both Wagner and Nietzsche and is essential to an understanding of Nietzsche's view of tragedy, where Schopenhauer's notions of the phenomenon and of will are associated with the Apollonian and the Dionysian impulses respectively.

Contemporary developments in music do not provide the sole

aesthetic context for the notions of the Apollonian and the Dionysian. In spite of the absence of any explicit link, it seems clear that the opposition between Apollonian and Dionysian echoes the eighteenth-century distinction between the beautiful (*das Schöne*) and the sublime (*das Erhabene*), as first proposed by Edmund Burke in his *Philosophical Enquiry into the Origin of our Ideas of the Sublime and the Beautiful* (1756) and later elaborated by Kant in the *Critique of Judgement* (1790). In opposition to the finite and symmetrical nature of the beautiful, whose experience elicits pleasure in the viewer, the sublime induces fear through its lack of limits and recognizable form. This contrast between form and formlessness constitutes one of the keys to the relationship between the Apollonian and Dionysian as defined by Nietzsche, and in some respects the Dionysian might even be described as a radicalized version of the sublime.

Perhaps the most explicit context for Nietzsche's early work, however, is that of German attitudes to the classical civilizations of Greece and Rome. Nietzsche was by training and profession a classicist, but he was just as influenced by the artistic as by the academic uses to which the classical past was put. In general, these uses were twofold—either the classical past could be used to justify and reinforce the present culture by suggesting an identity and continuity between past and present, or the past could be used to criticize the present by stressing the difference and distance between them. Something of the former approach can be seen in the neo-classical architecture of Karl Friedrich Schinkel which in the early nineteenth century helped to give monumental form to the growing political power of post-Napoleonic Prussia and thus to prepare Berlin for its ultimate role as imperial capital after unification. The Doric revival in architecture, with its emphasis on the earliest and supposedly purest artistic forms, coincided with the theories of the classicist Karl Otfried Müller, who argued that the Dorians were ethnically different from the other Greek tribes and were in fact of northern Germanic origin, thus providing a flattering precedent for the Prussian state. In contrast to this appropriation of the past for the purposes of aggrandizing the present, there existed in parallel the literary tradition of German Hellenism. From the late eighteenth century, a distinguished line of German writers began to use the example of the classical civilization of Greece not only as a source of literary inspiration but also as a model for cultural renewal. Such writing often took the form of a critique of the deficiencies of contemporary culture when compared with the accomplishments of the past. This use of the classical past to criticize the present is an important element in the work of such diverse writers as Winckelmann, Goethe, Schiller, Hölderlin, and Heine, and represents an important attempt to counter the official use of the past to justify the present. In the poetry of Hölderlin, for example, the project of mapping Greek culture onto German culture takes the form of a linguistic and topographical displacement—the German language is forced into Greek verse forms, while the geography of Germany is reconfigured as Greek landscape. In the process, the identity of German culture is estranged from itself and brought into question rather than simply confirmed by past precedent. Elements of both of these contrasting attitudes to the classical tradition exist in Nietzsche's early work—as in Müller, there is a strong suggestion of a special and exclusive relationship between German and Greek culture, but at the same time, the Greek example is used to criticize the low level of contemporary German achievement. Nietzsche's ambivalence to the critical tradition of German Hellenism surfaces also in his view of the presentation of Greek culture to be found in writers such as Winckelmann and Schiller.

In writing of Greek culture, the German Hellenists tended to present Greece as an idyllic lost world of innocence and harmony standing in stark contrast to the conflict and self-consciousness of modern life. So, for Winckelmann in his *Reflections on the Imitation of Greek Works in Painting and Sculpture* (1755), Greek art was characterized above all by 'noble simplicity and quiet grandeur' (*edle Einfalt und stille Größe*). In a similar vein, Schiller in his *On Naïve and Sentimental Poetry* (1795) distinguished between the free and spontaneous (naïve) creativity of the Greeks and the problematic and self-conscious (sentimental) sensibility of the modern artist. Both writers thus contributed to the creation of the image of Greek 'serenity' (*Heiterkeit*), which Nietzsche is at pains to revise in *The Birth of Tragedy*. For Nietzsche, the alleged 'serenity' of Greek culture is not some happy prelapsarian state, and so the product of an original innocence which has since been lost, but rather the end result of a difficult and protracted struggle to come to terms with the suffering caused by life, the hard-won triumph of Apollonian form over Dionysian insight.

The distinctions drawn by the Hellenists between Greek and German culture depend implicitly or explicitly on cultural and ethnic typologies. The Greek and the German are envisaged as cultural and ethnic types which may or should be related. The tendency to construct arguments around such types is very strong in nineteenth-century European culture, which frequently sought a biological or racial justification for its cultural and political value judgements. Three such typologies are important for an understanding of *The Birth of Tragedy*. The first of these is the distinction elaborated by the poet Heinrich Heine between the Nazarene (i.e. Judaeo-Christian) and the Hellene in his essay on Ludwig Börne (1840). For Heine, this was essentially an opposition between an ascetic culture of guilt and morality on the one hand and a sensual culture of innocent hedonism in the face of suffering on the other. This opposition was to enter anglophone culture, with local Victorian inflections, through the criticism of Matthew Arnold, with its distinction between Hebrew and Hellene (*Culture and Anarchy*, 1867), and the fiction of George Eliot (*Daniel Deronda*, 1876), before ultimately providing one of the structuring principles of the work of James Joyce (in the twin figures, for example, of the Hellenic Stephen Dedalus and the Hebraic Leopold Bloom in *Ulysses*, 1922). In terms of the development of Nietzsche's work, *The Birth of Tragedy* does not yet present the fully fledged critique of Judaeo-Christian morality which was to become such an important element of the later texts (he notes as much in the 1886 preface to the second edition), but the relationship between Greek hedonism and suffering suggested by Heine is already in place by 1872.

The second typology which surfaces in *The Birth of Tragedy* represents to some extent a variation on the first, although it is based on an opposition which is more disturbing in the light of the course of twentieth-century German history—that between Aryan and Semitic. Aryan and Semitic were originally terms used to designate two language families—the Aryan Indo-European peoples and languages of India, Persia, and Western Europe and the Semitic peoples and languages of the Middle East and North Africa (the speakers of Hebrew and Arabic). Gradually, the terms came to be applied less to the languages in question and more exclusively to the ethnic groups which spoke those languages and, in the late nineteenth century, this ethnic sense narrowed further into a racist opposition between European (Aryan) and Jew (Semitic), echoing the cultural typology opposing Hellene and Hebrew. In *The Birth of Tragedy*, Nietzsche makes use of this opposition between Aryan and Semitic in the distinctions he draws between Greek and biblical foundation myths (§ 9). For Nietzsche, the Greek notion of sacrilege communicated in the myth of Prometheus summarizes the active and masculine characteristics of the Aryan races, while the Judaic notion of sin conveyed in the story of the Fall embodies the passive and feminine characteristics of the Semitic races. Here Nietzsche is assuming a racial basis for cultural difference which brings him close to predecessors like Karl Otfried Müller. This assumption was widely held in nineteenth-century Europe, but it none the less signals Nietzsche's complicated relationship to contemporary racist discourses which were ultimately to feed into the ideology of National Socialism. In general, Nietzsche tended to use the prevailing racial oppositions of the time in his work, and it is certainly possible to find many examples of anti-Semitic remarks in his later work. It should be remembered, however, that the aggregate of his comments on Judaism is ambivalent and that his critique of Judaism is accompanied by equally ambiguous critiques of Christianity and socialism. Furthermore, Nietzsche remained vehemently opposed to political anti-Semitism throughout his life, albeit rather on grounds of its vulgar populism than because of its racism.

The third major typological opposition at work in *The Birth of Tragedy* is that between the Germanic on the one hand and the

Romanic or French on the other, an opposition which might also be formulated as one between culture (*Kultur*) and civilization (*Civilisation*). While the Germanic is identified with a deeply rooted indigenous culture, the Romanic is associated with a superficial and cosmopolitan rational civilization (§ 23). In political terms, the German emphasis on culture represents a resistance to the expansionist territorial ambitions of post-revolutionary Napoleonic France. In intellectual terms, it represents a kind of indigenous Romantic reaction to the 'foreign' values of the Enlightenment. This is a tradition which stretches from the Romantic cultural nationalism of eighteenth-century figures such as Johann Gotfried Herder to Wagner's polemics against French music and beyond. Such a context explains Nietzsche's early enthusiastic welcome for the recent German victory in the Franco-Prussian War, which appeared to herald the triumph of culture over civilization, the end of the domination of French rationalism and the possibility of a full and authentic development of German culture. All three of these existing typologies, the Judaeo-Christian versus the Hellenic, the Semitic versus the Aryan, and the Romanic versus the Germanic, are translated by Nietzsche into the terms of the new typological opposition at the centre of the argument of *The Birth of Tragedy*—that between the Apollonian and the Dionysian.

What is at issue in all of these typologies is a critique of what Nietzsche perceives as the decadence of modern life. Each of the oppositions cited above possesses a positive and a negative term, and for Nietzsche it is the negative term which gains the upper hand with the decline of Greek tragedy and which overshadows contemporary German culture. This critique of decadence, which Nietzsche at this stage of his career associates essentially with an excessive rationalism, was later to come to dominate his work and to acquire a new vocabulary in the form of a physiological discourse of health and sickness, a development demonstrated by the language of the 1886 preface.

As outlined above, Nietzsche employs existing cultural typologies and even invents a new one in the service of a critique of decadence. For Nietzsche, one of the clearest representatives of the contemporary culture of decadence was contemporary historiographical scholarship. Essentially, Nietzsche rejects the rationalist and factual approach to history represented by contemporaries such as Leopold Ranke in Germany and Ernest Renan in France. For Nietzsche, attempts at a scientific and objective historiography effectively suppress the vitality of the past, fail to discriminate between the values of different cultures and lead ultimately to an endless empty cataloguing of past cultures and events. The result is what Nietzsche in *The Birth of Tragedy* calls Alexandrian culture, a lifeless culture of librarians, curators, and scholars who waste their lives collecting and classifying the remains of other civilizations instead of ensuring the vitality of their own. As an alternative, Nietzsche suggests that the past should be remembered and celebrated through myths rather than history, since myths create a sense of spiritual community which analytic history only works to dispel. This is an argument which Nietzsche was to elaborate in his second *Untimely Meditation, On the Use and Disadvantage of History for Human Life* (1874). There Nietzsche distinguishes between three types of history: the antiquarian, the monumental and the critical. Antiquarian history seeks to preserve the past, monumental history seeks to emulate the past, and critical history seeks to liberate the present from the past. Each of these types of history is identified with a particular attitude: the historical, the suprahistorical, and the unhistorical respectively. For Nietzsche, the historical attitude has degenerated into an unhealthy obsession with the past which disables action in the present, and is clearly identified with his earlier notion of Alexandrian culture. In order to maintain what he calls the 'hygiene of life', the capacity to maintain a vital culture in the present, Nietzsche advocates a combination of, on the one hand, a suprahistorical search for useful past precedents and, on the other hand, an unhistorical forgetting of anything which hinders action in the present. Here Nietzsche is developing the critique of cultural decadence he began in *The Birth of Tragedy* in the terms of a new biological idiom, thus establishing the subject–matter and language of much of his later work.

The Argument

As suggested earlier, Nietzsche is conducting a double argument in *The Birth of Tragedy*. On the one hand, he is advancing a controversial academic argument about the origin and decline of Greek tragedy. On the other hand, he is also writing an impassioned manifesto for the regeneration of contemporary German culture. What links the two is the central role ascribed to music— as the title of the first edition makes clear from the outset, Nietzsche argues that Greek tragedy is born of music, while his hopes for German cultural renewal look to Wagnerian opera for their fulfilment. It is music and the Dionysian spirit embodied in it which for Nietzsche establishes the link between Greek and German culture.

Although Nietzsche's title suggests that Greek tragedy possesses a single origin in the spirit of music, it is clear from the outset of the book that this apparently single origin is in fact a double origin. Nietzsche opens his argument by defining two competing but complementary impulses in Greek culture—the Apollonian and the Dionysian. The Apollonian takes its name from Apollo, the god of light, dream, and prophecy, while the Dionysian takes its name from Dionysus, the god of intoxication. Apollo is associated with visible form, rational knowledge, and moderation, Dionysus with formless flux, mysticism, and excess. The world of Apollo is made up of distinct moral individuals, while Dionysus presides over the dissolution of individual identity into a universal spiritual community uniting human beings with nature. In artistic terms, Apollo is the god of the plastic or representational arts of painting and sculpture, and has a strong association with architecture, while Dionysus is the god of music, the art which is essentially non-representational and without physical form. The Apollonian artist is the visual dream-artist, while the Dionysian artist is the musical artist of intoxication. For Nietzsche, it is the Apollonian element of Greek culture which is responsible for the image of Greek serenity passed down to posterity, while the Dionysian offers an insight into a darker side of the culture, a confrontation with the pain and destruction of existence which horrifies but also consoles by demonstrating the lack of importance of the individual (§§ 1–3). The calm Apollonian surface of Greek art is thus the product of a long struggle against the tragic insights of the Dionysian state.

According to Nietzsche, Attic tragedy of the fifth century BC (essentially the work of Aeschylus and Sophocles) represents a fusion of the Apollonian and the Dionysian, a combination of the plastic art of sculpture with the formless art of music which produces a powerful visible representation of a spiritual state. In literary terms, it constitutes the fusion of the two major currents of Greek poetry represented by Homer on the one hand and Archilochus and Pindar on the other. According to Nietzsche, Homer's epic art consisted in using language to imitate the visible physical world, the world of phenomena, while the lyric poetry of Archilochus and the odes of Pindar sought rather to use language to imitate music (§§ 5–6). In combining both tendencies, the Apollonian and Dionysian elements of Greek poetry, Attic tragedy represents the culmination of both traditions.

Much of the early part of the book is taken up with a discussion of the role of the chorus in Greek tragedy. Nietzsche outlines the classical Aristotelian theory that tragedy finds its origins in the chorus and then proceeds to investigate more modern views of its function. For the German Romantic critic A. W. Schlegel, the chorus is envisaged as the representative of the spectators on stage, while Schiller argues that the chorus should rather act as a barrier between the real world and the tragic action depicted on stage. Nietzsche agrees that the chorus represents the origin of tragedy, and that it should act as a barrier between the stage and real life, but sees it as a representation of the Dionysian state rather than of the spectators understood as Apollonian individuals. For Nietzsche, the chorus incarnates what he calls the 'metaphysical consolation' of tragedy, the reassuring insight that life itself remains fundamentally indestructible and pleasurable in spite of the suffering and death implied in individual existence (§ 7). It follows that the original protagonist of tragedy is the god

Dionysus, veiled in the form of mortal heroes such as Prometheus or Oedipus and subject to the pain of individuation, which is the real meaning of the myth of the dismemberment of Dionysus (§ 10).

In spite of the promise of the title (*The Birth of Tragedy from the Spirit of Music*), detailed discussion of the role of music in the birth of tragedy is delayed until the second half of the book, where Nietzsche relates Schopenhauer's theory of music to the development of Greek tragedy (§ 16). Many commentators have made the point that the book might have ended with Section 15 (as an early draft did), since Nietzsche's argument about the birth of tragedy is essentially complete at this point. However, the remaining sections of the book are essential to Nietzsche's project of establishing a link between Greek tragedy and the predicament of contemporary German culture. This he seeks to do through the theme of music and an engagement with the work of Schopenhauer and Wagner. As we have seen, Schopenhauer argued that music, unlike the other arts, could bypass the superficial empirical world of phenomena or representations and offer direct access to the underlying fundamental reality of the thing in itself or will. For Nietzsche, music provided immediate insight into the Dionysian truth of existence, the knowledge that the underlying life of the will continues in spite of the annihilation of the individual. Music then has the capacity to generate myth by translating its Dionysian intuition into an allegorical image. It is at this point that the Dionysian takes on Apollonian form, and that the Apollonian seeks to provide its own consolation for the pain of individuation through the creation of beautiful forms.

Nietzsche tended to view the history of Greek civilization as the product of a struggle between the Apollonian and the Dionysian. In these terms, the Apollonian was initially able to fight off external or barbaric Dionysian forces, a triumph which produced Doric art and the Doric state, but it was eventually forced to compromise with the Dionysian elements within Greek culture itself, so giving rise to Attic tragedy (§§ 2, 4). For Nietzsche, this struggle found expression in the myths relating the conflict between the Olympians and the Titans. According to these myths, the new Olympian gods eventually managed to usurp the power of the Titanic demigods, although Titans such as Prometheus continued to defy their authority and eventually forced a compromise (§§ 3, 4, 9). The struggle between Olympians and Titans is a common motif of Romantic poetry, employed by Goethe, Keats, Shelley, and Byron among others, and generally stands for justified revolt against oppressive or usurped power, with defiant Titans such as Prometheus cast as heroes. In his dedication to Richard Wagner, Nietzsche even identified himself with the unbound Prometheus, a Dionysian figure in revolt against the rule of the Olympian Apollo.

The Apollonian and Dionysian drives are, however, as complementary as they are antagonistic, and it is the shifting balance of their combination which produces the ultimate art of Greek tragedy. Without the other to hold it in check, each drive would tend to the extreme. Unrestrained by the Dionysian, the Apollonian produces the secular and militaristic culture of ancient Rome, concerned purely with the imposition of form and discipline. Without the counterbalance of the Apollonian, the Dionysian results in the pessimism and passivity of Indian Buddhism, convinced of the ultimate futility of individual existence (§ 20).

As the argument progresses, it becomes clear that the real enemy of the Dionysian spirit is not the Apollonian form which complements it but the Socratic rationalism which comes to the fore in the dramatic work of Euripides. For Nietzsche, the appearance of Euripides marks the beginning of the end for Greek tragedy. Euripides and his contemporary Socrates inaugurate a new period in Greek art and philosophy, the rise of an aggressive rationalism which will ultimately undermine the mythical basis of tragedy and so destroy it. Unable to appreciate the Dionysian element in tragedy, Euripides seeks to eliminate it and reconstruct tragedy on a purely Apollonian basis. In Euripides, tragedy becomes transparent, logical and realistic in plot and dialogue, while the profound metaphysical response produced by the work of earlier dramatists is replaced by striving for effect through emotional extravagance and intellectual paradox (§ 12). In dramatic terms, the result is the end of tragedy as such and the origins of the later New Attic Comedy. In philosophy, a similar process leads from the often obscure Dionysian insights of the pre-Socratic thinkers to the limpid rationalism of the Platonic dialogues.

According to Nietzsche, Socratic culture destroys myth and tragedy in the name of reason and science, thus preparing the advent of the next phase in the decline of Greek civilization, the Alexandrian age. As indicated earlier, Alexandrian culture is a culture of dry scholarship, dedicated to amassing and cataloguing the achievements of the past. Its own cultural production is characterized by imitation and eclecticism. For Nietzsche, it offers a parallel with the German culture of his day—overly historicist and anxious to imitate and collect the forms of the past rather than to develop a vital contemporary culture. In Alexandrian culture, the Socratic impulse reaches its limits, demonstrating how science and rationalism ultimately result in a dissatisfied and dissatisfying culture which produces in turn a desire for the neglected pursuits of art and myth.

For Nietzsche, as we have seen, contemporary German culture is analogous to the Greek Alexandrian age, and a persuasive parallel exists between the decline of Greek tragedy and the development of modern Western music, particularly in the field of opera. According to Nietzsche, opera represents the modern form of Socratic culture, a kind of equivalent to Euripidean tragedy. This is because from its origins it has tended to subordinate music to text, its Dionysian potential to Apollonian intelligibility. In German music, however, Nietzsche sees an alternative tradition, stretching from the Lutheran chorales to Beethoven, where music is allowed greater autonomy. At the end of this tradition stands Wagner, whose work represents the possibility of an imminent return of a culture based on myth and the Dionysian. Throughout the book, Nietzsche refers to a range of Wagner's work, but the most sustained discussion is reserved for *Tristan and Isolde* (1865). For Nietzsche, *Tristan* represents a return to the spirit of Greek tragedy. In it, the suffering of individual existence is given the consolation of both Apollonian form and, more significantly, of Dionysian insight into the indestructible life of the will. The function of the Apollonian element is to render the Dionysian intuition tolerable (§ 21). The formal means which Wagner uses to communicate a sense of the Dionysian is dissonance, and it is with a discussion of dissonance that the book concludes for the first time—for just as it has two beginnings, *The Birth of Tragedy* in its completed form has two endings.

For Nietzsche, the aesthetics of dissonance finds its ultimate justification in the fact that man is 'dissonance in human form' (§ 25), torn and divided through the process of individuation and separation from an original unity. Musical dissonance then becomes the most effective artistic means of representing the pain of individual existence and its divided nature, the most expressive Apollonian form assumed by Dionysian loss of identity, form pushed to the limits of dissolution into formlessness. This emphasis on dissonance provides the book with its Dionysian conclusion. The final paragraph of the text, however, offers the more serene, and Apollonian, evocation of an imagined encounter between modern man and Greek culture in ancient Athens, concluding with an invitation to attend a tragedy and so to give an offering to its twin presiding deities, Apollo and Dionysus.

The argument of *The Birth of Tragedy* is constructed around a series of parallels and oppositions. As indicated earlier, Nietzsche is conducting a double argument about the origins and decline of Greek tragedy and about the possible regeneration of German culture through music. The overall case thus depends upon a parallel between the development of Greek and German culture. Broadly speaking, the first two-thirds of the book are devoted to an investigation of Greek tragedy (§§ 1–18), while the remaining third proceeds to examine the development of opera and modern German music (§§ 19–25). The link between the two sections is provided by the role of music. For Nietzsche, music is the womb of myth and tragedy, the source of the greatest period of Greek cultural achievement and, potentially, of German cultural revival.

But if music is supposedly the single origin of Greek tragedy, Nietzsche also seems to suggest that its source lies elsewhere, in the combination of the Apollonian and the Dionysian, the two forces which form the central opposition around which the book is structured. Furthermore, the uncertain relationship between single and double origins is exacerbated by the values ascribed to the Apollonian and the Dionysian. Nietzsche frequently seems to suggest that it is the Dionysian drive which takes precedence over the Apollonian, that it represents the more original impulse, possessing a privileged relation to music and to the truth of existence. But, as Nietzsche elsewhere concedes, Greek culture in general, and tragedy in particular, is inconceivable without Apollonian form, which renders the otherwise inchoate intuitions of the Dionysian visible and intelligible. The Dionysian may possess a certain priority in philosophical matters, but the origin of Greek tragedy is necessarily a double one, where Apollonian and Dionysian are fused.

A central paradox flows from this dual origin, one directly related to Nietzsche's argument about the decline of Greek culture and the decadence of contemporary Germany. Essentially, the cause of this decline is identified as the rationalism of Socrates and Euripides in the first instance and the historicism of scholars such as Ranke in the second instance. And yet in *The Birth of Tragedy*, Nietzsche conducts an argument which is both rational and historicist, constructing an argument in terms of causes and effects and illustrating it with examples drawn from a close knowledge of cultural history. In that sense, the book participates in the Alexandrian culture it criticizes. But it might also be said to use rationalism against rationalism and historicism against historicism, turning their methods against them in the service of other interests, in so far as Nietzsche advocates the replacement of reason and history by Dionysian mysticism and myth. This ambiguous inversion of cultural trends is a central feature of Nietzsche's analysis of the complex relationship between Apollonian and Dionysian, as each drive seeks to use the other to achieve its aims.

The relationship between the argument and the language in which it is presented is essential to an understanding of the book. While much of the argument takes the form of fairly sober if engaged exposition, there are also many passages of lyrical evocation, moral exhortation and disdainful invective. The tone of the book is very uneven as it shifts between description of the past, criticism of the present, and anticipation of the future. The central terms in which the argument is conducted are, while rationally deployed, concepts based on mythical figures or gods such as Apollo and Dionysus, the Olympians and the Titans, and the mythical reference is further sustained by references to the German *Nibelungenlied* which was the source for Wagner's *Ring* cycle of operas. This use of mythical terms allows Nietzsche to avoid giving precise definitions of his terminology. While it is clear what the respective characteristics of the Apollonian and Dionysian are, their fundamental essence remains obscure—they are variously described as powers, forces, impulses, drives. What is clear is that they represent forces larger than individuals, forces capable of compelling individuals to behave in certain ways regardless of their own volition. In later years, Nietzsche would come to describe them as surface manifestations of an underlying Will to Power, and *The Birth of Tragedy* anticipates this in its frequent references to the Hellenic 'will'.

If we turn our attention to the figurative language used in the book, then the central metaphor is surely that of the title—birth. Throughout the book, Nietzsche uses the imagery of organic procreation and birth to describe the origin of cultural phenomena such as tragedy. References to birth are unsurprisingly accompanied by references to wombs and mothers, and the text seems to depend largely on metaphors of female fertility. But the women of the text are ambiguous figures, as the Faustian Mothers of Being (§ 16) are accompanied by the malevolent Lamiae (§ 18), and the innocent victim Iphigenia (§ 20) contrasted with the Medusa's head, wielded by Apollo as a weapon (§ 2). Furthermore, the use of gendered terms to describe the characteristics of the opposition between Aryan and Semitic outlined above presents femininity as essentially passive and easily led astray, rather than as the original source of strength. In fact, the birth of tragedy itself, as described at the very beginning of the book, seems less the product of a female womb than the impossible child of a homosexual union between Apollo and Dionysus (§ 1). Nietzsche's use of gendered language points once again to the problem of origins, as well as suggesting a homoerotic subtext shared with other elements of the German Hellenist tradition, notably in the work of Winckelmann.

A further significant metaphor, albeit one which surfaces late in the text, is that of the tree. In describing the relationship between German and Romanic (French) culture, Nietzsche writes of a tree onto which another foreign species has been grafted (§ 23). The survival of the integrity of the original tree and culture depends upon the excision of the graft. Here Nietzsche is employing the standard Romantic image of the tree as a metaphor for indigenous cultural development, a culture with roots in a particular place which grows and develops naturally through time. The tree image represents a rejection of mixed or hybrid cultures, a refusal of the outside influences of rootless Enlightenment thought.

As befits a book about the importance of music, the form and sound as well as the content of Nietzsche's language is of key importance. Throughout the book, Nietzsche relies on a profusion of imagery to lend his arguments greater persuasiveness. The imagery deployed falls into two categories, which might be called Romantic and Symbolist. The Romantic rhetoric manifests itself in images of organic growth, as in the example of the tree just discussed, and of the storm and stress of fire and shipwreck, images of life-threatening crisis borrowed to a certain extent from Schopenhauer and Wagner. But also present in the text are a number of images which might rather be described as Symbolist. The Apollonian and Dionysian impulses and drives are often rendered as swirling vortices or spraying arcs (Foreword to Richard Wagner, §§ 5, 6, 15), visual motifs familiar from *Jugendstil* or *art nouveau* design. Furthermore, this movement of Dionysian energy is often concealed beneath an Apollonian mask, an image offered by the subject-matter of Greek theatre, but also echoing the interrogation of stable identity undermined by deeper forces found in writers such as Rainer Maria Rilke, Oscar Wilde, and W. B. Yeats. Moreover, since the argument of *The Birth of*

Tragedy seeks to replace reason with myth and language with music, it comes as no surprise that Nietzsche frequently seeks to exploit in his writing the sound effects available through assonance, alliteration, and internal rhyme. Associations between ideas are often established through sound-effects rather than argument. This emphasis on sound, together with the lyrical tone of certain passages, at moments produces a text which reads like a Symbolist prose-poem. In these formal respects, *The Birth of Tragedy* represents a transitional piece of writing, late Romantic in certain regards, but in other respects early modernist, both echoing the similar ambiguity of Wagner's music and gesturing towards the later more independent development of Nietzsche's style and ideas, when, to paraphrase the 1886 preface, he begins to sing in his own voice.

Subsequent Development

In the preface to the second edition of *The Birth of Tragedy* of 1886 entitled 'Attempt at a Self-Criticism', Nietzsche offers a critique of his first book from the perspective of his mature work. For the later Nietzsche, *The Birth of Tragedy* appears overwritten and Romantic, hopelessly in thrall to the illusion that Wagner's music might inaugurate the renewal of German culture. In retrospect, it also seems to fail to identify what should have been its real targets—Christianity and modern science, the religious and secular forms of the belief in a single and exclusive truth. So the later Nietzsche rewrites the opposition between Dionysus and Apollo as one between Dionysus and Christ, and discusses the problem of decadence in terms of signs and symptoms whose meaning and truth depend upon the point of view from which they are perceived. In the process, the preface sketches a contrast between the early and late work which stresses the differences rather than the continuities between the periods concerned. But it is clear that *The Birth of Tragedy* contains elements which will remain important in Nietzsche's later work as well as elements which are soon to be discarded.

In terms of presentation, Nietzsche's early works took the form of sustained arguments, while his mature work tended rather towards collections of aphoristic or fragmentary forms, with the important exception of _On the Genealogy of Morals_ (1886). The major shift in form came about with the publication of the first volume of _Human, All Too Human_ in 1878. As well as experimenting with shorter self-contained forms, _Human, All Too Human_ introduced a new language into Nietzsche's work which was to become more important in the years to come, that of the physical sciences. _Human, All Too Human_ famously relies chiefly on metaphors from chemistry to describe cultural change (most notably that of sublimation), but later works would draw on optics, biology, and medicine to elaborate a view of human life which was openly perspectival and physiological, insisting on the dependence of 'truth' on point of view and on the role of the body and physical constitution in the development of philosophy and culture. So the Romantic rhetoric of _The Birth of Tragedy_ gave way to another rhetoric of perspective and the body, the very terms in which Nietzsche chooses to criticize his early work in the preface of 1886.

In addition to these changes in style (which are also changes in substance, since they reflect a mode of thought), Nietzsche's intellectual and artistic allegiances shifted markedly in the course of the 1870s. In particular, the status of his early mentors Schopenhauer and Wagner changed radically. While the later Nietzsche retained Schopenhauer's idea that all human life is ultimately driven by an underlying will, the two thinkers differed considerably on how this insight should affect human life. For Schopenhauer, will manifests itself in the individual in the form of an insatiable desire, which condemns him or her to a life of suffering and dissatisfaction if it is not suppressed and negated. For the later Nietzsche, however, the will as it manifests itself through the individual should be expressed and affirmed, in spite of suffering, in the interests of maximizing the creative forces of life. In Nietzsche's view, Schopenhauer became a pessimist and hater of life, seeking consolation in a Buddhist-like state of desire-lessness. Nietzsche's rejection of Schopenhauer in the name of an affirmation of will at all costs was eventually to form the basis of the theory of the Will to Power.

In spite of significant divergences, the later Nietzsche retained a certain grudging respect for the work of Schopenhauer which is completely absent from his subsequent writings on Wagner. After the still sympathetic fourth *Untimely Meditation*, *Richard Wagner in Bayreuth* (1876), Nietzsche broke with Wagner, and subsequent references to him are almost always intensely critical. The core of Nietzsche's later critique of Wagner is to be found in the pamphlet *The Wagner Case* and the anthology of earlier remarks collected under the title *Nietzsche contra Wagner* (both 1888). Where once Nietzsche saw the heady prospect of a renewal of German culture, he now sees merely a symptom of decadence, a late Romantic artist whose work is marred by theatricality and religiosity. Instead of giving music the autonomy necessary to communicate Dionysian insight, Wagner subordinates music to text and dramatic posturing, presenting a pessimistic view of human existence whose only hope lies in Christian redemption. In formal terms, furthermore, Wagner's work is fragmentary and lacks an overall organic structure, and as such symbolizes the decadence of art. Nothing could be further from the formal and spiritual integrity of Greek tragedy as it was understood by Nietzsche in 1872.

Nietzsche's disillusionment with his early mentors was matched by his disenchantment with the development of German culture as a whole after unification. If victory in the Franco-Prussian War of 1870 initially seemed to promise the return to an authentic German essence, Nietzsche swiftly became a bitter critic of the Wilhelmine Empire. Throughout his later writings, he consistently attacked what he regarded as the philistine pomposity and stupidity of the new Germany, with its thoughtless pursuit of economic growth and international influence and prestige. Nietzsche soon rejected the Romantic ideal of a rediscovery of the roots of an organically pure German culture in favour of a celebration of certain aspects of the style and intelligence of French civilization, thus reversing the polarity established in *The Birth of Tragedy*.

In spite of the major changes in Nietzsche's outlook which took place after 1872, *The Birth of Tragedy* none the less introduces a number of themes and procedures which were to remain important throughout the later work. Perhaps the most obvious of these, in a book so concerned with origins, is the tendency to seek a hidden or unknown origin behind the avowed or accepted one. So tragedy originates in music, not in the chorus, and serenity is not the origin but simply a product of Greek culture. This suspicion with respect to origins is matched by a conviction that origins are not single points of departure but complex and ramified intersections of multiple forces. So Greek tragedy is not simply born of music, but produced by the conjunction of the Apollonian and the Dionysian. In this respect, the model of origin as birth used throughout the book is already developing towards the understanding of origin as genealogy which was to characterize Nietzsche's later work.

A further element already in place by 1872 was the critique of decadence, although Nietzsche's understanding of the term and his attitude towards it were to change. In 1872, Nietzsche viewed decadence from the outside essentially as a process of cultural decline which was on the point of being reversed. In later years, Nietzsche's standpoint shifted considerably, as illustrated by the analysis of decadence presented in *The Wagner Case*. There, Nietzsche presents decadence as less a matter of decline in purely cultural standards than as a process of biological degeneration which includes and explains such a decline. For the later Nietzsche, the human race is divided into two physiological types, the strong who affirm life in spite of suffering and the weak who seek to flee suffering and thus negate life. In the late nineteenth century it is the weak who have come to dominate Western culture and thus inaugurate a process of decline. This domination has been made possible by the fact that the weak have by necessity become more intelligent than the strong, who can afford to rely on instinct rather than reason to survive. The cultural predominance of rationalism is thus the rule of the weak. So in the later Nietzsche, the early critique of rationalism as the cause of decadence is supported in part by an argument based on a crude biological determinism. The dubious nature of this scientistic speculation, with its disturbing racist overtones, is qualified by a number of factors. In the first place, Nietzsche's insistence on the fact that all those in positions of power and 'strength' in contemporary society are in fact constitutionally 'weak' and owe their status merely to the decadent values of that society effectively blurs the distinction established between the physiological types—it is no longer immediately clear who is strong and who is weak. Secondly, Nietzsche positions himself ambiguously with regard to the opposition—on the one hand, in spite of physical weakness and chronic ill health, he is a strong critic of 'weak' decadence; on the other hand, in spite of his criticism, he maintains that he remains fully a part of the decadent culture he attacks. This is because the conflict between 'weak' and 'strong' types has actually been internalized in each individual. In this sense, Nietzsche's apparent physiology turns out to be a kind of psychology, and decadence a phenomenon which implicates all the members of a culture, not only a single group which might be isolated and expelled through a racist politics.

This movement back and forth between a physiological and a psychological discourse to account for the complexities of decadence signals a key aspect of Nietzsche's later work, namely the difficulty of finding a grounding principle or origin for his arguments. As in the instance outlined above, Nietzsche has a tendency to shuffle and re-shuffle the terms in which he conducts an argument, relying on first one and then another set of often incompatible ideas. As a result, it becomes impossible to locate a single explanation for cultural change. So the later Nietzsche radicalizes the questioning of origins begun in *The Birth of Tragedy* and applies it not just to the phenomena he criticizes but also to the foundations of his own work.

In spite of his suspicion of origins and foundations, Nietzsche's late work does ultimately appear to propose one founding explanatory principle—the Will to Power. This is essentially Nietzsche's affirmative version of Schopenhauer's insatiably desiring will, a primordial force which drives all natural and human activity. In *The Birth of Tragedy*, Nietzsche already refers

at points to 'will' and 'life' as interchangeable terms for the ultimate force which determines human behaviour and cultural forms.
These notions are clear precursors of the Will to Power, the single
underlying will which manifests itself on the surface of life in a
diversity of competing forms. The struggle between these rival
forms serves to maximize the expenditure of energy and so to
affirm the underlying will to the utmost. As a result, in assuming
the form of more superficial forces, the will frequently splits and
opposes itself, as in the case of the struggle between the Apollonian and the Dionysian, where the Dionysian may appear to be the
impulse most closely related to the will through the spirit of
music, but the Apollonian proves just as indispensable to the
production of tragedy by rendering the effects of the will more
accessible and tolerable to human spectators. The example of the
relationship between the Apollonian and the Dionysian illustrates
the way in which the will infiltrates and uses apparently opposed
or unsympathetic forces to express and affirm itself, a phenomenon which Nietzsche frequently analyses in his late work, most
notably perhaps in *On the Genealogy of Morals*.

Legacy

The Birth of Tragedy has become one of Nietzsche's best-known
and most influential books, but its initial reception was mixed. It
was welcomed in Wagnerian circles as a worthy contribution to
the cause, but many viewed it as simply the work of one of the
master's many acolytes. In academic circles, it provoked a bitter
polemic about scholarship and appropriate style which effectively
marked the end of Nietzsche's academic career. The book was
attacked by the classicist Ulrich von Wilamowitz-Möllendorf on
the grounds of inaccuracy, distortion, lack of objectivity, and its
attack on contemporary research methods. It was defended by
Wagner as a 'musical' attempt to re-imagine the past and by Ernst
Rohde, a friend and fellow classicist, for its application of contemporary philosophical ideas to the classical past. But in his
attack on rational historical scholarship, Nietzsche had succeeded

in alienating the vast majority of his professional colleagues, with the result that the book had little impact on academic circles. Ironically, perhaps, Nietzsche's view of the importance of ritual in the development of Greek tragedy is now widely accepted among classicists, even if his philosophical argument about the metaphysics of music and his contempt for scrupulous historical research is not.

In spite of the largely negative reception of *The Birth of Tragedy* in academic circles, the book has proved over time to have had a much greater resonance in the fields of aesthetics and art. To turn first to the aesthetics of music, Nietzsche's view of Wagner was to set the terms for some of the most influential subsequent interpretations of Wagner and the development of modern music. Nietzsche's characterization of Wagner's music as a combination of dissonant form and mythical content provides the outline for the parallel movements of formal experiment and atavistic primitivism which Theodor Adorno saw as defining the parameters of modern music in his study of the work of the composers Schoenberg and Stravinsky respectively (*Philosophy of Modern Music*, 1948).

In literature, many writers across Europe developed themes and approaches opened up by Nietzsche. In poetry, Rainer Maria Rilke explored the themes of loss and dissonance in his late elegiac work, while Stefan George drew instead on the aristocratic exclusivity and prophetic tone of Nietzsche's cultural criticism. Many novelists elaborated fictional variations of the opposition between Apollo and Dionysus. In André Gide's *The Immoralist* (1902), the historian protagonist, while recovering from a life-threatening illness, rejects the formal discipline and dry scholarship of his past life and embarks on an exploration of previously repressed sexual impulses which lead him to the edge of Western civilization, symbolically relinquishing Apollo for Dionysus. In Thomas Mann's *Death in Venice* (1912), deep Dionysian forces break through the Apollonian façade of a respectable writer who becomes obsessed by a young boy to the point of acquiescing in his own death. Both novels use the Apollo–Dionysus opposition as the framework for exploring decadence—in Gide's case, the perceived inadequacies of European culture provoke a vitalistic rejection of stifling convention, while in Mann's novel, the gradual recognition of unconscious forces beyond the control of the individual leads to a melancholy resignation in the face of disease and death.

While *The Immoralist* and *Death in Venice* examine the problem of decadence through its impact on individuals, later novels were to widen the question and investigate the possible political consequences of a rejection of reason and convention in the name of deeper cultural forces. After exploring some of the psychological implications of the confrontation between the Apollonian and the Dionysian in the personal relationships of *Women in Love* (1921), D. H. Lawrence was to turn explicitly to the theme of a Dionysian politics in *The Plumed Serpent* (1926). Set in Mexico, the novel relates the story of a regional uprising centred on a charismatic leader who aims to overthrow Christianity and the modern state and return to a more authentic religion and social organization based on pre-Columbian beliefs. The work of Thomas Mann shows a similar development from the personal to the political, albeit in a more critical vein. In *The Magic Mountain* (1924), a novel whose title is itself derived from *The Birth of Tragedy*, Mann uses the setting of a remote Alpine sanatorium to examine a cross-section of the European intelligentsia in terms of the relationship between Apollonian and Dionysian impulses, embodied in the novel in the relationship between the protagonist Hans Castorp and his two competing mentors, Settembrini and Naphtha. Mann's later novel *Doctor Faustus* (1947) explores the links between irrationalism and primitivism in art and the politics of European fascism. In this story of an opportunistic composer who makes a diabolical pact with National Socialism in order to further his artistic career, biographical elements from Nietzsche's life are combined with ideas on music drawn from the work of Schoenberg and Adorno. In the process the composer's aesthetic, which involves a return to atavistic forms of music in an attempt to escape the impasse of dissonance and atonality, is shown to be complicit with the barbaric politics of fascism.

In its use of a Nietzschean framework to explore the

psychology of decadence and the powerful effects of irrational forces, Mann's work points to how *The Birth of Tragedy* appeared to anticipate many of the insights of psychoanalysis. Nietzsche's early comments on dreams and on the opposition between the Apollonian and the Dionysian, form and intuition, imply that the relationship between them is analogous to that between conscious and unconscious, between manifest and latent content, as outlined by Freud in *The Interpretation of Dreams* (1899). Furthermore, Nietzsche's use of the term drive (*Trieb*) to describe the Apollonian and the Dionysian impulses also anticipates Freud in his attempt to develop a model of the psyche which could not be reduced immediately to the organic functioning of the body. Finally, the relationship between the Apollonian and Dionysian drives, the opposition and interdependence which means that each can reach its goals through the other, looks forward to the ambiguous intertwining of Eros and Thanatos, the sexual impulse and the desire for stasis and death, two forces which also bear the name of Greek gods, in Freud's *Beyond the Pleasure Principle* (1920).

The opposition between Apollo and Dionysus recurs also with inflections across a number of texts on German and European cultural history. In exploring the relationship between Nietzsche and Thomas Mann, Georg Lukács reads the tension between Apollonian and Dionysian as the essential predicament of the Wilhelmine intellectual, attempting to suppress and repress disruptive impulses in the name of Prussian 'composure' (*Essays on Thomas Mann*, 1957). As such it epitomizes not only individual psychological conflict, but also the sensibility of a specific historical moment combining the ruthlessness of accelerated capitalist development with the effort to project an assured image of imperial authority. In his monumental *The Decline of the West* (1918/22), Oswald Spengler rewrites the opposition between Apollo and Dionysus as one between Apollo and Faust, between classical Greek and modern German periods of cultural history, characterized by stasis and dynamism respectively. For Spengler, writing during and after the First World War, Faustian or modern capitalist civilization is drawing to a close and will be succeeded by the authoritarian and warlike age of Caesarism. In a sense, Spengler's vision of cultural decline is a late Weimar successor to the critique of Wilhelmine decadence begun in 1872 by Nietzsche, without the optimistic hopes for imminent regeneration.

Closer to Nietzsche's terminology if not to his sentiments is the use of the Apollo–Dionysus opposition by the American anthropologist Ruth Benedict in her *Patterns of Culture* (1936). Influenced by the work of her German-born teacher Franz Boas and also by D. H. Lawrence's essays on New Mexico, Benedict proposed a distinction between two different types of native American culture in the southwestern United States, the Apollonian culture of the sedentary and agrarian Pueblo Indians and the Dionysian culture of the nomadic hunter-gatherer Plains Indians. While the Pueblo dwellers practised their religion in a sober and restrained way, the tribes of the Plains tended to cultivate states of ritual frenzy. In employing Nietzsche's terms thus, Benedict sheds light on the anthropological elements of Nietzsche's interpretation of classical culture which have often been eclipsed by his philosophical concerns, as well as revealing the broader literary and cultural affiliations of anthropological enquiry itself.

In fact, Nietzsche's work anticipates the conjunction of literary and anthropological concerns in twentieth-century modernism, as in the work of Lawrence mentioned above, or in modern theories of the theatre such as Antonin Artaud's *The Theatre and its Double* (1938), perhaps the only work to develop some of the preoccupations of *The Birth of Tragedy* in a dramatic as opposed to a musical direction—insisting on the ritual function of theatre and on the importance of liberating stage performance from the restraints of language. Nietzsche's emphasis on the importance of ritual and myth was also to resonate in the work of other French writers such as Georges Bataille and Roger Caillois, who sought to cure the malaise of modern alienated society through the re-invention of the sacred.

If Nietzsche's work demonstrates strong affinities with the literary modernism of the first half of the twentieth century, perhaps the most obvious contemporary legacy is to be found in Continental philosophy. Since the Second World War, Nietzsche's work has been in effect rediscovered by philosophy. After a long period during which his writing was seen by many philosophers as at best perceptive cultural criticism which occasionally strayed into philosophy and at worst as a kind of proto-fascist rant against rationalism, Nietzsche is now securely part of the philosophical canon, at least within the Continental tradition, and his influence is manifest in many quarters. This influence may be divided into two periods. In the first period, following the war, Nietzsche was widely seen as a precursor of the existentialism of figures such as Karl Jaspers, Jean-Paul Sartre, and Albert Camus. His insistence on the absurdity of existence and on the need to invent meaning independently of the claims of the past seemed to anticipate the concerns of the post-war generation. In the second period, Nietzsche has been associated less with existentialism and more with post-structuralism. The work of Jacques Derrida, for example, depends on the incessant questioning of origins and on the reversal and displacement of conceptual oppositions, and in that sense repeats the tortuous and ambiguous reversals and displacements of the opposition between Apollo and Dionysus traced in *The Birth of Tragedy*. Furthermore, the Apollonian and the Dionysian principles are themselves analogous to the notions of structure and force (principles of formal containment and dynamic transgression) which Derrida employs and investigates in his reading of structuralism as outlined in the essays of *Writing and Difference* (1967). A further echo of the Apollonian and the Dionysian in Continental philosophy is provided by the work of Julia Kristeva. One key element of Kristeva's early work is the exploration of the relationship between what she calls the symbolic and the semiotic, the realm of meanings and stable identities on the one hand and the realm of rhythmic instinctual drives on the other. While the symbolic is identified with the interactions and communication of adult life, the semiotic is associated with life in the womb before birth. This opposition recalls once again that between the Apollonian and the Dionysian, echoing the musical themes and

imagery of birth in Nietzsche's book. So, in the work of contemporary Continental philosophers, distinctions and methods
first developed in *The Birth of Tragedy* are reworked and
developed.

This brief survey of some elements of the legacy of
Nietzsche's first book indicates its importance as a key document
of both modernism and post-modernism. From its resonance
with contemporary Symbolism to its influence on the critique of
rational Western civilization, *The Birth of Tragedy* enjoyed a close
relationship with many of the movements of early twentieth-
century modernism, particularly those with a vitalist or primitiv-
ist strain. From the mid-century, the emphasis has been rather on
the philosophical implications of the work, first on the late modernist and existentialist themes of freedom and responsibility in a
world devoid of meaning, and more recently on the interrogation
of origins which characterizes much post-modern art and
thought.

The Birth of Tragedy is a complex book which deals with much
more than the origins of Greek classical drama. It engages with
some of the major philosophical and aesthetic questions of its day
and continues to provide a framework for approaching the analysis of cultural phenomena. As an early work, it contains elements
which Nietzsche was to discard and disavow as his thought
developed, but it also clearly signals the emergence of some of his
characteristic concerns. In particular, the problems of origins and
of decadence were to remain important throughout his later
work. As a major event in cultural criticism, it pioneered both the
modernist critique of rootless rationalism and the post-modern
suspicion of origins and roots. A complex but compelling book,
The Birth of Tragedy represents a series of intertwined beginnings and endings, which begin and end incessantly with each
new reading.

NOTE ON THE TRANSLATION

The present translation is based on the text of the standard German edition (*Kritische Gesamtausgabe*) edited by Giorgio Colli and Mazzino Montinari (Berlin: De Gruyter, 1967). For the notes, I have consulted the apparatus to this edition, Peter Pütz's extremely useful paperback edition (Munich: Goldmann Klassiker, 1984), and Barbara von Reibnitz, *Ein Kommentar zu Friedrich Nietzsche 'Die Geburt der Tragödie aus dem Geist der Musik'* (Stuttgart/Weimar: J. B. Metzler, 1992).

As for the translation itself, I have retained the paragraphing and, except in one or two instances, the sentence length of the original, in order to give a sense of the rhetorical structure of the German text. Wherever possible, I have also sought to render the musical side of the text through equivalences in rhyme, alliteration, and assonance. Particular difficulties of translation are signalled in the notes.

I would like to thank the following people for their advice and help in the course of completing this translation: Saskia Brown, Toby Deller, Peter Haugh, Ian James, Philip Johnston, Catherine O'Beirne, Tony Phelan, Hugh Ridley. I am also indebted to the editorial team at OUP: Catherine Clarke, Susie Casement, Joanna Rabiger and, on this project in particular, Judith Luna for her patience and helpful advice on the Introduction. Last but not least, I would like to thank my copy-editor Elizabeth Stratford for her careful scrutiny and useful suggestions, which have improved the clarity and accuracy of the text, resulting in a more readable version. Any remaining errors or infelicities are entirely my own.

SELECT BIBLIOGRAPHY

On The Birth of Tragedy

De Man, Paul, 'Genesis and Genealogy (Nietzsche)', in *Allegories of Reading: Figural Language in Rousseau, Nietzsche, Rilke and Proust* (New Haven: Yale University Press, 1979), 79–102.

May, Keith M., *Nietzsche and the Spirit of Tragedy* (London: Macmillan, 1990).

Silk, M. S., and Stern, J. P., *Nietzsche on Tragedy* (Cambridge: Cambridge University Press, 1981).

Soll, Ivan, 'Pessimism and the Tragic View of Life: Reconsiderations of Nietzsche's *Birth of Tragedy*', in Robert C. Solomon and Kathleen M. Higgins (eds.), *Reading Nietzsche* (Oxford and New York: Oxford University Press, 1988), 104–31.

Staten, Henry, '*The Birth of Tragedy* Reconstructed', in *Nietzsche's Voice* (Ithaca, NY: Cornell University Press, 1990), 187–216.

Young, Julian, 'The Birth of Tragedy', in *Nietzsche's Philosophy of Art* (Cambridge: Cambridge University Press, 1982), 5–24.

General Criticism

Ahearn, Daniel, *Nietzsche as Cultural Physician* (University Park, Penn.: Pennsylvania State University Press, 1995).

Allison, David B. (ed.), *The New Nietzsche: Contemporary Styles of Interpretation* (Cambridge, Mass.: MIT Press, 1985).

Burgard, Peter J. (ed.), *Nietzsche and the Feminine* (Charlottesville, Va.: University Press of Virginia, 1994).

Deleuze, Gilles, *Nietzsche and Philosophy* (London: Athlone Press, 1983).

Gillespie, Michael Allen, and Strong, Tracey B. (eds.), *Nietzsche's New Seas: Explorations in Philosophy, Aesthetics, and Politics* (Chicago: University of Chicago Press, 1988).

Hayman, Ronald, *Nietzsche: A Critical Life* (London: Weidenfeld and Nicolson, 1980).

Hollingdale, R. J., *Nietzsche: The Man and his Philosophy* (London: Routledge & Kegan Paul, 1965).

Kaufmann, Walter, *Nietzsche: Philosopher, Psychologist, Antichrist* (Princeton: Princeton University Press, 1968).

Kofman, Sarah, *Nietzsche and Metaphor* (London: Athlone Press, 1993).

Levine, Peter, *Nietzsche and the Modern Crisis of the Humanities* (Albany, NY: State University of New York Press, 1995).

Magnus, Bernd, and Higgins, Kathleen M. (eds.), *The Cambridge Companion to Nietzsche* (Cambridge: Cambridge University Press, 1996).

Nehamas, Alexander, *Nietzsche: Life as Literature* (Cambridge, Mass.: Harvard University Press, 1985).

Pasley, Malcolm (ed.), *Nietzsche: Imagery and Thought* (London: Methuen, 1978).

Patton, Paul (ed.), *Nietzsche, Feminism and Political Theory* (London: Routledge, 1993).

Schacht, Richard, *Nietzsche* (London and New York: Routledge, 1983).

Stern, J. P., *Nietzsche* (London: Fontana, 1978).

Tanner, Michael, *Nietzsche* (Oxford: Oxford University Press, 1994).

Contexts and Reception

Adorno, Theodor W., *Philosophy of Modern Music*, trans. Anne Mitchell and Wesley Blomster (London: Sheed and Ward, 1987).

Aschheim, Steven E., *The Nietzsche Legacy in Germany 1890–1990* (Berkeley, Calif.: University of California Press, 1992).

Bernal, Martin, *Black Athena: The Afroasiatic Roots of Classical Civilization I: The Fabrication of Ancient Greece 1785–1985* (London: Free Association Books, 1987).

Bowie, Andrew, *Aesthetics and Subjectivity from Kant to Nietzsche* (Manchester: Manchester University Press, 1989).

Bridgwater, Patrick, *Nietzsche in Anglosaxony: A Study of Nietzsche's Impact on English and American Literature* (Leicester: Leicester University Press, 1972).

Easterling, P. E. (ed.), *The Cambridge Companion to Greek Tragedy* (Cambridge: Cambridge University Press, 1997).

Fischer-Dieskau, Dietrich, *Wagner and Nietzsche*, trans. Joachim Neugroschel (London: Sidgwick and Jackson, 1976).

Foster, John Burt, *Heirs to Dionysus: A Nietzschean Current in Literary Modernism* (Princeton: Princeton University Press, 1981).

Károlyi, Ottó, *Introducing Modern Music* (London: Penguin, 1995).

Kaufmann, Walter, *Tragedy and Philosophy* (New York: Doubleday, 1968).

Large, D. C., and Weber, W. (eds.), *Wagnerism in European Culture and Politics* (Ithaca, NY: Cornell University Press, 1984).

Pick, Daniel, *Faces of Degeneration: A European Disorder, c.1848– c.1918* (Cambridge: Cambridge University Press, 1989).

Sedgwick, Eve Kosofsky, *Epistemology of the Closet* (London: Penguin, 1994).

Steiner, George, *The Death of Tragedy* (London: Faber, 1961).

Torgovnik, Maria, *Gone Primitive: Savage Intellects, Modern Lives* (Chicago: University of Chicago Press, 1990).

Weidling, P. J., *Health, Race and German Politics between National Unification and Nazism* (Cambridge: Cambridge University Press, 1989).

White, Hayden, *Metahistory: The Historical Imagination in Nineteenth-Century Europe* (Baltimore: Johns Hopkins University Press, 1973).

Williams, Raymond, *Modern Tragedy* (London: Chatto and Windus, 1969).

Further Reading in Oxford World's Classics

Freud, Sigmund, *The Interpretation of Dreams*, trans. Joyce Crick, ed. Ritchie Robertson.

Lawrence, D. H., *Women in Love*, ed. David Bradshaw.

Nietzsche, Friedrich, *Beyond Good and Evil*, trans. and ed. Marion Faber, with an introduction by Robert C. Holub.

—— *On the Genealogy of Morals*, trans. and ed. Douglas Smith.

—— *Twilight of the Idols*, trans. and ed. Duncan Large.

A CHRONOLOGY OF FRIEDRICH NIETZSCHE

1844   Friedrich Wilhelm Nietzsche born in Röcken (Saxony) on 15 October, son of Karl Ludwig and Franziska Nietzsche. His father and both grandfathers are Protestant clergymen.

1846   Birth of sister Elisabeth.

1849   Birth of brother Joseph; death of father.

1850   Death of brother; family moves to Naumburg.

1858–64 Attends renowned boys' boarding-school Pforta, where he excels in classics. Begins to suffer from migraine attacks which will plague him for the rest of his life.

1864   Enters Bonn University to study theology and classical philology.

1865   Follows classics professor Ritschl to Leipzig University, where he drops theology and continues with studies in classical philology. Discovers Schopenhauer's philosophy and becomes a passionate admirer.

1867   Begins publishing career with essay on Theognis; continues publishing philological articles and book reviews till 1873.

1867–8 Military service in Naumburg, until invalided out after a riding accident.

1868   Back in Leipzig, meets Richard Wagner for the first time and quickly becomes a devotee. Increasing disaffection with philology: plans to escape to Paris to study chemistry.

1869   On Ritschl's recommendation, appointed Extraordinary Professor of Classical Philology at Basle University. Awarded doctorate without examination; renounces Prussian citizenship. Begins a series of idyllic visits to the Wagners at Tribschen, on Lake Lucerne. Develops admiration for Jacob Burckhardt, his new colleague in Basle.

1870   Promoted to full professor. Participates in Franco–Prussian War as volunteer medical orderly, but contracts dysentery and diphtheria at the front within a fortnight.

1871   Granted semester's sick leave from Basle and works intensively on *The Birth of Tragedy*. Germany unified; founding of the Reich.

1872   Publishes *The Birth of Tragedy from the Spirit of Music*, which earns him the condemnation of professional colleagues. Lectures 'On the Future of our Educational Institutions'; attends laying of foundation stone for Bayreuth Festival Theatre.

1873   Publishes first *Untimely Meditation: David Strauss the Confessor and the Writer*.

1874   Publishes second and third *Untimely Meditations: On the Use and Disadvantage of History for Human Life* and *Schopenhauer as Educator*. Relationship with Wagner begins to sour.

1875   Meets musician Heinrich Köselitz (Peter Gast), who idolizes him.

1876   Publishes fourth and last *Untimely Meditation: Richard Wagner in Bayreuth*. Attends first Bayreuth Festival but leaves early and subsequently breaks with Wagner. Further illness; granted full year's sick leave from the university.

1877   French translation of *Richard Wagner in Bayreuth* published, the only translation to appear during his mentally active lifetime.

1878   Publishes *Human, All Too Human: A Book for Free Spirits*, which confirms the break with Wagner.

1879   Publishes supplement to *Human, All Too Human, Assorted Opinions and Maxims*. Finally retires from teaching on a pension; first visits the Engadine, summering in St Moritz.

1880   Publishes *The Wanderer and His Shadow*. First stays in Venice and Genoa.

1881   Publishes *Daybreak: Thoughts on the Prejudices of Morality*. First stay in Sils-Maria.

1882   Publishes *The Gay Science*. Infatuation with Lou Andreas-Salomé, who spurns his marriage proposals.

1883   Publishes *Thus Spake Zarathustra: A Book for Everyone and No One*, Parts I and II (separately). Death of Wagner. Spends the summer in Sils and the winter in Nice, his pattern for the next five years. Increasingly consumed by writing.

1884   Publishes *Thus Spake Zarathustra*, Part III.

1885   *Thus Spake Zarathustra*, Part IV printed but circulated to only a handful of friends. Begins in earnest to amass notes for *The Will to Power*.

1886   Publishes *Beyond Good and Evil: Prelude to a Philosophy of the Future*. Change of publisher results in new expanded editions of

> *The Birth of Tragedy* and *Human, All Too Human* (now with a second volume comprising the *Assorted Opinions and Maxims* and *The Wanderer and His Shadow*).

1887   Publishes *On the Genealogy of Morals: A Polemic*. New expanded editions of *Daybreak* and *The Gay Science*.

1888   Begins to receive public recognition: Georg Brandes lectures on his work in Copenhagen. Discovers Turin, where he writes *The Wagner Case: A Musician's Problem*. Abandons *The Will to Power*, then completes in quick succession: *Twilight of the Idols, or How to Philosophize with a Hammer* (first published 1889), *The Antichrist: Curse on Christianity* (f.p. 1895), *Ecce Homo, or How One Becomes What One Is* (f.p. 1908), *Nietzsche contra Wagner: Documents of a Psychologist* (f.p. 1895), and *Dionysus Dithyrambs* (f.p. 1892).

1889   Suffers mental breakdown in Turin (3 January) and is eventually committed to asylum in Jena. *Twilight of the Idols* published 24 January, the first of his new books to appear after his collapse.

1890   Discharged into the care of his mother in Naumburg.

1894   Elisabeth founds Nietzsche Archive in Naumburg (moving it to Weimar two years later).

1897   Mother dies; Elisabeth moves her brother to Weimar.

1900   Friedrich Nietzsche dies in Weimar on 25 August.

THE BIRTH OF TRAGEDY
OR:
HELLENISM AND
PESSIMISM

New Edition
with an Attempt at a
Self-Criticism*

ATTEMPT AT A SELF-CRITICISM

I

Whatever may lie at the bottom of this questionable book: it must have been a question of the greatest interest and appeal, as well as a deeply personal question—as witnessed by the time in which it was written, *in spite of* which it was written, the exciting time of the Franco-Prussian War of 1870–1. While the thunder of the battle of Wörth died away over Europe, the exasperated friend of perplexing puzzles who was to father this book sat in some corner or other of the Alps, very perplexed and puzzled, at once very careworn and carefree, and wrote down his thoughts on the *Greeks*—the core of this wonderful and difficult book to which this belated foreword (or afterword) is to be added. Some weeks later: he found himself beneath the walls of Metz, still pursued by the question marks which he had added to the alleged 'serenity'* of the Greeks and of Greek art; until finally in that month of the greatest tension, as peace was being negotiated in Versailles,* he made his peace with himself and, during a slow convalescence from an illness brought home from the field of battle, completed the definitive version of the 'Birth of Tragedy from the Spirit of *Music*'.—From music? Music and tragedy? The Greeks and the music of tragedy? The Greeks and the pessimistic work of art? The most accomplished, most beautiful, most envied type of men so far, the most persuasive of life's seductions, the Greeks— what? they were the very people who *needed* tragedy? Even more—art? To what end—Greek art? . . .

One may surmise where all this places the great question mark of the value of existence. Is pessimism *necessarily* the sign of decline, decay, of the failure of the exhausted and weakened instincts?—as it was for the Indians,* as it is to all appearances for us 'modern' men and Europeans? Is there such a thing as a *strong* pessimism? An intellectual preference for the hard, horrific, evil, problematic aspects of existence which stems from well-being, from overflowing health, from an *abundance* of existence? Might

it even be possible to suffer from this over-abundance? A tempt-
ing courage of the most intense gaze, which yearns for the fearful,
as for the enemy, the worthy enemy, on whom it can test its
strength? from whom it wants to learn what 'fear'* is? What is the
meaning, for the Greeks of the best, strongest, bravest period in
particular, of the *tragic* myth? And of the tremendous phenomenon of the Dionysian? What, tragedy born of that?—And on the
other hand: that which killed tragedy, the Socratism* of morality,
the dialectic, the modesty and serenity of the theoretical man—
what? might this very Socratism itself not be a sign of decline, of
exhaustion, of ailing health, of the anarchic dissolution of the
instincts? So the 'Greek serenity' of the late Hellenic period
would be nothing more than a sunset? The Epicurean* will
against pessimism only a precaution on the part of the suffering
man? And science itself, our science—yes, what is the meaning of
all science anyway, viewed as a symptom of life? To what end,
even worse, from what *source*—does all science proceed? What? Is
the scientific approach perhaps only a fear and an evasion of
pessimism? A refined means of self-defence against—the *truth*?
And, in moral terms, something like faint-heartedness and false-
hood? In amoral terms, a sly move? O Socrates, Socrates, might
this have been *your* secret? O most secret ironist, might this have
been your—irony?——

2

What I began to grapple with at that time was something fearful and dangerous, a problem with horns, not necessarily a bull
exactly, but in any case a *new* problem: today I would call it the
problem of science itself—science grasped for the first time as
problematic, as questionable. But the book in which my youthful
courage and suspicion found expression at that time—what
an *impossible* book had to grow out of a task so uncongenial to
youth! Constructed from nothing but precocious and under-ripe
personal experiences, all of which bordered on the inexpressible,
and erected on the ground of *art*—since the problem of science

cannot be recognized on its own ground—it is a book perhaps for artists with an inclination to retrospection and analysis (that is, for an exceptional kind of artist, who is not easy to find and whom one would not care to seek out . . .), full of psychological innovations and artistic furtiveness, with a background of artistic metaphysics, a youthful work full of the exuberance and melancholy of youth, independent, defiantly self-reliant even where it seems to defer to an authority and personal reverence, in short a first work also in the bad sense of the term, a work afflicted, in spite of the ancient nature of its problem, with the pen of youth, above all with its 'excessive length', its 'Storm and Stress':* on the other hand, with respect to the success it enjoyed (particularly with the great artist to whom it was addressed as in a dialogue, Richard Wagner*), a book which has *proven* itself, I mean one which has in any case measured up to the 'best of its time'.* As a result, it should be handled with some consideration and discretion; nevertheless, I have no desire to suppress entirely how disagreeable it appears to me now, how unfamiliar it looks to me now after sixteen years—to an older eye, an eye grown a hundred times more discriminating, but an eye grown no colder, no less familiar with the audacious task first undertaken by this daring book—that of *viewing science through the optic of the artist, and art through the optic of life* . . .

3

To say it once again, today I find it an impossible book—I find it badly written, clumsy, embarassing, furious and frenzied in its imagery, emotional, in places saccharine to an effeminate degree, uneven in pace, lacking in a will to logical hygiene,* a book of such utter conviction as to disdain proof, and even to doubt the *propriety* of proof as such, a book for initiates, 'music' for such as are baptized in music, for those who are from the very beginning bound together in a strange shared experience of art, a password by means of which blood relations *in artibus** can recognize one another—an arrogant and infatuated book which from the outset

sought to exclude the *profanum vulgus** of the 'educated' even
more than the 'people', but which, as its influence proved and
continues to prove, must be capable enough of seeking out its
fellow infatuated enthusiasts and of luring them in a dance along
new secret paths. What found expression here in any case—and
this was conceded with as much curiosity as aversion—was an
unfamiliar voice, the disciple of a still 'unknown god',* who concealed himself under the cap of the scholar, the ponderousness
and dialectical ill humour of the German, and even under the bad
manners of the Wagnerian; what was encountered here was a
spirit with unfamilar needs, as yet unnamed, a memory bursting
with questions, experiences, hidden reaches, to which the name
Dionysus* was added as another question mark; what spoke
here—as one remarked suspiciously—resembled the soul of a
mystic or a Maenad* almost, stammering as it were randomly and
with great effort in an unfamiliar tongue, almost uncertain
whether to communicate or conceal itself. It should have *sung*,
this 'new soul'—rather than spoken!* What a pity that I did not
dare to say what I had to say then as a poet: I might have managed
it! Or at least as a philologist:*—even today, almost everything
has yet to be discovered and excavated by the philologist!
Above all, the problem *that* there is a problem here—and
that the Greeks, as long as we have no answer to the question
'what is Dionysian?' still remain completely unknown and
unimaginable . . .

4

Yes, what is Dionysian?—This book provides an answer—'a man
who knows' speaks in it, the initiate and disciple of his god.
Nowadays, perhaps, I would choose my words more carefully and
speak less eloquently about such a difficult psychological question
as the origin of tragedy among the Greeks. A fundamental question is the Greek's relationship to pain, his degree of sensitivity—
does this relationship remain constant? or did it undergo
a reversal?—the question of whether his increasingly strong

yearning for beauty, for festivals, amusements, new cults, was rooted in lack, privation, melancholy, pain. Assuming that this were in fact true—and Pericles (or Thucydides)* gives us to understand as much in the great funeral orations—: where must the opposite and chronologically earlier yearning have originated, the *yearning for the ugly*, the earlier Hellene's good severe will towards pessimism, towards the tragic myth, towards the image of everything fearful, evil, enigmatic, destructive, disastrous at the basis of existence—where must tragedy have originated? Perhaps in *joy*, in strength, in overflowing health, in an excess of abundance? And what then is the meaning in physiological terms of that madness from which tragic and comic art grew, the Dionysian madness? What? Is madness perhaps not necessarily a symptom of degeneration, of decline, of a culture in its final stages? Are there perhaps—a question for psychiatrists—such things as *healthy* neuroses?* Neuroses of a people's youth and youthfulness? In what direction does that synthesis of god and goat in the satyr* point? What personal experience, what impulse forced the Greek to imagine the Dionysian enthusiast and original man as satyr? And, as far as the origin of the Greek chorus is concerned, were there perhaps in the centuries when the Greek body flourished, when the Greek soul bubbled over with life, such things as endemic raptures? Visions and hallucinations shared by entire communities, entire cult assemblies? What? What if the Greeks in the very prime of their youth possessed the will *to* the tragic and were pessimists? What if it were madness itself, to use an expression of Plato's,* which bestowed the *greatest* blessings on Hellas?* And what if, conversely, it were precisely at the moment of their dissolution and weakness that the Greeks became increasingly optimistic, superficial, theatrical, increasingly fervent in their logic and in making the world logical, and so at the same time more 'serene' and more 'scientific'? What? Could perhaps, in spite of all 'modern ideas' and prejudices of democratic taste, the victory of *optimism*, the achieved predominance of *reason*, practical and theoretical *utilitarianism*,* like democracy itself, its contemporary—be a symptom of failing strength, of approaching old age, of physiological exhaustion? And precisely *not*—pessimism? Was Epicurus an optimist—precisely because he *suffered*?——As we can see, this book has loaded itself down with a whole sheaf of difficult questions—but it still remains for us to add the most difficult question of all! Viewed through the optic of *life*, what is the meaning of—morality? . . .

5

Already in the foreword addressed to Richard Wagner, art—and *not* morality—is established as the real *metaphysical* activity of man; in the book itself the suggestive proposition that the existence of the world is only *justified* as an aesthetic phenomenon recurs several times. In fact, the whole book recognizes only an ulterior artistic meaning hidden behind everything which happens—a 'god', if you like, but certainly only a completely thoughtless and amoral artist-god, who wishes to experience the same pleasure and self-satisfaction in building as in destroying, in good as in bad, who by means of creating worlds frees himself from the *distress* of *abundance* and *over-abundance*, from the *suffering* caused by the pressing contradictions within him. The world envisaged in that moment as the *achieved* redemption of god, as the eternally changing, eternally new vision of the greatest suffering, greatest contradiction, richest inconsistency, which can only redeem itself in *appearance*:* one may call this whole artistic metaphysics arbitrary, idle, fantastic—what is essential is that it already betrays a spirit which will regardless of the danger oppose the *moral* interpretation and meaningfulness of existence. It is here, perhaps, for the first time that a pessimism 'beyond good and evil'* announces itself, here that 'perversity of mind' gets a chance to speak and formulate itself, the perversity of mind against which Schopenhauer* tirelessly directed the curses and thunderbolts of his greatest wrath—a philosophy which dared to belittle morality itself by relegating it to the world of the phenomenon,* and not only to 'phenomena' (in the sense of the idealistic *Terminus technicus*,* but also to the realm of 'illusions', as appearance, madness, error, interpretation, contrivance, art.

Perhaps the depth of this *anti-moral* tendency can best be measured by the circumspect and hostile silence with which Christianity is handled throughout the whole book—Christianity as the
most extravagant working through of the moral theme yet
encountered by humanity. In truth, there is no greater contradiction of the purely aesthetic interpretation and justification of the
world as it is taught in this book than the Christian doctrine
which is and wants to be exclusively moral and, with its absolute
standards—already for example with the truthfulness of God—
exiles art, *each and every* art, to the realm of *lies*—that is, denies,
damns, condemns it. Behind such a way of thinking and evaluat-
ing, which must be hostile to art, if it is at all genuine, I always
sensed *hostility to life*, the wrathful and vengeful disgust at life
itself: for all life is founded on appearance, art, illusion, optic, the
necessity of the perspectival and of error. Christianity was from
the very beginning essentially and fundamentally the disgust and
aversion felt by life towards itself, merely disguised, concealed,
and masquerading under the belief in an 'other' or 'better' life.
Hatred of the 'world', a curse on the affects,* fear of beauty and
sensuality, a world beyond, invented in order better to slander
this world, basically a yearning for nothingness, for the end, for
rest, for the 'sabbath of sabbaths'—all this always seemed to me,
just like the absolute will of Christianity to recognize *only* the
validity of moral values, as the most dangerous and most
uncanny* form possible of a 'will to decline', at very least a sign of
the deepest sickness, fatigue, disgruntlement, exhaustion, impoverishment of life—since before morality (in particular Christian,
that is absolute, morality), life *must* continually and inevitably be
condemned, because life is something essentially amoral—life,
crushed under the weight of contempt and of the eternal No,
must finally be felt unworthy of desire, intrinsically without
value. Morality itself—what? might morality itself not be a 'will
to negate life', a secret instinct of annihilation, a principle of
decay, belittlement, slander, a beginning of the end? And consequently the danger of dangers? . . . So my instinct at that
time turned itself *against* morality with this questionable book, as
an instinct speaking on behalf of life, and invented for itself a

fundamental counter-doctrine and counter-evaluation of life, a purely artistic, an *anti-Christian* one. What should it be called? As a philologist and man of words I baptized it, not without taking a certain liberty—for who knows the true name of the Antichrist?—with the name of a Greek god: I called it the *Dionysian.*—

6

Is the nature of the task which I first undertook in this book clear? . . . How much I now regret that at that time I lacked sufficient courage (and arrogance?) to allow myself to express such personal and risky views throughout in my *own personal language*—that instead I laboured to express in the terms of Schopenhauer and Kant new and unfamiliar evaluations, which ran absolutely counter to the spirit, as well as the taste, of Schopenhauer and Kant! What after all were Schopenhauer's thoughts on tragedy? 'What gives tragedy its curious uplifting momentum,' he says in *World as Will and Representation*, II, 'is the dawning of the knowledge that the world, that life can offer no real satisfaction and as a result does *not merit* our devotion: this is the essence of the tragic spirit—it leads accordingly to *resignation*.'* Oh, how differently Dionysus spoke to me! Oh, how far removed I was at that time from precisely this whole attitude of resignation!—But there is something much worse about the book which I now regret even more than having darkened and debased its Dionysian presentiments by using Schopenhauer's terms: namely, that I *debased* the grandiose *Greek problem* as it occurred to me by introducing the most modern things! That I placed hopes where there was nothing to hope for, where everything all too clearly pointed towards an end! That on the basis of recent German music I began to spin fables about the 'German character', as if it were just on the point of rediscovering itself and finding itself once again—and all this at the very moment when the German spirit, which not long before had still possessed the will to dominate and the strength to lead Europe, was drawing up its last will and testament, its definitive *abdication*, and under the grandiose pretext of the foundation of an empire, was making its transition to mediocrity, democracy, and 'modern ideas'!* In fact, since then, I have learnt to think despairingly and mercilessly enough of this 'German character', likewise of contemporary *German music*, which is Romantic through and through and the most un-Greek* of all forms of art: and what is more, a first-rate destroyer of nerves, doubly dangerous for a people which loves drink and reveres obscurity as a virtue, namely in its double property as a narcotic which both delights and *dazes*.—Apart from all the over-hasty hopes and erroneous applications to the present which debased my first book at that time, the great Dionysian question mark which it put in place endures still, also with respect to music: what would music have to be like to be no longer of Romantic origin, like German music—but *Dionysian*? . . .

7

But, sir, if *your* book is not Romantic, then what in the world is? Is it possible to pursue any further the profound hatred of the 'present', 'reality', and 'modern ideas' than you do in your artistic metaphysics?—which would rather believe in nothingness, rather believe in the Devil than in the 'present'? Does a deep bass note of wrath and desire for annihilation not sound through your whole contrapuntal* vocal art and seduction of the ear, a decisive and raging refusal of everything which is 'contemporary', a will which borders on practical nihilism* and which seems to say, 'I would rather that nothing were true than that *you* were right, than that *your* truth were accepted as right!' Listen to yourself, Mister Pessimist and Deifier of Art, with a more open ear, listen to a single selected passage from your book, that not uneloquent passage about the dragon-slayer,* which might sound to young ears and hearts insidiously like the melody of the Pied Piper:* what? is this not the tried and true Romantic confession of 1830, behind the pessimistic mask of 1850?* behind which the usual Romantic finale is already introduced—break-up, break-down, return to and collapse before an old belief, before *the* old God . . . What? is your pessimistic book itself not a piece of anti-Hellenism and Romanticism, itself something 'which delights as much as it dazes', a narcotic in any case, even a piece of music, a piece of *German* music? But listen:

Let us imagine a future generation with this fearless gaze, with this heroic predisposition towards the tremendous, let us imagine the bold stride of these dragon-slayers, the proud audacity with which they turn their back on all the weakling doctrines of optimism, in order to 'live resolutely'* as completely as possible: *would it not be necessary* for the tragic man of this culture in the process of his self-education in seriousness and terror to desire a new art, the *art of metaphysical consolation*, to desire tragedy as his own Helen and to cry out with Faust:

> And should I not, most yearning power,
> Bring this most unique form to life?*

'Would it not be necessary?'. . . No, three times no! you young Romantics: it would *not* be necessary! But it is very probable that it will *end* this way, that *you* will end this way, namely, 'consoled', as it is written,* in spite of all self-education in seriousness and terror, 'metaphysically consoled', in short, as Romantics end, *Christian* . . . No! You should first learn the art of the consolation of *this world*—you should learn to *laugh*, my young friends, if you are determined to remain thorough pessimists; perhaps you might then at some stage or other laughingly send all petty metaphysical consolation to the Devil—with metaphysics leading the way! Or, to express it in the language of that Dionysian monster called *Zarathustra*:

Lift up your hearts, my brothers, high, higher! And do not forget your legs! Lift up your legs also, you good dancers, and even better: stand on your heads!

This crown of the man who laughs, this crown of roses: I myself placed this crown upon my head, I myself proclaimed my laughter holy. I could find no one else strong enough today.

Zarathustra the dancer, Zarathustra the man light on his feet, who beckons with his wings, poised for flight, beckoning to all the birds, poised and prepared, the man blessed and light-headed:—

Zarathustra the sooth-sayer, the sooth-laugher, the man who is not impatient, the man who is not absolutist, the man who loves to leap and to leap sideways: I myself placed this crown upon my head!

This crown of the laughing man, this crown of roses: I throw this crown to you, my brothers! I proclaimed laughter holy: you higher men, *learn* from me how to—laugh! (*Thus Spake Zarathustra*, Part Four*)

THE BIRTH OF TRAGEDY
FROM THE
SPIRIT OF MUSIC*

FOREWORD TO RICHARD WAGNER

In order to ward off any apprehensions, excitements, and mis-understandings, which the ideas assembled in this book might occasion on the part of the peculiar character of our aesthetic public, and also in order to enable me to write the words of its introduction with the same contemplative bliss, which is imprinted on its every page as the petrefact of good and uplifting hours, I imagine the moment in which you, my highly esteemed friend, will receive this book: as you, perhaps after an evening walk in the winter snow, contemplate the unbound Prometheus* on the title-page, read my name, and are immediately convinced that whatever this book might contain, the author has something serious and pressing to say, and likewise that he was communicat-ing all his thoughts to you as they came to him as if you were present, and that he was permitted to commit to writing only that which was appropriate to this presence. You will in the process recall that at the same time as your magnificent commemorative text on Beethoven* was being written, that is amid the horrific and sublime events of the war* which had just broken out, I was collecting myself and these thoughts of mine. And yet those readers would be mistaken who approach this collection of ideas with an opposition between patriotic excitement and aesthetic indulgence in mind, an opposition between bold seriousness and the serenity of play: if they were really to read this book, they might learn to their astonishment what a serious German prob-lem is being dealt with here, one which we place right in the centre of German hopes, as the point around which they twist and turn.* But perhaps such readers are in any case the kind who will take offence at the sight of an aesthetic problem being taken so seriously, if they can see in art nothing more than an amusing sideshow, a readily dispensable tinkling of bells to accompany the 'seriousness of existence': as if no one knew what is at issue in this contrast with the 'seriousness of existence'. May it serve as a lesson to these serious people that I am convinced that art is the highest task and the real metaphysical activity of this life in the sense of the man to whom, as my sublime pioneer on this trail, I wish to dedicate this book.

Basle, end of 1871

We will have achieved much for the discipline of aesthetics when we have arrived not only at the logical insight but also at the immediate certainty of the view that the continuing development of art is tied to the duality of the *Apollonian* and the *Dionysian*:* just as procreation depends on the duality of the sexes, which are engaged in a continual struggle interrupted only by temporary periods of reconciliation. These names are borrowed from the Greeks who revealed the profound secret doctrines of their view of art to the discerning mind precisely not in concepts but rather in the insistently clear forms of their pantheon. To both of their artistic deities, Apollo* and Dionysus, is linked our knowledge that in the Greek world there existed a tremendous opposition, in terms of origin and goals, between the Apollonian art of the sculptor and the imageless Dionysian art of music: these two very different drives run in parallel with one another, for the most part diverging openly with one another and continually stimulating each other to ever new and more powerful births, in order to perpetuate in themselves the struggle of that opposition only apparently bridged by the shared name of 'art'; until finally, through a metaphysical miracle of the Hellenic 'will',* they appear coupled with one another and through this coupling at last give birth to a work of art which is as Dionysian as it is Apollonian—Attic tragedy.*

In order to acquaint ourselves more closely with both of these drives, let us think of them first of all as the opposed artistic worlds of *dream* and *intoxication*; the opposition between these physiological phenomena corresponds to that between the Apollonian and the Dionysian. According to Lucretius,* it was in dreams that the magnificent forms of the gods first appeared before the souls of men, it was in dreams that the great sculptor first beheld the delightful anatomy of superhuman beings, and the Hellenic poet, if questioned about the secret of poetic creation, would likewise have referred to dreams and given a similar explanation to that of Hans Sachs in *The Mastersingers*:

> My friend, it is the task of the poet
> To note dreams and interpret.
> The truest delusion of man seems,
> Believe me, revealed to him in dreams:
> All the art of poetry and versification
> Is nothing but the true dream-interpretation.*

The beautiful appearance of the worlds of dream, in whose creation every man is a consummate artist, is the precondition of all plastic art, even, as we shall see, of an important half of poetry. We take pleasure in the direct understanding of form, all shapes speak to us, there is nothing indifferent or superfluous. And yet even in the most intense life of this dream-reality, the sense of its status as *appearance* still shimmers through: this at least is my experience, for whose frequency, even normality, I could adduce much evidence, including the sayings of the poets. The philosophical man even senses that under this reality in which we live and exist, there lies hidden a second and completely different reality, and that this surface reality is therefore also an appearance. Schopenhauer designates precisely the gift of occasionally seeing men and all things as mere phantoms or dream-images* as the distinctive characteristic of the capacity for philosophy.* So the artistically sensitive man responds to the reality of the dream in the same way as the philosopher responds to the reality of existence; he pays close attention and derives pleasure from it: for out of these images he interprets life for himself, in these events he trains himself for life. He experiences not only the agreeable and friendly images with that universal understanding: but also the serious, the gloomy, the sad, the dark aspects of life, the sudden inhibitions, the teasing of chance, the fearful expectations. In short the whole 'divine comedy' of life, including the Inferno,* passes before him, not only as a game of shadows— since he participates in the life and suffering of these scenes—yet also not without that fleeting sense of their status as appearance. And perhaps many will remember, as I do, calling out to themselves in encouragement amid the dangers and terrors of the dream, not without success: 'This is a dream! I want to dream on!' I have likewise heard of people who were able to extend the causal sequence of one and the same dream over three consecutive nights and more: facts which clearly prove that our innermost being, the substratum common to us all, experiences the dream with profound pleasure and joyful necessity.

The Greeks have likewise expressed this joyful necessity of the dream experience in their Apollo: Apollo, as the god of all plastic energies is at the same time the god of prophecy. He, who according to the etymological root of his name is the 'one who appears shining',* the deity of light, is also master of the beautiful appearance of the inner world of the imagination. The higher truth, the perfection of these states in contrast to the only partial comprehensibility of everyday reality, the deep consciousness of nature as it heals and helps in sleep and dream is at the same time the symbolic analogue of the capacity for prophecy and of the arts as a whole, which make life possible and worth living. But our image of Apollo must include that delicate and indispensable line which the dream image may not overstep if it is not to have pathological effects, otherwise appearance would deceive us as clumsy reality: that measured restraint, that freedom from the wilder impulses, that calm wisdom of the image-creating god. His eye must 'shine like the sun',* in accordance with his origins; even when it rages and looks displeased, it remains consecrated by the beauty of appearance. And so what Schopenhauer says about man caught in the veil of Maya* might apply to Apollo in an excentric sense—*World as Will and Representation*, I: 'As a sailor sits in a small boat in a boundless raging sea, surrounded on all sides by heaving mountainous waves, trusting to his frail vessel; so does the individual man sit calmly in the middle of a world of torment, trusting to the *principium individuationis*.'* In fact, it might be said of Apollo that in him the unshaken trust in that *principium* and the calm repose of the man caught up in it has found its most sublime expression, and Apollo might even be described as the magnificent divine image of the *principium individuationis*, through whose gestures and looks all the pleasure and wisdom and beauty of 'appearance' speak to us.

In the same passage, Schopenhauer has depicted the tremendous *horror* which grips man when he suddenly loses his way among the cognitive forms of the phenomenal world, as the principle of reason* in any of its forms appears to break down. When we add to this horror the blissful rapture which rises up from the innermost depths of man, even of nature, as a result of the very same collapse of the *principium individuationis*, we steal a glimpse into the essence of the *Dionysian*, with which we will become best acquainted through the analogy of *intoxication*. Either under the influence of the narcotic drink of which all original men and peoples sing in hymns, or in the approach of spring which forcefully and pleasurably courses through the whole of nature, those Dionysian impulses awaken, which in their heightened forms cause the subjective to dwindle to complete self-oblivion. In mediaeval Germany, too, increasingly large throngs of singing and dancing people surged from place to place under the influence of the same Dionysian force: in these St John's and St Vitus's dancers* we recognize again the Bacchic choruses of the Greeks, with their prehistory in Asia Minor, stretching all the way back to Babylon and the orgiastic Sacaea.* There are men who from lack of experience or from stupidity turn away in contempt and pity from such phenomena as they would from 'folk diseases'* with a greater sense of their own good health: but these poor men do not suspect how cadaverous and ghostly their 'health' looks, compared to the glowing life of Dionysian enthusiasts which roars past them.

Under the spell of the Dionysian it is not only the bond between man and man which is re-established: nature in its estranged, hostile, or subjugated forms also celebrates its reconciliation with its prodigal son,* man. The earth voluntarily gives up its spoils while the predators of cliffs and desert approach meekly. The chariot of Dionysus overflows with flowers and wreaths: beneath its yoke tread the panther and the tiger.* If one were to allow one's imagination free rein in transforming Beethoven's 'Hymn to Joy'* into a painting, particularly the moment when the multitudes kneel down awestruck in the dust:* then one might come close to an idea of the Dionysian. Now the slave is a free man, now all the inflexible and hostile divisions which necessity, caprice, or 'impudent fashion'* have established between men collapse. Now, with the gospel of world-harmony, each man feels himself not only reunified, reconciled, re-incorporated, and merged with his neighbour, but genuinely one, as if the veil of Maya had been rent and only its shreds still fluttered in front of the mysterious original Unity.* In song and dance man expresses himself as a member of a higher communal nature: he has forgotten how to walk and speak and is well on the way to dancing himself aloft into the heights. His gestures communicate an entranced state. Just as now the animals speak and the earth gives forth milk and honey,* so something supernatural sounds forth from him: he feels himself as god, now he himself strides forth as enraptured and uplifted as he saw the gods stride forth in dreams. Man is no longer an artist, he has become a work of art: the artistic force of the whole of nature, to the most intense blissful satisfaction of the original Unity, reveals itself here in the shudder of intoxication. Here the noblest clay, the most expensive marble, man, is kneaded and hewn, and the chisel-blows of the Dionysian artist of worlds are accompanied by the sound of the Eleusinian Mysteries* calling: 'Do you fall to your knees, multitudes? World, do you sense the creator?'*—

2

Until now we have considered the Apollonian and its opposite, the Dionysian, as artistic powers, which burst forth from nature itself, *without the mediation of the human artist*, and in which their artistic drives at first satisfy themselves directly: first as the image-world of the dream, whose perfection is wholly unconnected to the intellectual level of artistic education of the individual, and then as intoxicated reality, which again pays no heed to the individual, and even seeks to annihilate the individual and to redeem him through a mystical feeling of unity. In relation to these direct artistic states of nature, every artist is an 'imitator', that is, either Apollonian dream-artist or Dionysian artist of intoxication, or finally—as for example in Greek tragedy— simultaneously artist of dream and intoxication: such as we have to imagine him as he stands alone to one side of the infatuated choruses before sinking to his knees in Dionysian drunkenness and mystical self-abandonment and as, through the effect of the Apollonian dream, his own state, that is, his unity with the innermost ground of the world, is revealed to him *in an allegorical dream-image*.*

Having established these general preconditions and comparisons, let us now approach the *Greeks* in order to learn the degree and extent to which those *artistic drives of nature* have developed in them: this will then enable us to understand and appreciate more deeply the relation of the Greek artist to his archetypes,* or, to use the Aristotelian term, 'the imitation of nature'.* In spite of all the dream literature recounting their countless dream anecdotes, we can only speculate as to the *dreams* of the Greeks, but with some confidence none the less: given the incredibly precise and sure plastic capacity of their eye, with its vivid and honest pleasure in colour, we must, to the shame of all succeeding generations, presuppose also for their dreams a causality and logic of lines and outlines, colours and groups, a sequence of scenes resembling one of their finest reliefs, whose perfection would justify, were a comparison possible, our describing the dreaming Greeks as Homers and Homer* as a dreaming Greek: in a more profound sense than that in which the modern man in speaking of his dreams dares to compare himself to Shakespeare.*

On the other hand, we have no need to speculate with regard to the huge chasm which separates the *Dionysian Greeks* from the Dionysian barbarian. In all corners of the ancient world—to leave the modern one to one side here—from Rome to Babylon, we can prove the existence of Dionysian festivities, whose type is at best related to the Greek type as the bearded satyr,* to whom the goat lent its name and attributes, is to Dionysus himself. Almost everywhere the centre of these festivities lay in an effusive transgression of the sexual order, whose waves swept away all family life and its venerable principles; none other than the wildest beasts of nature were unleashed here to the point of creating an abominable mixture of sensuality and cruelty which has always appeared to me as the true 'witches' brew'.* Against the feverish impulses of these festivities, knowledge of which reached them across land and sea, the Greeks were, it seems, for a while completely sheltered and shielded by the figure of Apollo who stood tall and proud among them and who with the Medusa's head* warded off this grotesque barbaric Dionysian force, the most dangerous power it had to encounter. That majestic repudiation of Apollo has immortalized itself in Doric art.* This resistance became more questionable and even impossible as, from the deepest roots of the Hellenic character itself, similar drives finally broke through: now the influence of the Delphic god* was limited to avoiding annihilation by disarming the powerful adversary through a well-timed reconcilation. This reconciliation is the most important moment in the history of Greek religion: wherever one looks, one sees the revolutions wrought by this event. It was the reconciliation of two adversaries, clearly defining the boundaries to be respected from now on and instituting periodic exchanges of tokens of esteem; at bottom the chasm which separated them remained unbridged. If, however, we see how the Dionysian power revealed itself under the pressure of that peace settlement, then we recognize in the Dionysian orgies of the Greeks, in contrast to those Babylonian Sacaea and their regression of man to the tiger and the ape, the meaning of festivities of world redemption and days of transfiguration. Here nature first attains its artistic exultation, here the tearing asunder of the *principium individuationis* first becomes an artistic phenomenon. That horrific witches' brew of sensuality and cruelty was powerless here: only the peculiar mixture and duality of the emotions on the part of the Dionysian enthusiasts recalls it—as cures recall lethal poisons—the phenomenon that pain arouses pleasure, that exultation tears cries of agony from the breast. Out of the most intense joy the scream of terror or the yearning lament for an irreplaceable loss sounds forth. In those Greek festivities a sentimental* trait of nature breaks through, so to speak, as if it has reason to lament its dismemberment into individuals. The song and gestures of such ambivalent enthusiasts were something new and unheard-of in the Homeric Greek world: and Dionysian *music* in particular awakened its fear and horror. If music was apparently already known as an Apollonian art, this was strictly speaking only as the wave-like beat of rhythm, whose plastic force was developed for the representation of Apollonian states. The music of Apollo was Doric architecture rendered in sound,* but in the merely suggestive notes characteristic of the cithara.* Carefully kept at a distance is precisely that element which defines the character of Dionysian music and so of music itself, the shattering force of sound, the unified flow of melody and the utterly incomparable world of harmony. In the Dionysian dithyramb,* all the symbolic faculties of man are stimulated to the highest pitch of intensity; something never before experienced struggles towards expression, the annihilation of the veil of Maya, unity as the spirit of the species, even of nature. Now the world of nature is to be expressed in symbols; a new world of symbols is necessary, a symbolism of the body for once, not just the symbolism of the mouth, but the full gestures of dance, the rhythmic movement of all the limbs. Then the other symbolic forces will develop, particularly those of music, suddenly impetuous in rhythm, dynamism, and harmony. In order to grasp this complete unleashing of all symbolic forces, man must already have reached that height of self-abandonment which seeks to express itself symbolically through those forces: so the dithyrambic servant of Dionysus will only be understood by those like him! With what astonishment the Apollonian Greek must have regarded him! With an astonishment which was all the greater for being accompanied by the horror that all this was really not so unfamiliar to him after all, even that his Apollonian consciousness did no more than cast a veil over this Dionysian world before him.

3

In order to understand this, we must as it were dismantle stone by stone the elaborate edifice of *Apollonian culture* until we can see the foundations upon which it is built. Here we see first the magnificent figures of the *Olympian* pantheon* which stand on the gables of this building and whose deeds adorn its friezes in brilliant reliefs visible from a great distance. If Apollo too stands among them as one deity among others without claiming a pre-eminent place, we should not allow ourselves to be led astray by this. The same drive which took on concrete form in Apollo has given birth to the whole Olympian world, and in this sense Apollo may serve for us as its father. From what great need did such a brilliant company of Olympian beings spring?

Whoever approaches these Olympians with another religion at heart, in search of moral elevation, even saintliness, disembodied spirituality, glances of compassion and love, will soon be obliged to turn his back on them. There is nothing here to remind us of asceticism, spirituality, and duty: everything here speaks to us of a sumptuous, even triumphant, existence, an existence in which everything is deified, regardless of whether it is good or evil. And so the spectator might stand full of consternation before this fantastic exuberance of life, wondering what magic potion these arrogant men took in order to have enjoyed life in such a way that wherever they look, Helen, the ideal image of their own existence 'hovering in sweet sensuality',* smiles back at them, laughing. But to this spectator who has already turned to leave we must shout: Do not leave just yet, but listen first to what Greek folk wisdom says about this same life, which stretches out before you here with such inexplicable serenity. According to an ancient legend, King Midas had long hunted the forest for the wise *Silenus*,* the companion of Dionysus, without catching him. When Silenus finally fell into his hands, the king asked him what is the very best and most preferable of all things for man. The stiff and motionless daemon refused to speak; until, forced by the king, he finally burst into shrill laughter and uttered the following words: 'Miserable ephemeral race, children of chance and toil, why do you force me to tell you what it is best for you not to hear? The very best of all things is completely beyond your reach: not to have been born, not to *be*, to be *nothing*. But the second best thing for you is—to meet an early death.'

How is the Olympian pantheon related to this folk wisdom? As the delightful vision of the tortured martyr is to his torments.

Now the Olympian magic mountain* opens itself up to us as it were and shows us its roots. The Greek knew and felt the terrors and horrors of existence: in order to be able to live at all, he had to use the brilliant Olympians, born of dream, as a screen. That great mistrust of the Titanic powers of nature,* those ruthless Moira* ruling over all knowledge, that vulture of the great friend of man, Prometheus,* that fearful fate of the wise Oedipus,* that curse on the house of the Atrides which drove Orestes* to matricide, in short that whole philosophy of the forest god,* together with its mythical examples, on which the melancholy Etruscans* foundered, was continually overcome anew, in any case veiled and removed from view by the Greeks through that artistic *middle world* of the Olympians. In order to be able to live, the Greeks were obliged to create these gods, out of the deepest necessity: a process which we should probably imagine in the following way—through the Apollonian drive towards beauty, the Olympians' divine reign of joy developed in a slow series of transitions from the original Titans' divine reign of terror: as roses burst forth from the thorn-bush. How else could that people, so sensitive in its emotions, so impetuous in its desires, so uniquely equipped for *suffering*, have tolerated existence, if the very same existence had not been shown to it surrounded by a higher glory in its gods. The same drive which calls art into life as the completion and perfection of existence which seduces the living into living on, also brought into being the Olympian world in which the Hellenic 'will' holds up before itself a transfiguring mirror. So the gods justify the life of men by living it themselves—the only adequate theodicy!* Existence under the bright sunlight of such gods will be felt to be in itself worth striving for, and the real *pain* of the Homeric men relates to their taking leave of it, above all in the near future: so that now it could be said of them in a reversal of the wisdom of Silenus that 'the very worst thing of all would be to meet an early death, the second worst to die at all'. Once lament sounds forth, it is heard again for the premature death of Achilles,* for the continual passing of mankind, like leaves in the

*) "reversal", now, living is *fervently* desired

wind, for the decline of the age of heroes. It is not unworthy of
the greatest heroes to yearn to live on, even as a day labourer.* So
impetuously does the 'will' in its Apollonian form desire this
existence, so at one does the Homeric man feel with it, that even
lament becomes its hymn of praise.

It must be said here that this harmony which more modern
men view with such yearning, this unity of man with nature,
whose designation by the artistic term 'naïve' was popularized
by Schiller,* is a by no means simple, self-evident, as it were
unavoidable state, which is *necessarily* to be found at the gate of all
cultures, as paradise for mankind: only an age which sought to
imagine Rousseau's *Émile** as an artist and imagined that it had
found in Homer such an artistic Émile, brought up in the heart of
nature, could believe this. Wherever we encounter the 'naïve' in
art, we must recognize the greatest effect of Apollonian culture:
which must always first overthrow a realm of Titans, slay mon-
sters, and triumph over a horrific depth of contemplation of the
world and the most sensitive capacity for suffering by resorting to
powerful misleading delusions and pleasurable illusions. But how
seldom is that naïve state, that complete embrace by the beauty of
appearance achieved! How inexpressibly sublime *Homer* is, therefore, who as a single individual relates to that Apollonian folk
culture as the single dream-artist to the dream-capacity of the
people and of nature itself. Homeric 'naïveté' is only to be understood as the complete triumph of the Apollonian illusion: this is
such an illusion as nature so often uses to realize her intentions.
The true goal is concealed by a hallucinatory image: we stretch
out our hands towards the latter and nature achieves the former
by deceiving us. In the Greeks, 'will' wanted to contemplate
itself, in the transfiguration of the genius and the world of art; in
order to glorify itself, its creatures had to feel themselves worthy
of glorification, they had to see themselves again in a higher
sphere, without this perfect world of contemplation acting as an
imperative or a reproach. This is the sphere of beauty, in which
they saw their mirror-images, the Olympians. With this mirroring of beauty, the Hellenic 'will' struggled against the artistically
correlative talent for suffering and for the wisdom of suffering:

and as a monument to its triumph Homer stands before us, the
naïve artist.

4

The dream analogy goes some way towards explaining this naïve
artist. Let us imagine the dreamer, as in the middle of the illusion
of the dream-world and without disturbing it he shouts to himself: 'This is a dream, I want to dream on.' If we must deduce
from this a deep inner joy in contemplating the dream, or if, on
the other hand, in order to be able to dream with this inner joy in
looking at all, we must first forget the present with its horrific
urgency, then, under the guidance of Apollo the interpreter of
dreams, we may interpret all these phenomena in the following
way. Although of the two halves of life, the waking half and the
dreaming half, the first appears to us incomparably preferable,
more important, more worthy, more worth living, even as the
only half which is really lived, I would still like, however paradoxical it may seem, to assert precisely the opposite evaluation of
the dream on behalf of the secret ground of our essence, whose
phenomenal appearance we are. For the more I become aware of
those omnipotent artistic drives in nature and in them of a fervent yearning for appearance, for redemption through appearance, the more I feel myself compelled to make the metaphysical
assumption that that which truly exists and the original Unity,*
with its eternal suffering and contradiction, needs at the same
time the delightful vision, the pleasurable appearance, for its continual redemption: the very appearance which we, completely
enmeshed in it and consisting of it, are forced to experience as
that which does not truly exist,* to experience then as a continual
becoming in time, space, and causality, to experience in other
words as empirical reality.* So if for once we look away from our
own 'reality' for a moment, if we grasp our empirical existence,
like that of the world as a whole, as a concept produced at each
moment by the original Unity, then the dream must seem to us
now as the *appearance of appearance** and therefore as an even

higher satisfaction of the the original desire for appearance. It is for this same reason that the innermost core of nature takes that indescribable pleasure in the naïve artist and the naïve work of art, which is likewise only the 'appearance of appearance'. In an allegorical painting, *Raphael*,* himself one of those immortal naïves, has represented this relegation of appearance to the status of appearance, the original process of the naïve artist and also of Apollonian culture. In his *Transfiguration*,* the lower half with the possessed boy, his despairing bearers, and the helplessly fearful disciples, shows us the reflection of the eternal original suffering, of the sole ground of the world: 'appearance' here is the reflection of the eternal contradiction, of the father of things. Now out of this appearance rises like the scent of ambrosia* a new vision-like world of appearance, which remains invisible to those who are caught in the first world of appearance—a brilliant hovering in purest bliss and painless contemplation through beaming wide-open eyes. Here we have before our eyes, rendered in the highest symbolism of art, that Apollonian world of beauty and its substratum, the horrific wisdom of Silenus, and we understand intuitively their reciprocal necessity. But Apollo appears to us again as the apotheosis of the *principium individuationis*, in which the eternally achieved goal of the original Unity, its redemption through appearance, is alone completed: he shows us with sublime gestures how the whole world of torment is necessary in order to force the individual to produce the redeeming vision and then to sit in calm contemplation of it as his small boat is tossed by the surrounding sea.

This apotheosis of individuation, if we think of it as at all imperative and prescriptive, knows only *one* law, the individual, that is, respect for the limits of the individual, *moderation* in the Hellenic sense. Apollo, as an ethical deity, demands of his disciples moderation and in order to maintain it, self-knowledge. And so in parallel with the aesthetic necessity of beauty runs the imperative of the 'know thyself'* and the 'nothing to excess!',* while arrogance and lack of moderation are regarded as the really hostile daemons of the non-Apollonian sphere, and hence as characteristics of the age before Apollo, of the age of the Titans, and of the world beyond the Apollonian, that is, the world of the barbarians. It was because of his Titanic love for men that Prometheus had to be torn apart by vultures, it was because of his arrogant wisdom, which solved the riddle of the Sphinx,* that Oedipus had to plunge into a bewildering spiral of atrocities: in such a way did the Delphic god interpret the Greek past.

The effect aroused by the *Dionysian* also seemed 'Titanic' and 'barbaric' to the Apollonian Greek: while he was at the same time unable to conceal from himself the fact that he was inwardly related to those fallen Titans and heroes. Indeed, he was obliged to sense something even greater than this: his whole existence, with all its beauty and moderation, rested on a hidden substratum of suffering and knowledge, which was once again revealed to him by the Dionysian. And look! Apollo was unable to live without Dionysus! The 'Titanic' and the 'barbaric' were ultimately as much a necessity as the Apollonian! And let us now imagine how the ecstatic sound of the Dionysian celebration rang in an ever more seductive and spellbinding way through this artificially dammed-up world built on appearance and moderation, how in these spells the whole *excess* of nature in pleasure, pain, and knowledge resounded to the point of a piercing scream: let us imagine what meaning the ghostly harp music and psalm-singing of the Apollonian artist could have when compared to this daemonic song of the people! The muses of the art of 'appearance' paled before an art which in its intoxication spoke the truth, in which the wisdom of Silenus cried out woe! woe! to the Olympians in their serenity. The individual, with all his limits and moderation, sank here into the self-oblivion of the Dionysian state and forgot the Apollonian principles. *Excess* revealed itself as the truth, and the contradiction, the bliss born of pain spoke out from the heart of nature. And so, wherever the Dionysian broke through, the Apollonian was cancelled, absorbed, and annihilated.* But it is equally certain that in the place where the first assault was successfully resisted, the reputation and majesty of the Delphic god expressed itself in more inflexible and more threatening forms than ever before. Indeed, I can only explain the *Doric* state and Doric art as the extension of the Apollonian war camp: only in a continual struggle against the Titanic-barbarian essence of the Dionysian could such a defiantly stubborn and heavily fortified art, such a warlike and severe education, such a cruel and ruthless state, survive for any length of time.

So far, I have been elaborating the remark made at the beginning of this essay: how the Dionysian and the Apollonian have dominated the essence of the Hellenic in an ongoing sequence of new births in a relationship of reciprocal stimulation and intensification: how under the influence of the Apollonian drive to beauty the Homeric world developed out of the 'bronze' age* with its struggles between the Titans and its severe folk philosophy, how this 'naïve' magnificence was again swallowed up by the encroaching flood of the Dionysian, and how in face of this new power the Apollonian elevated itself to the inflexible majesty of Doric art and the Doric world-view. If in this way the more ancient history of the Hellenic world falls into four great artistic periods* in the course of the struggle between these two hostile principles, then we are forced at this point to ask further questions about the last phase of this development and growth, unless the latest period, that of Doric art, is to stand as the culmination and intended goal of those artistic drives: and here the sublime and highly praised work of art of *Attic tragedy* and the dramatic dithyramb* offers itself to our eyes as the common goal of both drives, whose secret marriage, following a long struggle, has glorified itself in such a child—at once Antigone and Cassandra.*

5

We are now approaching the real goal of our enquiry, which is directed towards knowledge of the Dionysian–Apollonian genius and its work of art, or towards some sense of the mystery of that union. At this point we ask first where that new seed which later developed into tragedy and the dramatic dithyramb first attracted attention in the Hellenic world. On this matter the ancient world itself gives us an answer in visual form, when it places *Homer and Archilochus** side by side on sculptures, intaglios, and so on as the original fathers and torchbearers of Greek poetry, sure in the feeling that only these two completely and equally original natures merited consideration, these two from whom a torrent of fire streams forth into the whole of the later Greek world. Homer, the old self-absorbed dreamer, the type of the Apollonian naïve artist, gazes in astonishment at the passionate head of Archilochus, the warlike servant of the muses, as he is pursued wildly through existence: and modern aesthetics* could only add by way of interpretation that this was the moment when the 'objective' artist first confronts his 'subjective' counterpart. This interpretation is of little help to us, because we know the subjective artist only as a bad artist and demand above all in art the defeat of the subjective, redemption from the 'I' and the silencing of each individual will and craving, indeed we cannot conceive of the slightest possibility of truly artistic creation without objectivity, without pure disinterested contemplation.* For this reason our aesthetic must first solve the problem of how the 'lyric poet' is possible as an artist: he who according to the experience of all ages always says 'I' and sings out before us the whole chromatic scale* of his passions and desires. In comparison with Homer, it is precisely this Archilochus who terrifies us, with the scream of his hatred and scorn, with the drunken outburst of his desires: is he, the first artist to be called subjective, not therefore none other than the true non-artist? But in that case what explains the reverence shown to this poet by even the Delphic oracle itself, the hearth of 'objective' art, in a number of remarkable pronouncements?

Schiller shed light on the process of the composition of his poetry in a psychological observation which did not give him pause although he was at a loss as to how to explain it; for he admitted that in the preparatory state which precedes the act of writing poetry he did not have before him and within him a series of images and causally organized thoughts, but rather a *musical mood* ('In my case, the feeling lacks a definite and clear object to begin with; this only takes shape later. A certain musical and emotional mood develops and for me the poetic idea only follows subsequently'*). If we now include the most important phenomenon of the whole of ancient lyric poetry, the unity, even identity of the *lyric poet* and the *musician*, which was universally taken for granted—in comparison with which our more modern lyric poetry appears like the headless image of a god*—then we can now, on the basis of the aesthetic metaphysics presented earlier, explain the lyric poet in the following way. He has in the first place as a Dionysian artist become entirely fused with the original Unity, with its pain and contradiction, and produced the copy* of this original Unity in the form of music, assuming, that is, that it is correct to identify music as a repetition and cast of the world; but now this music becomes visible to him again, as in an *allegorical dream-image*, under the influence of the Apollonian dream. That reflection of original suffering in music, devoid of image and concept, with its redemption in appearance, now produces a second mirror-image, as a single allegory or example. The artist has already surrendered his subjectivity in the Dionysian process: the image which now shows him his unity with the heart of the world is a dream-scene which gives concrete form to the original contradiction and pain, along with the original pleasure in appearance. So the 'I' of the lyric poet sounds forth from the abyss of being: his 'subjectivity' in the sense of the more modern aestheticians is a delusion. When Archilochus, the first of the Greek lyric poets, simultaneously declares his raging love and contempt to the daughters of Lycambes,* it is not his passion which dances before us in orgiastic frenzy: we see Dionysus and the Maenads, we see the intoxicated enthusiast Archilochus sunk in sleep—sleep as Euripides describes it in the *Bacchae*,* sleep in high alpine meadows, in the midday sun—: and now Apollo draws near and touches him with the laurel.* The sleeping poet, enchanted by Dionysian music, now begins as it were to spray sparkling images around him, lyrical poems which at the height of their development are called tragedies and dramatic dithyrambs.

The sculptor, and also the related figure of the epic poet, is absorbed in the pure contemplation of images. Bereft of images, the Dionysian musician is himself wholly and exclusively original pain and original echo of that pain. The lyrical genius feels a new world of images and allegories grow forth from that state of mystical self-abandonment and unity, a world which is completely different in colouring, causality, and tempo from that of the sculptor and epic poet. While the epic poet lives in these images a life of comfort and joy otherwise impossible and never tires of contemplating them lovingly in their minutest details, while he regards even the fury of the raging Achilles as nothing more than an image, whose raging expression he enjoys with that dreamer's pleasure in appearance—so that he is protected by this mirror of appearance from unification and fusion with its forms—the images of the lyric poet are on the other hand nothing other than himself, are as it were only different objectivations* of himself, which is why he may as the moving centre of that world say 'I': only this 'self'* is not the same as that of the empirically real waking man, but rather the only I which truly exists, the eternal I, resting on the ground of things, the I by means of whose copies the lyrical genius sees through to the very ground of things. Let us now imagine how among these copies he regards *himself* as non-genius, that is, as 'subject', the whole throng of subjective passions and impulses of the will directed towards a definite object which appears real to him; and if it now appears as if the lyrical genius and the non-genius associated with him were one and the same and as if the former spoke of its own accord the little word 'I', then this apparent state of affairs will no longer lead us astray, as it has certainly led astray those who have designated the lyric poet as the subjective poet. In truth, Archilochus, who loves and hates and is consumed by burning passion, is only a vision of the genius which has long since ceased to be Archilochus but become instead the world-genius which expresses in symbolic form its original pain through that allegory of Archilochus the man, while Archilochus the man, who subjectively wills and desires, can never at any time be a poet. But it is not at all necessary for the lyric poet to see before him only the phenomenon of Archilochus the man as the reflection of eternal being; and tragedy proves how far removed the vision-world of the lyric poet can be from that least distant of phenomena.

Schopenhauer, who did not conceal from himself the difficulty which the lyric poet posed for the philosophical view of art, believed that he had found a way out of the impasse, one along which I cannot follow him. Yet it was into his hands alone that the means were given to deal decisively with this difficulty, in the form of his profound metaphysics of music: and here I believe I have accomplished this task in his spirit and in his honour. It was in the following terms, however, that he characterized the particular essence of song (*World as Will and Representation*, I): 'It is the subject of the will, that is, his own particular willing which fills the consciousness of the singer, often in the form of an unburdened, satisfied willing (joy) but probably even more often in the form of an inhibited willing (sorrow), always as affect, passion, agitated emotional state. But alongside this state, through looking at his natural surroundings, the singer at the same time becomes conscious of himself as the subject of pure knowledge devoid of will, whose unshakeable spiritual calm then comes into conflict with the pressure of the increasingly restricted, increasingly needy willing: the feeling of this contrast, of this alternation is really what is expressed in the whole of the song and what constitutes the lyrical state itself. In this state, pure knowledge as it were approaches us in order to redeem us from willing and its pressure: we follow, yet only momentarily: willing, the memory of our personal goals, tears us away again and again from calm contemplation; but equally the next beautiful surroundings in which pure knowledge devoid of will presents itself to us entice us away again from willing. For that reason, in the song and lyrical mood, willing (the personal interest in goals) and the pure contemplation of the available surroundings are blended together in a wonderful mixture: relations between both are sought and imagined; subjective mood, the affection of will communicates its colour to the contemplated surroundings and vice versa in a reflexive movement: the genuine song is the imprint of the mixed and divided feelings of this emotional state.'*

Who could fail to notice in this depiction the fact that lyric poetry is characterized as an incompletely achieved art, an art which as it were reaches its goal only seldom and sporadically, even as a half-art, whose *essence* should consist in the miraculous blending together of willing and pure contemplation, that is of the unaesthetic and the aesthetic state? We assert rather that the whole opposition between subjective and objective, which even Schopenhauer still used as a yardstick to classify the arts, is completely irrelevant to aesthetics, since there the subject, the willing individual who promotes his own ends, can only be conceived as the enemy and not as the origin of art. But in so far as the subject is an artist, he has already been redeemed from his individual will and become as it were a medium, through which the only subject which truly exists celebrates its redemption in appearance. For this above all must be clear to us, as a cause of both humiliation *and* exultation, that the whole comedy of art is not in any way performed for our benefit, for our improvement and edification, and that we are to an even lesser extent the real creators of that world of art: but we may assume that we are already images and artistic projections for the true creator of that world and have our greatest dignity in our meaning as works of art—for only as an *aesthetic phenomenon* are existence and the world *justified* to eternity:—while admittedly our consciousness of this meaning of ours scarcely differs from that which warriors in a painting have of the battle depicted on the canvas. Consequently, our whole knowledge of art is at bottom completely illusory, because we are not as knowing beings at one and identical with that essence, which as sole creator and spectator of that comedy of art prepares for itself an eternal pleasure. Only in so far as the genius in the act of artistic creation fuses with that original artist of the world does he know something about the eternal essence of art: for in that state he miraculously resembles the uncanny image of the fairy-tale, which can turn its eyes inside out and contemplate itself; now he is simultaneously subject and object, simultaneously poet, actor and spectator.

6

With respect to Archilochus, scholarly research has discovered that he introduced the *folk song** into literature, for which achievement he received the unique honour of a place at Homer's side in the universal appreciation of the Greeks. But what is the folk song in comparison to the fully Apollonian epic? What else but the *perpetuum vestigium** of a unification of the Apollonian and the Dionysian; its tremendous diffusion across all peoples, intensifying itself in ever new births, is witness to the strength of that dual artistic drive of nature: the drive which leaves its traces behind in the folk song in a similar way to that in which the orgiastic movements of a people immortalize themselves in its music. It should even be possible to demonstrate historically how that period which was so richly productive of folk songs has at the same time been aroused most powerfully by Dionysian currents, which we must always regard as the substratum and precondition of the folk song.

But the folk song represents for us in the very first instance a musical mirror of the world, an original melody, which now seeks a parallel phenomenon in dream and expresses this in poetry. *So the melody is the first and the universal principle*, which explains why it can sustain several objectivations, in several texts. It is also by far the more important and more necessary principle in the naïve appreciation of the people. Melody gives birth to poetry over and over again; this is exactly what the *verse-form of the folk song* tells us: a phenomenon which I had always regarded with astonishment until I finally came upon this explanation. Whoever examines a collection of folk songs, such as *Des Knaben Wunderhorn*,* on the basis of this theory, will find countless examples of how melody in the continual labour of birth sprays out sparkling images, which in their colourfulness, their sudden variation, even their mad tumbling succession reveal a force wildly unfamiliar to the calm continuous flow of epic appearance. From the standpoint of epic, the uneven and irregular world of images of lyric poetry is simply to be condemned: and the solemn epic rhapsodes* of the Apollonian festivals in the age of Terpander* certainly did just that.

So in the poetry of the folk song we see language stretched to the limit in order to *imitate music*: Archilochus, therefore, represents the beginning of a new world of poetry, one which contradicts the Homeric world in its deepest foundations. Here we find sketched out for us the only possible relationship between poetry and music, word and sound: the word, the image, the concept seeks an expression analogous to music and now feels the force of music in itself. In this sense we may distinguish two main currents in the history of the language of the Greek people, according to whether language imitates the world of phenomena and images or the world of music. We need only give some deeper consideration to the linguistic differences between Homer and Pindar,* differences in colour, in sentence structure, in vocabulary, in order to understand the significance of this opposition; it will become palpably clear that between the ages of Homer and Pindar the *orgiastic flute melodies of Olympus** must have sounded forth, melodies which, even in Aristotle's time, in the midst of an infinitely more developed music, continued to transport listeners in drunken enthusiasm and which in their original effect certainly stimulated contemporary man to imitate them with all the available means of poetic expression. Let me remind the reader here of a well-known phenomenon of our time which cannot but appear offensive to our aesthetics. Again and again, we witness how a Beethoven symphony compels individual listeners to describe it in images, even if, set side by side, the different image-worlds produced by a single piece of music would look fantastically multicoloured, even contradictory: to practise its wit on such comparisons and to overlook the phenomenon which is truly worthy of explanation is absolutely typical of this aesthetics. Even when the composer himself has described a composition in images, as when he describes a symphony as pastoral, one movement as a 'Scene by a Brook', and another as a 'Merry Gathering of Rustics',* these are likewise only allegorical notions born of music—and not somehow objects imitated by music—notions which can tell us nothing whatsoever about the *Dionysian* content of music, and which possess no exclusive value relative to other images. We now have to transfer this process of the discharge of music in images to the young and fresh, linguistically creative mass of a folk community in order to arrive at an idea of how the verse form of the folk song emerged and how the whole linguistic capacity is stimulated by the new principle of the imitation of music.

If we may regard lyric poetry as the imitative lightning burst* of music in images and concepts, then we can now ask: 'In what form does music *appear* in the mirror of images and concepts?' *It appears as will*, in the Schopenhauerian sense, that is, as the opposite of the aesthetic, purely contemplative mood, which is devoid of will. Let us here distinguish as sharply as possible between the concept of essence and that of phenomenon:* for it is, according to its essence, impossible for music to be will, because as such it would have to be completely excluded from the sphere of art—since will is the unaesthetic in itself—; but music appears none the less as will. For, in order to express the artistic phenomenon in images, the lyric poet needs all the impulses of passion, from whispering inclination to rumbling madness; subject to the drive to speak about music in Apollonian allegories,* he understands the whole of nature and himself in nature only as that which eternally wills, desires, longs. But in so far as he interprets music in images,* he himself remains at rest in the calm sea of Apollonian contemplation, however much what he sees through the medium of music is caught in the throes of urgent and forceful movement. Indeed, when he sees himself through that same medium, then his own image appears to him as a feeling of dissatisfaction: his own willing, longing, groaning, exulting is to him an allegory by means of which he interprets music to himself. This is the phenomenon of the lyric poet: as Apollonian genius he interprets music through the image of the will, while he himself, completely detached from the greedy craving of will, is the pure unclouded eye of the sun.

This whole discussion turns on the point that lyric poetry is dependent on the spirit of music, while music itself, in its full unrestricted form, has no *need* for the image and the concept, but rather only *tolerates* their proximity. Lyric poetry can express nothing which was not already present at the highest level of universality and validity in the music which compelled it to speak in images. The world symbolism of music utterly exceeds the grasp of language, because it refers symbolically to the original contradiction and pain at the heart of the original Unity, and therefore symbolizes a sphere which exists over and above all phenomena. In comparison with this, all phenomena are merely allegories:* so *language*, as organ and symbol of phenomena, can never reveal the innermost depths of music, and as soon as it engages in the imitation of music, can only ever skim the surface, while even the most eloquent lyric poetry is powerless to bring the deepest meaning of music as much as one step closer to us.

7

We must now avail ourselves of all the principles of art discussed so far in order to find our way in the labyrinth, for there is no other way to describe it, of the *origin of Greek tragedy*. I do not think I am speaking nonsense if I say that the problem of this origin has not yet even been seriously posed, let alone solved, no matter how many times before the torn and fluttering shreds of the ancient tradition have been sewn together and then torn asunder. This tradition* tells us decisively that *tragedy emerged from the tragic chorus* and was originally only the chorus and nothing but the chorus: which obliges us to look into the heart of the tragic chorus as the real original drama, without somehow satisfying ourselves with the current artistic clichés—that the chorus represents the ideal spectator or represents the princely area of the stage to the people. The latter explanation, which sounds sublime to many politicians—as if the immutable moral law of the democratic Athenians were represented in the people's chorus, which is always in the right in its dealings with the passionate excesses and extravagances of the kings—might well be suggested by a word of Aristotle's:* none the less, it has no influence whatsoever on the original formation of tragedy, since those purely religious origins exclude the whole opposition of people and prince and indeed any political-social sphere whatsoever; but with reference to the classical form of the chorus known to us from Aeschylus and Sophocles we might also regard it as blasphemy to speak of a presentiment of a 'constitutional representation of the people', a blasphemy from which others have not shrunk. The ancient state constitutions had no knowledge of constitutional representation of the people *in praxi** and hopefully did not even have so much as a 'presentiment' of it in their tragedy.

Much more famous than this political explanation of the chorus is A. W. Schlegel's thought which advises us to regard the chorus to a certain extent as the epitome and essence of the audience, as the 'ideal spectator'.* This opinion, when compared with that historical tradition which tells us that tragedy was nothing but the chorus, reveals itself for what it is, a crude, unscientific, yet brilliant assertion, whose brilliance derives exclusively from its concentrated form of expression, from the truly German prejudice in favour of everything going by the name of 'ideal', and from our momentary astonishment. We are indeed astonished once we compare the theatre public which we know so well with the chorus and ask ourselves if it would be at all possible to idealize this public into something analogous to the tragic chorus. We silently deny this and are no less surprised by the audacity of Schlegel's assertion than by the completely different nature of the Greek public. For we had always believed that the true spectator, whoever he might be, must always remain aware of the fact that he has before him a work of art and not an empirical reality: while the Greek tragic chorus is compelled to recognize incarnations of real existence in the figures of the stage. The chorus of Oceanides really believes that it sees the Titan Prometheus* before it and considers itself as real as the god of the stage. And we are asked to believe that this should be the highest and purest kind of spectator, one which like the Oceanides would consider Prometheus as physically present and real? And so it would be the sign of the ideal spectator that he would run onto the stage and free the god from his torture? We had believed in an aesthetic public and considered the individual spectator the better equipped the more he could regard the work of art as art, that is, aesthetically; and now Schlegel's expression suggests to us that the completely ideal spectator lets the world of the stage work its effect on him not at all in an aesthetic but in an embodied and empirical way. Oh these Greeks! we sighed; they overturn our aesthetics. But being used to that, we repeated Schlegel's aphorism every time the chorus came up in discussion.

But here the tradition, which is quite categorical, bears witness against Schlegel: the chorus in itself, without a stage, the primitive form of tragedy, is not consistent with the chorus of the ideal spectator. What sort of artistic genre would it be which was derived from the concept of the spectator, and which was represented in its true form by the 'spectator in himself'? The spectator without a play is a nonsensical concept. We fear that the birth of tragedy can be explained neither by reverence for the moral intelligence of the masses nor by the concept of the spectator without a play, and consider such shallow points of view incapable of even skimming the surface of this deep problem.

Schiller had already divulged an infinitely more valuable insight into the meaning of the chorus in the famous foreword to *The Bride of Messina*,* where he viewed the chorus as a living wall which tragedy built around itself in order to shut out the real world and to protect its ideal ground and poetic freedom.

Using this as his main weapon, Schiller engages in a struggle against the commonly held concept of the natural, against the illusion commonly demanded of dramatic poetry. According to Schiller, even if in the theatre the daylight is merely artificial, the architecture merely symbolic and the metrical language of an ideal character, the naturalist error still dominates overall: for Schiller, it is not enough that the very thing which constitutes the essence of all poetry be merely tolerated as a poetic licence. The introduction of the chorus is, for Schiller, the decisive step through which war with naturalism in art is openly and honestly declared.—It seems to me that this is the kind of point of view which our arrogant and condescending age dismisses with the catchword 'pseudo-idealism'.* I fear that with our contemporary reverence for the natural and the real we have arrived at the opposite pole of all idealism, that is, in the region of the wax museum. There too there is a kind of art, as in certain contemporary popular novels: only spare us the torture of asking us to believe that this art has overcome the 'pseudo-idealism' of Schiller and Goethe.

Admittedly, the ground upon which the Greek satyr chorus, the chorus of the original tragedy, used to tread, is, following Schiller's correct insight, an 'ideal' ground, a ground elevated high above the real paths trodden by mortals. For this chorus, the Greek has erected the scaffolding of an invented *state of nature* and placed upon it invented *creatures of nature*. Tragedy has grown up on this foundation and has of course from the very beginning dispensed with an embarrassing counterfeiting of reality. And yet this is not a world arbitrarily imagined into existence between heaven and earth; but rather a world of equal reality and credibility to that which Olympus and its inhabitants possessed for the Hellenic believer. The satyr as Dionysian chorist lives in a reality admitted by faith, under the sanction of myth and religion. The fact that tragedy begins with him, that the Dionysian wisdom of tragedy speaks through him is a phenomenon which disconcerts us as much as the original emergence of tragedy from the chorus. Perhaps we might gain a starting point for reflection if I make the assertion that the satyr, the invented creature of nature, has the same relationship to the man of culture as Dionysian music has to civilization. Richard Wagner said of the latter that it would be cancelled and absorbed by music as lamplight is by daylight.* The Greek man of culture, I believe, felt himself cancelled and absorbed in a similar way by the chorus of satyrs: and this is the most immediate effect of Dionysian tragedy, that state and society, indeed the whole chasm separating man from man, gives way to an overpowering feeling of unity which leads back to the heart of nature. The metaphysical consolation— with which, as I have already suggested here, all true tragedy leaves us—that life at the bottom of things, in spite of the passing of phenomena, remains indestructibly powerful and pleasurable, this consolation appears in embodied clarity in the chorus of satyrs, of creatures of nature who live on as it were ineradicably behind all civilization and remain eternally the same in spite of the passing of generations and of the history of peoples.

The profound Hellene, who is uniquely equipped for the most delicate and intense suffering, who has directed his acute gaze down into the middle of that fearful swirling compulsive process of annihilation which goes by the name of world history as well as into the cruelty of nature, and is in danger of longing for a Buddhist negation of the will,* finds consolation in this chorus. Rescued by art, he is rescued, for its own purposes, by—life.

The ecstasy of the Dionysian state, with its annihilation of the usual limits and borders of existence, contains for its duration a *lethargic* element in which all past personal experience is submerged. And so this chasm of oblivion separates the world of everyday reality from that of Dionysian reality. However, as soon as that everyday reality returns to consciousness, it is experienced for what it is with disgust: an ascetic mood which negates the will is the fruit of those conditions. In this sense the Dionysian man is similar to Hamlet:* both have at one time cast a true glance into the essence of things, they have acquired *knowledge*, and action is repugnant to them; for their action can change nothing in the eternal essence of things, they feel that it is laughable or shameful that they are expected to repair a world which is out of joint.* Knowledge kills action, to action belongs the veil of illusion—that is the lesson of Hamlet, not that cheap wisdom of Hans the Dreamer,* who fails to act because he reflects too much, as a result as it were of an excess of possibilities; not reflection, no!—but true knowledge, insight into the horrific truth, outweighs any motive leading to action, in Hamlet as well as in the Dionysian man. Now no consolation is accepted, the longing goes beyond the world after death, goes beyond even the gods, now existence, together with its glittering reflection in the gods or in an immortal other world, is negated. Conscious of the truth once glimpsed, man now sees all around him only the horrific or the absurd aspects of existence,* now he understands the symbolic aspect of Ophelia's fate,* now he recognizes the wisdom of the forest god Silenus: it disgusts him.

Here, at this point of extreme danger for the will, *art* draws near as the enchantress who comes to rescue and heal; only she can reshape that disgust at the thought of the horrific or absurd aspects of life into notions with which it is possible to live: these are the *sublime*, the artistic taming of the horrific, and the *comic*,* the artistic discharge of disgust at the absurd. The satyr chorus of the dithyramb is the rescuing deed of Greek art; those feelings previously described exhaust themselves in the middle world of these companions of Dionysus.

8

The satyr and the idyllic shepherd* of more modern times are both products of a longing for the original and the natural; but with what firm and fearless hands did the Greek reach out for his man of the forest, and how shamefully and timidly modern man dallies with the flattering image of a meek and mild flute-playing shepherd! Nature before knowledge has set to work on it, before the bolts of culture have been broken open—that is what the Greek saw in his satyr, which he did not yet identify with the ape.* On the contrary: what he saw was the archetype of man, the expression of his highest and strongest impulses, as excited enthusiast, delighted by the proximity of the god, as a compassionate comrade, in whom the suffering of the god is repeated, as wise prophet from the depths of the breast of nature, as symbol of the sexual omnipotence of nature, which the Greek habitually regards with reverence and astonishment. The satyr was something sublime and divine: he could appear no other way to the painfully broken gaze of the Dionysian man. The sanitized fabrication of the shepherd would have insulted him: his eye dwelt with sublime satisfaction on the magnificent handwriting of nature* as it flourished here in the open; here the illusion of culture was wiped away from the archetype of man, here the true man revealed himself, the bearded satyr, exulting in the worship of his god. Before him, the man of culture shrivelled up into a deceitful caricature. Schiller is right again as far as these beginnings of tragic art are concerned: the chorus is a living wall erected against the pounding storm of reality, because it—the satyr chorus—is a copy of a more truthful, more real, more complete image of existence than the man of culture who commonly considers himself the sole reality. The sphere of poetry does not lie outside the world, as the fantastic impossibility imagined by the brain of a poet: it wants to be the very opposite, the unadorned expression* of truth, and must therefore cast off the deceitful finery of the supposed reality of the man of culture. The contrast between this real truth of nature and the lie of culture which poses as the sole reality is similar to that between the eternal core of things, the thing in itself, and the whole world of phenomena: and just as tragedy with its metaphysical consolation points to the eternal life of that core of existence, in contrast to the continual decline of phenomena, so the symbolism of the satyr chorus already expresses in allegorical form that original relationship between thing in itself and phenomenon. That idyllic shepherd of modern man is only a counterfeit of the sum of cultural illusions which he regards as nature; the Dionysian Greek desires truth and nature in their highest power—he sees himself magically transformed into the satyr.

The infatuated crowd of servants of Dionysus exults under the influence of such moods and knowledge: the latter's power transforms them before their very eyes, so that they imagine themselves as recreated geniuses of nature, as satyrs. The later constitution of the tragic chorus is the artistic imitation of this natural phenomenon; one for which a separation of those who were Dionysian spectators from those under the Dionysian spell was admittedly necessary. Only it must be remembered at all times that the public of Attic tragedy rediscovered itself in the chorus of the orchestra,* that there was at bottom no opposition between public and chorus: for everything is only a great sublime chorus of dancing and singing satyrs or of people who let themselves be represented by these satyrs. Schlegel's description must reveal itself to us here in a deeper sense. The chorus is the 'ideal spectator' in so far as it is the sole *beholder*, the beholder of the stage's vision-world. A public of spectators as we know it was unknown to the Greeks: in their theatres, with their terraces rising in concentric circles around the auditorium, it was possible for everyone to have a real *overview* of the whole surrounding world of culture and in satisfied contemplation to imagine oneself a member of the chorus. Following this insight we may call the chorus in its primitive stage in the original tragedy a self-reflection of the Dionysian man: a phenomenon which can be most clearly demonstrated by the case of the actor who sees the image of the role he is to play hover before his eyes as if he could reach out and touch it. The satyr is in the very first place a vision of the Dionysian mass, as the world of the stage is in turn a vision of this satyr chorus: the force of this vision is strong enough to deaden the gaze to the impression of 'reality', to the surrounding rows of seated men of culture. The form of the Greek theatre recalls a secluded mountain valley: the architecture of the stage appears like a radiant image from the clouds, beheld from a mountain peak by the swirling crowd of Bacchic enthusiasts as the magnificent frame within which the image of Dionysus is revealed to them.

In the terms of our scholarly view of the elementary artistic processes, the original artistic phenomenon which we introduce here by way of explanation of the tragic chorus borders on the offensive; while nothing could be clearer than the fact that the poet is only a poet in so far as he sees himself surrounded by figures who act out their lives before him as he gazes into their innermost being. Through a peculiar weakness of our modern constitution, we tend to have an overly complicated and abstract conception of the original aesthetic phenomenon. For the true poet, metaphor is no rhetorical figure but rather an image which takes the place of something else, which really hovers before him in the place of a concept. A character is for him not something whole composed from an assembly of individual traits but rather a person who appears before his eyes with all the urgency of life, a person who differs from the same vision of the painter only through continual movement in life and action. What makes Homer's descriptions so much more vivid to the eye than those of all other poets? The fact that his eye sees so much more. We talk so abstractly about poetry because we are all used to being bad poets. At bottom, the aesthetic phenomenon is simple: if one has the capacity always to see before one a vivid play and to live continually surrounded by crowds of ghosts, then one is a poet; if one as much as feels the drive to transform oneself and to speak out of other bodies and souls, then one is a dramatist.

The Dionysian arousal is capable of communicating to a whole mass of people this artistic constitution which allows one to see oneself surrounded by such a crowd of ghosts, with which one knows oneself to be intimately at one. This process of the tragic chorus is the original *dramatic* phenomenon: to see oneself transformed before one's very eyes and now to act as if one had really entered into another body and another character. This process stands at the beginning of the development of the drama. Here there is something different from the rhapsode who does not fuse with his images, but like the painter sees them outside himself with an observing eye; here there is already a surrender of the individual through an entering into an unfamiliar nature. And indeed this phenomenon emerged in epidemic proportions; a whole crowd felt itself enchanted in this way. The dithyramb is therefore essentially different from any other chorus song. The virgins who ceremonially approach the temple of Apollo bearing laurel branches and singing a procession song remain who they are and retain their names as citizens: the dithyrambic chorus is a chorus of people who have been transformed, who have completely forgotten their past as citizens, their social position: they have become the timeless servants of their god, living outside all spheres of society. All the other choral lyric poetry of the Hellenes is only a great intensification of the individual Apollonian singer; while in the dithyramb a community of unconscious actors stands before us who even among themselves regard themselves as transformed.

Such enchantment is the precondition of all dramatic art. Under the influence of its spell, the Dionysian enthusiast sees himself as satyr, *and as satyr he in turn beholds the god*, that is, transformed in this way he sees a new vision outside himself, as the Apollonian completion of his state. With this vision, the drama is complete.

Following this insight, we must understand Greek tragedy as the Dionysian chorus which again and again discharges itself in an Apollonian world of images. So those chorus parts which are interwoven through tragedy are to a certain extent the maternal womb of the whole so-called dialogue, that is, of the whole world of the stage, of the real drama. In several successive discharges, this original ground of tragedy radiates that vision of drama: which is thoroughly dream-phenomenon and to that extent of an epic nature, but on the other hand, as objectivation of a Dionysian state, represents not the Apollonian redemption in appearance, but on the contrary the shattering of the individual and his union with the original being. Thus drama is the concrete Apollonian representation of Dionysian insights and effects and as a result a huge chasm separates it from epic.

This view of ours offers a full explanation of the *chorus* of Greek tragedy, the symbol of the whole mass in Dionysian arousal. While we, accustomed to the place of the chorus on the modern stage, and especially of the opera chorus,* could not understand how the Greek tragic chorus should be older, more original, even more important than the real 'action'—as this was yet so clearly transmitted by the tradition—while we in turn could not reconcile that great importance and originality as outlined in the tradition with the fact that the chorus was composed exclusively of lowly servant beings, even, in the first place, of goat-like satyrs, while the orchestra in front of the stage remained a constant enigma to us, we arrived at the insight that the stage together with the action was basically and originally conceived only as a *vision*, that the sole 'reality' is precisely the chorus, which produces the vision from itself and speaks of it with the whole symbolism of dance, music, and word. In its vision this chorus beholds its lord and master Dionysus and is therefore eternally the chorus of *servants*: it watches how the latter, the god, suffers and glorifies himself, and therefore itself refrains from *action*. But in this attitude of complete service to the god, the chorus is the highest, indeed Dionysian expression, of *nature* and speaks therefore, like nature, oracular words of wisdom in a state of enthusiastic excitement: as the *compassionate* chorus, it is at the same time the *wise* chorus, proclaiming the truth from the heart of the world. It is in this way then that the fantastic and apparently so offensive figure of the wise and enthusiastic satyr emerges, the satyr who is at the same time the 'stupid man' in contrast to the god: a copy of nature and its strongest drives, even their symbol and at the same time proclaimer of their wisdom and art: musician, poet, dancer, visionary in *one* person.

Dionysus, the real hero of the stage and centre of the vision, is, according to this knowledge and according to the tradition, at first, in the most ancient period of tragedy, not truly present, but is only imagined as present: that is, tragedy is originally only 'chorus' and not 'drama'. Later the attempt is made to show the god as real and to represent the figure of the vision together with its transfiguring frame as visible to every eye: this is the beginning of 'drama' in the narrower sense. Now the dithyrambic chorus is given the task of providing Dionysian stimulation to the mood of the listeners to the point that, when the tragic hero appears on stage, they do not see the awkwardly masked man, but rather a figure of the vision born as it were out of their own rapture. If we imagine Admetus, deep in remembrance and absorbed spiritual contemplation of his recently deceased wife Alcestis,*—if we imagine his sudden agitated trembling, his frantic comparison, his instinctive conviction, as a veiled image of a woman of similar build and gait is brought towards him—then we have an analogy for the feeling with which the spectator under the influence of Dionysian stimulation saw the arrival onstage of the god, with whose suffering he had already become as one. He involuntarily transferred the whole image of the god which trembles magically before his soul to that masked figure and as it were dissolved its reality in a ghostly unreality. This is the Apollonian dream-state, in which the world of the day veils itself and a new world, clearer, more intelligible, more gripping than the other and yet more shadowy, in constant flux, is born before our eyes. Accordingly we recognize in tragedy a far-reaching stylistic contrast: in the Dionysian lyric of the chorus and in the Apollonian dream-world of the stage, language, colour, mobility, dynamic of speech diverge into entirely separate spheres of expression. The Apollonian phenomena in which Dionysus takes on objective form are no longer, like the music of the chorus, 'an eternal sea, a changing weave, a glowing life',* they are no longer restricted to those forces which were only sensed but not condensed into images, in which the enthusiastic servant of Dionysus felt the proximity of the god: now, from the stage, the clarity and fixity of epic form speaks to him, now Dionysus no longer speaks through forces, but speaks as an epic hero, almost in the language of Homer.

9

Everything which rises to the surface in the Apollonian part of Greek tragedy, in the dialogue, looks simple, transparent, and beautiful. In this sense, the dialogue is a copy of the Hellene whose nature reveals itself in dance, because in dance the greatest force remains potential, but betrays itself in the suppleness and sumptuousness of movement. In this way, the language of the Sophoclean heroes surprises us by its Apollonian certainty and brightness, so that we immediately delude ourselves that we have looked into the innermost depths of their essence, with some surprise that the bottom of these depths lies so near the surface. But once we turn our gaze from the character of the hero as he approaches and visibly develops on the surface—a character which is at bottom nothing more than a projected image thrown onto a dark wall,* that is, phenomenon through and through— then we penetrate rather into the myth which projects itself in these bright reflections and we suddenly experience a phenom- enon which is the reverse of a well-known optical effect. If, after a powerful attempt to stare at the sun, we turn away blinded with dark spots before our eyes, as a remedy so to speak, then the projected images of the Sophoclean hero are the opposite of this—in short, the Apollonian qualities of the mask are the necessary results of a glance into the terrifying inner world of nature, bright spots so to speak to heal the eyes which have been damaged by the sight of the terrible darkness. Only in this sense are we entitled to believe that we have correctly understood the serious and significant concept of 'Greek serenity'; while, admit- tedly, the mistaken understanding of this concept of serenity is still to be encountered safe and sound on all highways and byways.

Sophocles understood the most painful figure of the Greek

stage, the hapless *Oedipus*,* as the noble man who is destined to error and misery in spite of his wisdom, but who finally through his great suffering casts a beneficial spell on those around him, a spell which endures beyond his death. The noble man does not sin, the profound poet wants to tell us: all law, all natural order, even the moral world may be destroyed by his actions, but precisely through these actions a higher enchanted circle of effects is drawn, which build a new world on the ruins of the old overturned one. This is what the poet, in so far as he is at the same time a religious thinker, wants to tell us: as poet he shows us first a wonderfully intricate knot* of a case, which the judge slowly unravels, twist by twist, in the process bringing about his own ruin; the genuine Hellenic joy at this dialectical unravelling is so great that in the process an element of superior serenity comes over the whole work, which everywhere blunts the horrific presuppositions of the case. In *Oedipus at Colonus** we meet the same serenity, but elevated and infinitely transfigured: opposite the old man afflicted by an excess of misery, the old man who is abandoned to everything which comes his way purely as a *suffering man*—stands the heavenly serenity which descends from the divine sphere and indicates to us that the hero reaches his highest activity, which extends far beyond his life, in this passive attitude, a passivity to which all the conscious hopes and endeavours of his earlier life have led in spite of themselves. In this way, the knot of the Oedipus fable, which seems inextricably intertwined to the mortal eye, is slowly unravelled—and the deepest human joy overcomes us as a result of this divine counterpart of the dialectic. Once we have done the poet justice with this explanation, the question remains if the content of the myth is thereby exhausted: and here it becomes clear that the whole view of the poet is nothing but that projected image which healing nature holds before us after a glance into the abyss. Oedipus the murderer of his father, the husband of his mother, Oedipus the solver of the riddle of the Sphinx! What does the secret trinity of these fateful deeds tell us? There is a very ancient, popular belief, particularly prevalent in Persia, according to which a wise magus* can only be born from incest: which we, with respect to the riddle-solving and mother-marrying Oedipus must immediately interpret as follows—that wherever prophetic and magic powers break the spell of present and future, the inflexible law of individuation, and above all the real enchantment of nature, this must have been brought about by a monstrous transgression of nature—as in this instance incest; for how could nature be forced to give up its secrets otherwise than by a triumphant violation, that is, through the unnatural? I see this knowledge stamped in that appalling trinity of the fate of Oedipus: the same man who solves the riddle of nature—of that ambiguous Sphinx—must also break the holiest principles of nature as the murderer of his father and the husband of his mother. Indeed, the myth seems to want to whisper to us that wisdom and especially Dionysian wisdom is an abomination against nature, that he who plunges nature into the abyss of annihilation must experience the dissolution of nature as it affects him personally. 'The point of wisdom turns against the wise man; wisdom is a crime against nature':* such are the terrifying principles which the myth cries out to us; but the Hellenic poet like a shaft of sunlight touches the myth's sublime and fearful column of Memnon,* so that it suddenly begins to sing—in Sophoclean melodies!

To the glory of passivity I now juxtapose the glory of activity, which radiates around the *Prometheus* of Aeschylus.* What Aeschylus had to say to us here as a thinker, what he as poet however could only intimate to us through his allegorical image, the youthful Goethe was able to reveal to us in the bold words of his Prometheus:

> Here I sit, make men
> In my image,
> A race the same as I,
> In order to suffer, to cry,
> To delight and to enjoy,
> And to show you no respect,
> Just the same as I!*

Man, as he raises himself to Titanic stature, wins a culture for himself through struggle and forces the gods to form an alliance

with him, because he holds their existence and limits in his hands
in the form of his very own wisdom. But the most miraculous
thing about that Prometheus poem, which according to its basic
conception is the real hymn of impiety, is the deep Aeschylean
predisposition towards *justice*: the immeasurable suffering of the
audacious 'individual' on the one side, and the divine need, even
presentiment of a twilight of the gods* on the other, the power of
both of these worlds of suffering which compels reconciliation,
metaphysical unity—all this recalls in the strongest way the
centre and highest principle of the Aeschylean view of the world,
which sees the Moira* reign over gods and men as eternal justice.
In considering the astonishing audacity with which Aeschylus
places the Olympian world on his scales of justice, we must recall
that the profound Greek had an irrevocably solid substratum of
metaphysical thought in his mysteries and that all his feelings of
scepticism could be discharged on the Olympians. The Greek
artist in particular experienced with respect to these deities an
obscure sense of mutual dependence; and this is precisely the
feeling symbolized in Aeschylus' *Prometheus*. The Titanic artist
found in himself the defiant belief in his capacity to create men
and at least to destroy Olympian gods: and this through his higher wisdom which he was admittedly forced to expiate through
eternal suffering. The magnificent 'ability' of the great genius,
which is cheap at the price of even eternal suffering, the severe
pride of the *artist*—that is the content and soul of Aeschylean
poetry, while Sophocles in his *Oedipus* intones a prelude to the
song of triumph of the *holy man*. But even Aeschylus' interpretation of the myth does not plumb the astonishing depths of its
horror: rather the artist's delight in change, the disaster-defying
serenity of artistic creation is only a bright image of clouds and
sky reflected in a dark lake of sadness. The story of Prometheus
belongs from the beginning to the entire Aryan community of
peoples* and is evidence of their gift for the profound and the
tragic, indeed it may not be beyond the bounds of probability that
this myth contains precisely the same characteristic meaning for
the Aryan character which the myth of the Fall* possesses for the
Semitic character, and that these two myths are related to one

another like brother and sister. The presupposition of the Prometheus myth is the extravagant value ascribed by the naïveté of mankind to fire as the true palladium* of every ascending culture: but that man should freely control fire and not merely receive it as a gift from heaven, sparked off by a bolt of lightning or ignited by the heat of the sun, appeared to the contemplative original man as a sacrilege, as a theft committed against divine nature. And so the first philosophical problem immediately establishes an embarrassing insoluble contradiction between man and god, placed like a boulder before the gate of every culture. The best and the highest blessing which humanity can receive is achieved through sacrilege and its consequences must be accepted, namely the whole flood of suffering and troubles with which the insulted gods have no other choice but to afflict humanity as it strives nobly upward: a severe thought which, through the *dignity* ascribed to the sacrilege, stands in strange contrast to the Semitic myth of the Fall, in which curiosity, dissimulation, the susceptibility to be led astray, lasciviousness, in short a series of eminently feminine feelings, are viewed as the origin of evil. What distinguishes the Aryan conception is the sublime view of the *active sin* as the real Promethean virtue: which at the same time reveals the ethical substratum of pessimistic tragedy as the *justification* of human evil, and even of human guilt as the suffering caused by it. The misfortune in the essence of things—which the contemplative Aryan is disinclined to interpret away—the contradiction in the heart of the world reveals itself to him as a collision of different worlds, for example of a divine and a human world, each of which individually has right on its side, but must suffer for its individuation as an individual world alongside others. In the heroic impulse towards the universal, in the attempt to step outside the spell of individuation and to become the *single* essence of the world, the individual suffers within himself the original contradiction hidden in things, that is, he commits sacrilege and suffers. In this way, sacrilege is understood by the Aryans as male, sin* by the Semites as female, just as the original sacrilege is committed by man and the original sin committed by woman. Moreover, as the witches' chorus says:

We do not mind so much:
With a thousand steps the woman arrives;
Yet no matter how she rushes,
With a single leap, the man gets there.*

Whoever understands the innermost core of the Prometheus story—namely, the necessity of sacrilege as it is imposed on the Titanically striving individual—must also immediately sense how un-Apollonian this pessimistic conception is, for Apollo wants to bring individual beings to rest precisely by drawing boundaries between them, boundaries which his demands for self-knowledge and moderation impress upon us again and again as the most sacred laws of the world. But lest under the influence of this Apollonian tendency form might harden into Egyptian inflexibility and coldness,* lest in the course of the effort to prescribe the path and range of the individual wave, the movement of the whole lake might die, from time to time the high tide of the Dionysian destroyed once again all those little eddies in which the spell cast by the one-sided Apollonian 'will' sought to confine Hellenic culture. The sudden surge of the Dionysian tide lifts the small individual mountains of waves on its back, as the brother of Prometheus, the Titan Atlas,* did the earth. This Titanic impulse, to become as it were the Atlas of all individuals and to carry them ever higher and further on a broad back, is the common element shared by the Promethean and the Dionysian principles. The Aeschylean Prometheus is in this regard a Dionysian mask, while in that previously mentioned predisposition towards justice Aeschylus betrays to the insightful observer his paternal descent from Apollo, the god of individuation and of just limits. So the essential duality of the Aeschylean Prometheus, his simultaneously Dionysian and Apollonian nature might be expressed in conceptual terms as follows: 'All that exists is just and unjust and equally justified in both.'

That is your world! That is a world indeed!*—

10

According to an incontrovertible tradition, the suffering of
Dionysus was the sole subject of the earliest form of Greek tragedy and for a long time there was no other available stage hero
than Dionysus himself. And we may maintain with equal assur-
ance that up to the time of Euripides Dionysus remained the
tragic hero, and that all the famous figures of the Greek stage,
Prometheus, Oedipus, and so on, are only masks of that original
hero Dionysus. That behind all these masks a deity is hidden
is the essential reason for the typical 'ideality' of those famous
figures, so often a source of wonder. Someone or other once
affirmed that all individuals taken as individuals are comic and
therefore untragic:* from which it might be deduced that the
Greeks were absolutely *incapable* of tolerating individuals on the
tragic stage. And in fact, this is how they seem to have felt: as
above all else that Platonic distinction and evaluation of the 'idea'
as opposed to the 'idol',* the copy, is deeply rooted in the Hellenic
character. But if we were to use Plato's terminology, then the
tragic figures of the Hellenic stage could be described in the
following terms: the one truly real Dionysus appears in a multiplicity of forms, in the mask of a hero engaged in struggle and as
it were entangled in the net of the individual will. In the form in
which the god now appears, speaks and acts, he resembles an
erring, striving, suffering individual: and that he *appears* at all
with such epic certainty and clarity is the effect of Apollo the
interpreter of dreams, who through this allegorical appearance*
interprets to the chorus its Dionysian state. In truth, however,
this hero is the suffering Dionysus of the mysteries, that god
experiencing in himself the agonies of individuation, the god of
whom marvellous myths speak, telling the story of how he as a
boy was dismembered by the Titans and is now worshipped in
that state as Zagreus:* which suggests that this dismemberment,
the properly Dionysian *suffering*, is similar to a transformation
into earth, wind, fire, and water,* and that we should regard
the state of individuation as the source and original cause of

suffering, as something objectionable in itself. From the smiles of this Dionysus sprang the Olympian gods, from his tears sprang man. In that existence as dismembered god, Dionysus possesses the dual nature of a cruel, wild daemon and of a meek and mild sovereign. The hope of the epopts* was directed towards a rebirth of Dionysus, a rebirth which we must begin to sense obscurely as the end of individuation: this third coming of Dionysus was greeted by the roar of the epopts' song of jubilation. And only in this hope does a ray of joy cross the face of the world which is torn asunder and broken into individuals: as represented in myth through the figure of Demeter,* sunk in eternal mourning, who only experiences *joy* once again when she is told that she may give birth to Dionysus *once more*. In the views cited here, we have already assembled all the components of a profound and pessim- istic view of the world and at the same time *tragedy's doctrine of the mysteries*: the fundamental knowledge of the unity of all that exists, the consideration of individuation as the original cause of evil, art as the joyful hope that the spell of individuation is to be broken, as the presentiment of a restored unity.

We have already suggested that the Homeric epic is the poetry of the Olympian culture, in which it sings its own song of tri- umph over the terrors of the struggle with the Titans. Now, under the overpowering influence of tragic poetry, the Homeric myths are reborn again and again in different form and their metempsychosis* shows that in the interim Olympian culture too has been defeated by an even more profound world-view. The defiant Titan Prometheus announced to his Olympian torturer that one day his rule would be threatened by the greatest danger, if he did not enter into an alliance with him at the right moment. In Aeschylus we recognize the alliance between the frightened Zeus, fearful of his demise, and the Titan. In this way, the earlier age of the Titans was retroactively brought back from Tartarus* into the light. The philosophy of wild and naked nature watches with the undisguised expression of truth the myths of the Homeric world as they dance past in procession: the myths grow pale, tremble before the lightning-like gaze of this goddess—until the powerful fist of the Dionysian artist forces them into the service of a new deity. The Dionysian truth takes over the whole domain of myth as a symbolic language for *its* insights and expresses these partly in the public cult of tragedy, partly in the secret rituals of dramatic mystery festivals, but always under the veil of the old myths. What power was this, which freed Prometheus from his vultures and transformed myth into a vehicle for Dionysian wisdom? It is the Herculean power of music: which, having reached its highest manifestation in tragedy, was able to interpret myth with a new and profound significance; a process which we had earlier already characterized as the most powerful capacity of music. For it is the fate of every myth gradually to creep into the narrow defile of an alleged historical reality and to be treated by a later period as a unique fact with historical claims: and the Greeks were already well on the way to changing the stamp of their entire youth, transforming it with acuity and whimsy from a mythical dream into a historico-pragmatic *history*.* For this is how religions usually die out: namely, when the mythical presuppositions of a religion are systematized as a finished sum of historical events under the strict rational eye of a dogmatic conviction and when one begins to mount an anxious defence of their credibility, when therefore the feeling for myth dies out and is replaced by religion's claim to historical foundations. The newly reborn genius of Dionysian music now took hold of this dying myth: and in its hands it bloomed once again, with colours never seen before, with a scent which aroused a longing presentiment of a metaphysical world. After this last radiant appearance, the myth collapses, its leaves wither, and soon its faded and ravaged flowers are scattered by the wind in all directions, pursued by the scornful Lucians* of the ancient world. Through tragedy, myth achieves its deepest content, its most expressive form; it rises once again, like a wounded hero, and the whole excess of its force, together with the calm wisdom of the dying man, burns in its eyes with a last powerful gleam.

What was it you wanted, sacrilegious Euripides, when you sought to force this dying myth once again into your service? It died at your violent hands: and now you needed a masked imitation myth,* which like Hercules' ape* could do no more than dress itself up in the old grandeur. And just as myth died on you, so too did the genius of music: even when you plundered with craven grasping hands all the gardens of music, you never managed to produce anything but a masked imitation music. And because you had abandoned Dionysus, you were abandoned by Apollo as well; rouse all passions from their camp and put them under the spell of your enchanted circle, sharpen and hone to perfection for the speeches of your heroes a sophistical dialectic*—even your heroes possess nothing more than masked imitation passions and deliver nothing more than masked imitation speeches.

II

Greek tragedy met her end in a different way from all her older sister-genres: she committed suicide,* as a result of an insoluble conflict, and so she died a tragic death, while all her sister-genres passed away beautifully and peacefully at an advanced age. For if it is fitting for a happy disposition to depart from life painlessly, leaving behind beautiful descendants, then the end of those older genres shows us such a happy disposition: they fade slowly, and before their dying gaze the even more beautiful new generation already stands with a courageous gesture, impatiently craning its neck. The death of Greek tragedy, on the other hand, left behind a deep feeling of great emptiness; as once Greek ships at the time of Tiberius* heard from an isolated island the shattering cry: 'The great Pan is dead',* so now like a painful note of lament, the following words rang out throughout the Hellenic world: 'Tragedy is dead! And along with her, poetry itself has perished. Away, away with you pale, emaciated epigones!* Away to Hades, so that there you can for once eat your fill on the crumbs of the masters of a previous age!'

But then, when another new artistic genre flourished nevertheless, one which honoured tragedy as her precursor and mistress, then we saw to our horror that she certainly bore the traits of her mother, but those which had come to the fore in the course of her long struggle with death. It was *Euripides** who fought this death struggle of tragedy; the later genre is known as the *New Attic Comedy*.* In it, the degenerate form of tragedy lived on, as a monument to her laborious and violent demise.

This context explains the passionate affection felt by the poets of the New Comedy towards Euripides; so we are no longer puzzled by Philemon's desire to have himself hanged immediately in order to seek out Euripides* in the underworld, if only he could be sure that the dead poet was still of sound mind. But if, without claiming to say something exhaustive, one wants to summarize briefly what Euripides has in common with Menander* and Philemon and what for them seemed so exciting and exemplary in his work, then one need only say that Euripides brought the *spectator* onto the stage. He who has recognized the stuff of which the heroes of the Promethean tragic poets were made before Euripides, and how far it was from their intentions to bring onstage the faithful mask of reality, will be clear about the completely deviant nature of the Euripidean tendency. Through him, the man of everyday life pushed his way from the auditorium to the stage; now the mirror, in which previously only the great and bold traits came to expression, showed that embarrassing fidelity which reproduces the botched lines of nature. Odysseus, the typical Hellene of the earlier art, was reduced now in the hands of the newer poets to the figure of the Graeculus,* who as the good-natured and mischievous house-slave, from now on stands at the centre of dramatic interest. What Euripides claims credit for in Aristophanes' *The Frogs*, that his household remedy had freed tragic art from its grandiose corpulence, can be sensed above all in his tragic heroes. Essentially, the spectator now saw and heard his double on the Euripidean stage and rejoiced that the latter could express himself so well. But joy was not the end of it; from Euripides one even learnt how to speak, and he prides himself on this in his contest with Aeschylus:* on how from him the people have learnt how to observe themselves, how to debate and to draw conclusions with art and the most cunning sophistries. Through this revolution of public language he made the New Comedy possible. For from now on there was no longer any secret as to how and with which aphorisms daily life could be represented on stage. The mediocrity of the citizen, upon which Euripides built all his political hopes, now got a chance to speak, while previously in tragedy it had been rather the demigod and in comedy the drunken satyr or the half-man who had determined the character of language. And so the Aristophanic Euripides stressed in praise of himself how he represented the everyday life and activity which was familiar and common to all, which everyone was capable of judging. And if now the masses in their entirety philosophized, administered land and property, and conducted their own legal cases with unprecedented prudence, then this was a credit to him and the successful result of the wisdom with which he had inoculated the people.

Thus prepared and enlightened, the masses could now be addressed by the New Comedy, for which Euripides had to a certain extent become the chorus leader; only that this time the chorus of spectators had to be rehearsed. As soon as the chorus had been trained to sing in the Euripidean key, that genre of drama which resembles chess,* the New Comedy, rose up, with its continual triumph of cunning and artfulness. But Euripides—the chorus leader—was incessantly praised; indeed, one would have committed suicide in order to learn even more from him, if one had not known that the tragic poets were as dead as tragedy itself. With the death of tragedy, however, the Hellene had relinquished his belief in immortality, not only the belief in an ideal past, but also the belief in an ideal future. The phrase from the famous epitaph 'in old age foolish and silly'* applied also to the ageing Hellenic world. The passing moment, the witticism, levity, whim are its highest deities; the fifth estate, that of the slaves, now comes to predominance,* at least in terms of mentality: and if one may now still speak of 'Greek serenity', then it is the serenity of the slave who is incapable of taking responsibility for anything serious, of striving for anything great, of valuing anything past or future more than the present. It was this appearance of 'Greek serenity' which so outraged the profound and fearful natures of the first four centuries of Christianity: to them this feminine flight from seriousness and fear, this cowardly complacency in comfortable pleasure appeared not only contemptible but also as the specifically anti-Christian mentality. And it is due to their influence that the view of the ancient Greek world which has survived down through centuries with almost insuperable tenacity has retained that pink hue of serenity—as if there had never been a sixth century with its birth of tragedy, its mysteries, its Pythagoras and Heraclitus,* indeed as if the works of art of the great period had not existed, none of which—in its own terms—can even begin to be explained on the basis of such a senile and slavish pleasure in existence and serenity but point rather to a completely different world-view as the foundation of their existence.

If finally it is argued that Euripides brought the spectator onstage in order for the first time truly to enable the spectator to reach a judgement about drama, then it appears as if the earlier tragic art never escaped from an inadequate relation to the spectator: and one might be tempted to praise the radical tendency of Euripides to aim at a corresponding relation between the work of art and the public as an advance over Sophocles. Far from being an homogeneous and stable mass, however, the 'public' is a mere word. Why should the artist be duty-bound to accommodate himself to a force whose only strength is in numbers? And if in terms of his gift and intentions he feels himself sublimely superior to every individual spectator, how might he feel greater respect for the common expression of all these capacities which are inferior to his than for the relatively most gifted individual spectator? In truth, no Greek artist has treated his public with greater audacity and complacency throughout than Euripides: he, who, even when the masses threw themselves at his feet, in sublime defiance publicly reversed his own tendency, the same tendency with which he had conquered the masses. If this genius had had the slightest respect for the pandaemonium* of the public, he would have collapsed under the cudgel blows of his failures long before reaching the middle of his career. These considerations show us that our suggestion that Euripides brought the spectator onstage in order to enable him truly to make judgements was only provisional and that we have to look for a deeper understanding of his tendency. Conversely, it is widely recognized that Aeschylus and Sophocles fully enjoyed the appreciation of the people throughout their lives and even well beyond them and so, with respect to Euripides' precursors, there can be no question of an inadequate relation between the work of art and the public. What drove this richly gifted artist with his incessant compulsion to create so violently from the path illuminated by the sun of the great names of poetry and the unclouded sky of the appreciation of the people? What strange consideration for the spectator turned him against the spectator? How could he, out of excessive respect for his public—despise his public?

Euripides—and this is the solution to the enigma just posed—felt himself as a poet sublimely superior to the masses, with the exception of two of his spectators: while he brought the masses onstage, he revered those two spectators as the only arbiters and masters capable of judging his art in its entirety: following their instructions and admonitions, he transferred the whole world of feelings, passions, and experiences, which up until now had sat in the auditorium at every festival production as an invisible chorus, into the souls of his stage heroes; he conceded to their demands, as he sought for these new characters also a new language and a new music; in their voices alone he heard valid judgements of his creations as well as the encouragement which promised triumph, when he saw himself once again condemned by the court of the public.

Of these two spectators, one is—Euripides himself, Euripides as *thinker*, not as poet. It could be said of him as of Lessing* that the extraordinary abundance of his critical talent continually fertilized a productively artistic drive, if it did not actually create it as a side effect. With this gift, with all the clarity and agility of his critical thinking, Euripides had sat in the theatre and made an effort to rediscover the masterpieces of his great precursors, feature by feature, line by line, as with paintings which have darkened over time. And here he encountered something which should come as no surprise to the initiate into the deeper secrets of Aeschylean tragedy: he perceived something incommensurable in every feature and every line, a certain deceptive certainty and at the same time an enigmatic depth, indeed infinity of background. Even the clearest figure still retained a comet's tail which seemed to point to the uncertain, to darkness beyond illumination. The same twilight lay over the structure of drama, especially over the meaning of the chorus. And how dubious the solution of ethical problems seemed to him! How questionable the treatment of myth! How uneven the distribution of good and bad fortune! Even in the language of the earlier tragedy there was much that offended or at least puzzled him; in particular he found too much grandeur for straightforward relationships, too many tropes* and monstrosities for the simplicity of the characters. So he sat agitated and brooding in the theatre, and, as spectator, admitted to himself that he failed to understand his great precursors. But if understanding represented for him the real root of all enjoyment and creation, then he had to ask and look around him to see if no one else thought as he did and likewise recognized that incommensurability. But most people, including the best individuals, only responded with a suspicious smile; no one, however, could explain to him why, in spite of his reservations and objections, the great masters were none the less correct. And in this painful state he found the *other spectator*, who failed to understand tragedy and therefore respect it. In alliance with this other spectator, he could dare to begin from his isolation the tremendous struggle against the works of art of Aeschylus and Sophocles—not through polemical writings, but as a dramatic poet who opposed *his* conception of tragedy to the traditional one.

12

Before we name this other spectator, let us pause here for a moment to remind ourselves of the impression of duality and incommensurability at the heart of Aeschylean tragedy as we have previously described it. Let us think how disconcerted we felt by the *chorus* and the *tragic hero* of that tragedy, both of which were as difficult to reconcile with our habits as with the tradition—until we rediscovered that duality itself as the origin and essence of Greek tragedy, as the expression of two interwoven artistic drives, the *Apollonian and the Dionysian*.

To excise that original and all-powerful Dionysian element from tragedy and to rebuild tragedy purely on the basis of an un-Dionysian art, morality, and world-view—that is the Euripidean tendency which now reveals itself to us in radiant clarity.

At the end of his life, Euripides himself posed the question of the value and meaning of this tendency to his contemporaries most emphatically in the form of a myth. Is the Dionysian entitled to exist at all? Should it not be forcibly eradicated from Hellenic soil? Certainly, the poet tells us, if only that were possible: but the god Dionysus is too powerful: his most intelligent opponent—such as Pentheus in the *Bacchae**—is unsuspectingly caught in his spell and subsequently plunges to his doom under its influence. The judgement of the two old men Cadmus and Tiresias* also seems to be the judgement of the aged poet: that the thought of the cleverest individuals cannot overthrow those old folk traditions, the eternally self-perpetuating veneration of Dionysus, and indeed that it is proper to show at least a cautious diplomatic interest in such miraculous forces: which still allows the possibility that the god might take offence at such a luke-warm interest and finally transform the diplomat—like Cadmus in this instance—into a dragon. This is said by a poet who with heroic strength resisted Dionysus throughout a long life—in order finally to conclude his career with a glorification of his opponent and a suicide, like someone who throws himself from a tower to escape the horrific dizziness of unbearable vertigo. The tragedy in question is a protest against the impossibility of implementing his tendency; ah, but it had already been implemented! The miraculous had happened: by the time the poet retracted, his tendency had already triumphed. Dionysus had already been driven from the tragic stage, and by a daemonic power which spoke through Euripides. Even Euripides was in a certain sense only a mask: the deity which talked through him was neither Dionysus nor Apollo but a newly born daemon called *Socrates*.* This is the new opposition: the Dionysian and the

Socratic, and the work of art of Greek tragedy foundered on it. In spite of Euripides' efforts to console us with his retraction, he fails: the most magnificent temple lies in ruins; of what use to us is the lament of the man who destroyed it and his admission that it had been the most beautiful of all temples? And even if Euripides has been punished by being transformed into a dragon by the artistic arbiters of all ages—whom might this pitiful compensation satisfy?

Let us now approach that *Socratic* tendency, with which Euripides fought and conquered Aeschylean tragedy.

What could have been the goal—this is the question which we must now ask ourselves—of the Euripidean intention, in the most ideal form in which it was implemented, to found drama exclusively on the un-Dionysian? What form of drama remained if it were not to be born from the womb of music, in that mysterious Dionysian twilight? Only the *dramatized epic*: in whose Apollonian artistic domain the *tragic* effect is admittedly unattainable. It is not a matter here of the content of the events represented; indeed I would like to argue that Goethe in his projected *Nausicaa**** would have found it impossible to make the suicide of that idyllic being—which was to constitute the fifth act—tragically moving; so tremendous is the power of the epic-Apollonian that it conjures away from before our very eyes the most horrific things through that pleasure in appearance and in redemption through appearance. The poet of the dramatized epic is as unable to fuse completely with his images as the epic rhapsode: he remains for ever calm and unmoved, a wide-eyed contemplation, which sees images *before* itself. The actor in his dramatic epic remains at the profoundest level for ever a rhapsode; the consecration of the inner dreaming settles over all his actions so that he is never completely an actor.

How then does the Euripidean play relate to this ideal of Apollonian drama? As the young rhapsode of Plato's *Ion* relates to the solemn rhapsode of an earlier age, describing his being in the following terms: 'When I say something sad, my eyes fill with tears: but if what I say is terrifying and horrific, then my hair stands on end and my heart pounds with fear.'* Here we no longer see that epic loss of the self in appearance, the cool absence of emotion of the true actor, who, particularly at the moment of his most intense activity, is completely appearance and pleasure in appearance. Euripides is the actor whose heart pounds and hair stands on end; as Socratic thinker, he elaborates his plan, as passionate actor he executes it. Neither in the planning nor in the execution is he a pure artist. Thus Euripidean drama is a thing at once cool and on fire, as likely to freeze as to burn; it is impossible for it to attain the Apollonian effect of epic, while on the other hand it has freed itself as much as possible from the Dionysian elements and now, in order to be able to have any effect at all, it needs new stimulants, which now no longer lie within the sphere of the two single artistic drives, the Apollonian and the Dionysian. These new stimulants are cool paradoxical *thoughts*—instead of Apollonian visions—and fiery *emotions*—in the place of Dionysian raptures—and they really are highly realistic imitations of thoughts and emotions devoid of any trace of the ether of art.

So, now that we have acknowledged that Euripides failed utterly to provide an exclusively Apollonian basis for drama, and that its un-Dionysian tendency developed rather into a naturalistic and unartistic aberration,* we may approach the essence of *aesthetic Socratism*, whose highest law runs approximately as follows: 'In order to be beautiful, everything must be intelligible'; as a counterpart to the Socratic principle 'Knowledge is virtue'.* With this doctrine in hand, Euripides measured all the individual elements of drama and rectified them accordingly: language, characters, the dramatic structure, the music of the chorus. What we are so often accustomed to considering in comparison to Sophoclean tragedy as poetic shortcoming and regression on Euripides' part is to a large extent the product of that penetrating critical process, of that audacious intelligence. May the Euripidean *prologue** serve as an example for the productivity of that rationalistic method. Nothing could be further from the technique of our own stage than the prologue in Euripidean drama. That a single character should emerge at the beginning of the play, say who he is, what precedes the action, what has happened up until now, indeed what will happen in the course of the play, would be condemned by a modern dramatist as a wilful and unpardonable renunciation of the effect of suspense. One knows what will happen; who will want to wait until it really happens?— since in this case there exists nothing of the exciting relationship between a prophetic dream and what happens subsequently in reality. Euripides did not think like that at all. The effect of tragedy was never based on epic suspense, on the stimulating uncertainty of what will happen now and afterwards: but rather on those great rhetorical-lyrical scenes in which the passion and the dialectic of the protagonists swelled up into a broad and powerful torrent. Everything served to enhance not plot but pathos:* and whatever did not serve to enhance pathos was regarded as reprehensible. But what disturbs the pleasurable devotion to these scenes most for the spectator is a missing link, a gap in the weave of the story so far; as long as the spectator is still obliged to work out what such and such a character represents, or the presuppositions of such and such a conflict of inclinations and intentions, full absorption in the suffering and actions of the main characters, in the breathless sympathy of compassion and fear* remains impossible. Aeschylean–Sophoclean tragedy used the most ingenious artistic means to give the spectator, as if by chance, all the strands necessary for understanding in the opening scenes: a process in which the noble artistry of masking formal *necessity* and letting it appear as accident proves itself. All the same, however, Euripides believed that he detected during those opening scenes a peculiar anxiety on the part of the spectator to solve the problem of the story so far, so that the poetic beauties and the pathos of the exposition were lost on him. So in Euripides' plays the prologue preceded even the exposition and was placed in the mouth of a character who could be trusted: often a deity had to guarantee so to speak the plot of the tragedy to the public and allay any doubt as to the reality of the myth: in a similar way to that in which Descartes* was only able to prove the reality of the empirical world through an appeal to God's truthfulness and his inability to lie. Euripides needed this same divine truthfulness once again at the end of his drama in order to assure the public of the future of his heroes: this is the task of the notorious *deus ex machina*.* Between the epic prologue and epilogue lies the dramatic-lyrical present, the 'drama' proper.

Euripides as a poet is therefore above all the echo of his conscious insights; and it is precisely this which gives him such a memorable place in the history of Greek art. Looking back on his critical and creative production he must often have felt that it was his duty to give dramatic life to the beginning of Anaxagoras' text: 'In the beginning all things were mixed together; then came understanding and created order.'* And if Anaxagoras with his *nous** appeared among the philosophers like the first sober man among a crowd of mere drunks, then Euripides too might have used a similar image to understand his relation to the other tragic poets. As long as the sole ordering and governing principle of all things, the *nous*, was excluded from artistic creation, then everything remained mixed together in a chaotic primal soup; this is the judgement Euripides had to make, as the first 'sober man' he had to condemn the 'drunken' poets in this way. What Sophocles said of Aeschylus, that he acted justly, albeit unconsciously, was certainly not said in the spirit of Euripides: who would at most have allowed that Aeschylus created something unjust *because* he created unconsciously. Even the divine Plato speaks almost always only ironically of the creative capacity of the poet, in so far as it is not conscious insight, and equates it with the gift of the soothsayer and interpreter of dreams;* as if the poet is only capable of composing poetry when unconscious and abandoned by reason. Euripides undertook the task, which Plato had also undertaken, to show to the world the reverse of the 'unreasonable' poet; his basic aesthetic principle 'in order to be beautiful, everything must be conscious' is, as I said, the counterpart to the Socratic 'in order to be good, everything must be conscious'. Accordingly, Euripides may stand for us as the poet of aesthetic Socratism. Socrates however was that *second spectator* who failed to understand and so to respect the earlier tragedy; in alliance with him, Euripides dared to be the herald of a new artistic creation. If it destroyed the earlier tragedy, then aesthetic Socratism is the lethal principle: but in so far as the struggle was directed against the Dionysus of the older art, we recognize in Socrates the opponent of Dionysus, the new Orpheus* who rises up against Dionysus and although destined to be torn apart by the Maenads of the Athenian court, still puts the more powerful god to flight: Dionysus, who, as when he fled from Lycurgus* king of the the Edoni, sought refuge in the depths of the sea, namely in the mystical tides of a secret cult which was gradually spreading over the whole world.

13

This close link between the Socratic and the Euripidean tendency did not escape the notice of the contemporary ancient world; and this felicitous intuition finds its most eloquent expression in the story which circulated in Athens according to which Socrates used to help Euripides with his writing.* The supporters of the 'good old days' mentioned both names in a single breath when they enumerated those contemporaries who were leading the people astray, whose influence was responsible for the fact that the old robust Marathonian efficiency* of body and soul was being increasingly sacrificed to a dubious enlightenment, accompanied by advancing atrophy of the strength of body and soul. It was in this tone, half indignant, half contemptuous, that Aristophanic comedy* used to speak of Socrates and Euripides, to the horror of modern men, who, if they are quite prepared to abandon Euripides, are continually surprised by the fact that Aristophanes always presents Socrates as the first and highest *sophist*,* as the mirror and epitome of all sophistical strivings: and their only available consolation was to pillory Aristophanes himself as nothing more than a dissolute and deceitful Alcibiades* of poetry. Without at this point defending Aristophanes' profound instincts against such attacks, I shall continue to deduce the close relationship between Socrates and Euripides from this intuition of the contemporary ancient world; with this in mind, we should remember in particular that Socrates as an opponent of the tragic art refrained from attending tragedies and only joined the audience when a new play by Euripides was performed. But most famous of all is the close conjunction of the two names in the pronouncement of the Delphic oracle which designated Socrates as the wisest of men, and at the same time decided that the second prize in the contest of wisdom should be awarded to Euripides.*

Sophocles was named as third in line; he, who in contrast to Aeschylus, might pride himself on the fact that he acted justly, because he *knew* what was just. Obviously it is precisely the degree of clarity of this *knowledge* which collectively distinguishes these three men as the three 'men of knowledge' of their time.

But the most acute word for that new and unprecedentedly high evaluation of knowledge and insight was spoken by Socrates, when he found himself to be the only person who admitted to *knowing nothing*; whereas, on his critical rambles through Athens, he encountered everywhere the self-delusion of knowledge in the greatest statesmen, orators, poets, and artists. He realized with astonishment that all those famous men lacked proper and sure insight even into their own professions and practised them exclusively from instinct.* 'Exclusively from instinct': with this expression we touch on the heart and centre of the Socratic tendency. With this expression Socratism condemns existing art as much as existing ethics: wherever it turns its searching gaze, it sees the lack of insight and the power of delusion and deduces from this lack the essentially perverse and reprehensible character of what exists. From this point on, Socrates believed that it was his duty to correct existence: he, alone, with an expression of contempt and superiority, as the precursor of a completely different culture, art, and morality, entered a world to touch whose hem with reverence we today would consider the greatest good fortune.

This is the great apprehension which seizes us each time we encounter Socrates and which again and again spurs us to discover the meaning and intention of this most questionable phenomenon of the ancient world. Who is this man who single-handedly dares negate the Greek character, which in the form of Homer, Pindar, and Aeschylus, of Phidias,* Pericles, Pythia,* and

Dionysus, as the deepest abyss and the highest peak is assured of our astonished adoration? What daemonic power is this which dares to spill this magic potion in the dust? What demigod is this, to whom the ghostly chorus of the noblest of humanity must shout: 'Woe! Woe! Your powerful fist has destroyed the beautiful world; it collapses, it falls apart!'*

That miraculous phenomenon which is described as the 'daemonium of Socrates'* offers us a key to the essence of Socrates. In certain circumstances, when his great powers of reason began to waver, a divine voice made itself heard and gave him a sure indication. This voice, when it comes, always *dissuades*. In this completely abnormal nature, instinctive wisdom only shows itself sporadically in order to oppose and *obstruct* conscious knowledge. While in all productive people it is precisely instinct which is the creative-affirmative force and it is consciousness which criticizes and dissuades, in Socrates, however, instinct becomes the critic and consciousness the creator—a true monstrosity *per defectum*!* Actually, we have before us here a monstrous *defectus** of that mystic disposition, so that Socrates might be characterized as the very type of the *non-mystic*, in whom the logical nature has through uncontrolled growth* developed itself to excess in the same way as instinctive wisdom has in the mystic. On the other hand, however, the logical drive which emerged in Socrates was utterly forbidden to turn against itself; in this boundless torrent it demonstrated a power of nature such as we encounter to our horrified surprise only in the greatest instinctive forces. Anyone who has received even the slightest hint of the divine naïveté and certainty of the Socratic way of life from Plato's writings will also feel how this huge driving wheel of logical Socratism is in motion *behind* Socrates as it were and how, in order to contemplate it, we must see through Socrates himself as if he were only a shadow. But that he himself had an sense of this relationship is expressed in the dignified seriousness with which he everywhere asserted his divine calling, continuing to protest it even before his judges. It was at bottom as impossible to refute him on this point as it was to approve his instinct-dissolving influence. In this insoluble conflict, once he had been summoned before the forum of the

Greek state, only one form of sentence was imperative—exile; as something completely enigmatic, unclassifiable, inexplicable, he might have been dispatched over the border, and no posterity could have rightfully accused the Athenians of a shameful deed. But that a sentence of death rather than one of exile only was passed seems to have been brought about by Socrates himself, with complete clarity and without the natural horror in the face of death: according to Plato's account, he approached death with the calm with which he left the symposium* in the early dawn as the last of the revellers; while behind him on the benches and on the floor his fellow carousers remained behind asleep, dreaming of Socrates, the true eroticist.* The *dying Socrates* became the new ideal, never seen before, of the noble Greek youth: above all the typical Hellenic youth, Plato, threw himself down before this image with all the fervent devotion of his enthusiast's soul.

14

Let us now imagine the single great Cyclops's eye* of Socrates turned towards tragedy, that eye which never glowed with the sweet madness of artistic enthusiasm—let us imagine how this eye was denied the pleasure of looking into the Dionysian abyss—what must it have really seen in the 'sublime and much praised' tragic art, as Plato* calls it? Something utterly unreasonable, where causes appear to lack effects and effects appear to lack causes; and moreover the whole so colourful and diverse that it could only repel a balanced constitution, while it might dangerously inflame touchy and sensitive souls. We know what single genre of poetry Socrates understood, the *Aesopian fable*:* and this certainly occurred with that same smiling accommodation with which the good old honest Gellert sings the praises of poetry in the fable of the bee and the hen:

> You see from me how useful it can be
> To use an image to tell the truth
> To someone who is not very bright.*

But to Socrates tragic art did not even appear to tell 'the truth': quite apart from the fact that it addresses the man who 'is not very bright', rather than the philosopher: two reasons for avoiding it. Like Plato, he counted it among the flattering arts, which portray the pleasing rather than the useful* and therefore demanded of his disciples abstinence and strict segregation from such unphilosophical stimulants; with such success that the youthful tragic poet Plato* first burnt his poetry in order that he might become a pupil of Socrates. And even where unconquerable constitutions fought against the Socratic maxims, their power, together with the force of his tremendous character, was still great enough to force poetry itself into new and unprecedented positions.

An example of this is Plato, whom we have just mentioned: in his condemnation of tragedy and of art as a whole, he certainly did not lag behind the naïve cynicism of his master, and yet he was obliged by full artistic necessity to create an art-form essentially related to the existing art-forms which he had rejected. The main reproach which Plato addressed to the older art—that it is the imitation of an apparent image, and so belongs to an even lower sphere than the empirical world—certainly could not be directed against the new work of art: and so we see Plato's efforts to go beyond reality and to represent the idea which lies at the basis of that pseudo-reality. But in this way Plato the thinker arrived by a circuitous route at the place which had always been his home as an artist and from where Sophocles and the whole of the earlier art mounted their solemn protest against such a reproach. If tragedy had absorbed all earlier artistic genres, so the same might be said in an eccentric sense of the Platonic dialogue, which, created from a mixture of all available styles and forms, is suspended between narrative, lyric, and drama, between prose and poetry, and so broke the strict older law of the unity of linguistic form; this was taken much further in the writings of the *Cynics*,* who with the greatest stylistic diversity, in the oscillation between prosaic and metric forms, realized the literary image of the 'raving Socrates' whom they represented in life. The Platonic dialogue was the raft as it were on which the earlier poetry rescued itself and all its children from shipwreck: huddled together in a confined space and fearfully subservient to the single helmsman Socrates, they now sailed into a new world which never tired of the fantastic image passing before it. Plato really gave to all posterity the model for a new art-form, the *novel*: which may be characterized as the infinitely intensified Aesopian fable, in which poetry lives in a hierarchical relation to dialectical philosophy similar to that in which for centuries this same philosophy lived with theology: namely as *ancilla*.* This was the new position into which poetry was forced by Plato under the pressure of the daemonic Socrates.

At this point, art is overgrown by *philosophical thought* and forced to cling closely to the trunk of dialectic. The *Apollonian* tendency has disguised itself in logical schematism: just as we were obliged to perceive something similar in Euripides, accompanied by a translation of the *Dionysian* into naturalistic emotion. Socrates, the dialectical hero in the Platonic drama, reminds us of the related nature of the Euripidean hero, who must defend his actions by argument and counter-argument and in the process so often risks forfeiting our tragic compassion: for who could fail to recognize the *optimistic* element in the essence of the dialectic, which celebrates exultantly in each conclusion and needs the cool radiance of consciousness in order to breathe: the optimistic element which, once it has penetrated tragedy, gradually overgrows its Dionysian regions and must necessarily drive it to self-annihilation—to the lethal plunge into bourgeois drama.* Let us consider the consequences of the Socratic principles: 'Knowledge is virtue; sin is the result of ignorance; the virtuous man is the happy man': in these three basic forms of optimism lies the death of tragedy. For now the virtuous hero must be a dialectician, now there must be a necessary visible link between virtue and knowledge, belief and morality, now Aeschylus' solution of transcendental justice is degraded to the shallow and impudent principle of 'poetic justice'* with its usual *deus ex machina*.

How does the *chorus* and above all the whole musical-Dionysian substratum appear when faced with this new Socratic-optimistic stage-world? As something accidental, as an in all probability dispensable memory of the origin of tragedy; while we, however, have seen that the chorus can only be understood as the *cause* of tragedy and of the tragic itself. This embarrassment with respect to the chorus is already evident in Sophocles—an important sign that the Dionysian ground of tragedy is already beginning to crumble in his work. Sophocles no longer dares to entrust to the chorus the main share of the effect, but restricts its domain to such an extent that it now appears almost co-ordinated with the actors, just as if it were lifted out of the orchestra onto the stage: in the process, of course, its essence is completely destroyed, even if Aristotle approves precisely this definition of the chorus.* This displacement of the chorus, which Sophocles in any case recommended through his practice and according to tradition even in a treatise, is the first step towards the *annihilation* of the chorus, whose phases follow one another with frightening rapidity in Euripides, Agathon,* and the New Comedy. The optimistic dialectic drives *music* out of tragedy with the whip of its syllogisms:* that is, it destroys the essence of tragedy, which can only be interpreted as a manifestation and transformation into images of Dionysian states, as visible symbolization of music, as the dream-world of a Dionysian intoxication.

If as a result we must assume the existence of an effective anti-Dionysian tendency even prior to Socrates, in whom it merely achieved unprecedented greatness of expression, then we must not shrink from the question of the direction in which a phenomenon such as Socrates points: a phenomenon which we, in the face of the Platonic dialogues, are not yet in a position to understand as an exclusively negative dissolving power. And while the most immediate effect of the Socratic drive was undoubtedly to bring about a disintegration of the Dionysian tragedy, a profound experience undergone by Socrates himself forces us to ask whether the relationship between Socratism and art is *necessarily* only an antipodal one and whether the birth of an 'artistic Socrates' is actually a contradiction in terms.

For, with respect to art, that despotic logician experienced sporadically the feeling of a gap, a void, a half reproach, perhaps of a neglected duty. As he told his friends in prison, there often came to him the same recurring dream phenomenon, which always said the same thing: 'Socrates, make music!'* Up to his last days, he comforted himself with the thought that his philosophizing was the highest art of the muses and did not really believe that a deity wished to remind him of that 'common popular music'. Finally, in prison, in order completely to unburden his conscience, he even agreed to make the music for which he had so little respect. And in this frame of mind, he composed a *proemium**   to Apollo and rewrote some Aesopian fables in verse. It was something resembling a daemonic warning voice which forced him to undertake these exercises, it was his Apollonian insight that he, like a barbarian king, was failing to understand a noble image of a god and was, through his failure to understand, in danger of sinning against its deity. This mention of the Socratic dream-phenomenon is the only sign of an apprehension on his part about the limits of the logical nature: he must have asked himself the following question—perhaps whatever is not intelligible to me is not necessarily immediately unintelligent? Perhaps there is a domain of wisdom which excludes the logician? Perhaps art is even a necessary correlative of and supplement to science?

15

In the spirit of these last suggestive questions, it must now be said how the influence of Socrates has extended down through posterity to this very moment and indeed stretches out into the future in its entirety, like a shadow which grows in the evening sun, as the same influence again and again necessitates the re-creation anew of *art*—of art in the already metaphysical, broadest, and deepest sense—and how its own infinity guarantees the infinity of art also.

Before this could be recognized, before the innermost dependence of all art on the Greeks from Homer to Socrates had been convincingly demonstrated, we were obliged to undergo the same experience with these Greeks as the Athenians were obliged to do with Socrates. Almost every period and stage of cultural development has at one time or another with profound moroseness sought to free itself from the Greeks, because in comparison with the latter everything which has been achieved on one's own account, everything which appeared completely original and was admired with proper honesty suddenly seemed to pale and flag, shrivelling to a failed copy, even to a caricature. And so there broke out again and again that heart-felt wrath against that presumptuous little people which had the audacity to characterize everything non-indigenous as 'barbaric': who are these people, one wonders, who, with only an ephemeral historical brilliance, only ridiculously limited institutions, only a dubious moral competence to show for themselves and who are even marked by ugly vices, yet lay claim to the dignity and exceptional status among peoples which is accorded to the genius among the masses? Unfortunately, one was not sufficiently fortunate to find the cup of hemlock* which could do away with such a being: for all the poison which envy, slander, and wrath produced was not enough to annihilate that self-sufficient splendour. And one feels ashamed and fearful before the Greeks; unless one respects truth in all things and so also dares to admit to oneself that the Greeks as charioteers hold the reins of our and every other culture in their hands, but that almost always the chariot and horses are too slight and frail to live up to the glory of their drivers, who then consider it a jest to spur such a team into the abyss: while they themselves jump to safety with a leap of Achilles.*

In order to show the dignity which such a position of leadership held for Socrates, one need only recognize in him the type of an unprecedented form of existence, the type of the *theoretical man*, whose meaning and goal it is our next task to investigate. Like the artist, the theoretical man takes an infinite pleasure in that which exists, a pleasure which likewise protects him from the practical ethic of pessimism with its eyes of Lynceus* which glow only in the dark. For if in the course of all unveiling of the truth the delighted gaze of the artist remains perpetually fixed on the truth which has been unveiled but remains even now a veil, the theoretical man derives delight and satisfaction rather from the discarded veil and finds his greatest pleasure in a happy process of unveiling which always succeeds through its own efforts. There would be no science, if science were concerned exclusively with that *single* naked goddess* and with nothing else. For then her disciples would have to feel like those men who wanted to dig a tunnel right through the earth: each individual realizes that the greatest lifelong effort will merely scratch the surface of the vast depths and that before his very eyes his own work will be undone by the efforts of the next man digging alongside, so that a third man appears to do well when he chooses on his own initiative a new site for his tunnelling attempts. If at this point someone persuasively demonstrates that the goal of the Antipodes cannot be reached in this direct way, who will want to continue working in the old depths, unless he has in the mean time settled for the satisfaction of discovering precious stones or the laws of nature? For this reason, Lessing,* the most honest theoretical man, dared to express the idea that he was more concerned with the search for truth than with truth itself: in the process, the fundamental secret of science was exposed, to the astonishment, even annoyance of the scientists. Now admittedly this isolated insight, as an excess of honesty, if not of arrogance, is accompanied by a profound *delusion*, which first came into the world in the person of Socrates—the unshakeable belief that, by following the guiding thread of causality, thought reaches into the deepest abysses of being and is capable not only of knowing but also even of *correcting* being. This sublime metaphysical madness accompanies science as an instinct and leads it again and again to its limits, where it must transform itself into *art: which is the real goal of this mechanism*.

By the torchlight of this thought, let us now take a look at Socrates: he appears to us now as the first man who was able not only to live according to that instinct of science, but—what is more significant by far—also to die according to it: and so the image of the *dying Socrates*, the man elevated above the fear of death through knowledge and reasoning, is the heraldic shield hung above the entrance gate to science in order to remind everyone of its purpose, namely to make existence appear intelligible and so justified: and, if reasons prove insufficient, even *myth* must finally serve this end, myth which I have just characterized even as the necessary consequence, indeed as the intended goal of science.

Once one imagines how after Socrates, the mystagogue* of science, one school of philosophy succeeded another, wave after wave, how the craving for knowledge attained a never suspected universality in the widest domain of the educated world, established itself as the real task for those with higher abilities, and steered science onto the high seas, from which it has never since been driven completely, how through this universality a shared net of thought was first cast over the whole globe, holding out the prospect of discovering the law-governed nature of the whole solar system; once one imagines all this, including the astonishingly high pyramids of present knowledge, one is obliged to see in Socrates the single point around which so-called world-history turns and twists.* For if one were to imagine the whole incalculable sum of energy which has been consumed by this world tendency, employed *not* in the service of knowledge but instead to the practical, that is, egoistic ends of individuals and peoples, then the instinctive pleasure in life would probably have been so weakened in widespread struggles of annihilation and ongoing emigrations that, with suicide having become habitual, the individual would perhaps feel driven to strangle his parents and friends by the last vestige of a sense of duty towards them, like the inhabitants of the Fiji islands: a practical pessimism which could produce a horrific ethic of genocide from compassion—a pessimism which moreover exists and has existed everywhere in the world, where art in some form or other, particularly as religion and science, has not appeared as a remedy and defence against that miasma.

In contrast to this practical pessimism, Socrates is the archetype of the theoretical optimist who in his belief in the fathomability of the nature of things ascribes to knowledge and insight the strength of a panacea and understands error as evil in itself.* To fathom those reasons and to separate true knowledge from appearance and error seemed to the Socratic man to be the noblest, even the sole truly human vocation: just as, from Socrates on, that mechanism of concepts, judgements, and conclusions was valued above all other capacities as the highest activity and the most astonishing gift of nature. Even the most sublime moral deeds, the impulses of compassion, of sacrifice, of heroism, and that oceanic calm of the soul which is so difficult to achieve and which the Apollonian Greek calls *sophrosyne*,* were deduced from the dialectic of knowledge and accordingly designated as teachable by Socrates and his like-minded successors down to the present. Anyone who has personally experienced the pleasure of Socratic knowledge and feels how it seeks through ever widening circles to encompass the whole world of phenomena, will feel no more intense spur to existence than the desire to complete the conquest and to draw the net impenetrably tight. To someone so disposed, the Platonic Socrates then appears as the teacher of a completely new form of 'Greek serenity' and blissful existence, which seeks to discharge itself in actions and will find this discharge mostly in maieutic* and educational influences on noble youths for the purpose of the final production of genius.

But now science, spurred on by its powerful delusion, hurtles inexorably towards its limits where the optimism hidden in the essence of logic founders. For the periphery of the circle of science has an infinite number of points and while there is no telling yet how the circle could ever be fully surveyed, the noble and gifted man, before he has reached the middle of his life, still inevitably encounters such peripheral limit points and finds himself staring into an impenetrable darkness. If he at that moment sees to his horror how in these limits logic coils around itself and finally bites its own tail*—then the new form of knowledge breaks through, *tragic knowledge*, which in order to be tolerated, needs art as a protection and remedy.

If we look with eyes strengthened and refreshed by the sight of the Greeks at the highest spheres of that world which surges around us, then we perceive how the craving of an insatiable optimistic knowledge, which appears in an exemplary form in Socrates, is transformed into tragic resignation and need for art; while admittedly this same craving in its lower stages must express itself as hostile to art and must have a particular inner aversion to Dionysian-tragic art, as illustrated earlier for example in the struggle of Socratism against Aeschylean tragedy.

At this point, we knock with stirred emotions at the gates of the present and the future: will this 'transformation' lead to ever new configurations of genius and precisely of *Socrates as maker of music*? Will the net of art which is cast over existence, whether under the name of religion or science, be woven ever more tightly and delicately or is it destined to be torn to shreds in the swirling restlessness and barbaric turmoil which now calls itself the 'present'?—Anxious yet not disconsolate, we stand to one side for a moment, as contemplative bystanders to whom it has been granted to witness these great struggles and transitions. Oh! it is the magic of these struggles that whoever observes them must also enter into the fray!*

16

By way of the historical example set out here we have sought to clarify how tragedy dies with the disappearance of the spirit of music as surely as it can only be born from that same spirit. In order to mitigate the unusual nature of this assertion and to demonstrate the origin of this knowledge, we must now cast an unprejudiced eye on the analogous phenomena of the present; we must plunge right into the middle of those struggles which, as I said, are being waged in the highest spheres of our contemporary world between knowledge with its insatiable optimism and the tragic need for art. In the process, I want to leave to one side all the other opposing drives which are always working against art and against tragedy in particular and which are at present expanding with such certainty of victory that, of the theatrical arts for example, only farce and ballet* blossom and flourish with any lavishness, and their fragrance perhaps smells not so sweet to some. I want to speak only of the most *illustrious opponent* of the tragic world-view, and by that I mean science, which is optimistic in its deepest essence, with its ancestor Socrates to the forefront. And presently I shall name the powers which seem to me to guarantee a *rebirth of tragedy*—and other blissful hopes for the German character!

Before we plunge into the middle of these struggles, let us shield ourselves in the armour of the knowledge which we have acquired so far. In contrast to all those who conscientiously seek to deduce the arts from a single principle as the necessary source of life for every work of art, my gaze remains fixed on those two artistic deities of the Greeks, Apollo and Dionysus, and recognizes in them the living and clearly visible representatives of *two* worlds of art which differ in their deepest essence and their highest goals. Apollo stands before me as the transfiguring genius of the *principium individuationis*, through which alone true redemption in appearance can be attained, while under the mystical cry of exultation of Dionysus the spell of individuation is burst apart and the path to the Mothers of Being,* to the innermost core of things, lies open. The revelation of this tremendous opposition which stretches like a yawning abyss between the Apollonian plastic arts and the Dionysian art of music has been granted to only one of the great thinkers to the extent that, even without this clue to the Hellenic symbolism of the deities, he recognized that music possessed a character and origin different from all other arts, because music, unlike all the other arts, is not an copy of the phenomenon but an unmediated copy of the will itself, and so represents the *metaphysical in relation to the whole physical world* and the thing in itself in relation to the phenomenal world (Schopenhauer, *The World as Will and Representation*, I*). On this most important insight of aesthetics, which, in a more serious sense, represents the beginning of all aesthetics, Richard Wagner stamped his seal of approval, strengthening its eternal truth, when in his *Beethoven** he asserts that music is to be judged according to aesthetic principles completely different from those of the plastic arts and absolutely not according to the category of beauty: although a mistaken aesthetic, along with a misguided and degenerate art* has on the basis of that concept of beauty which is valid in the world of the visual arts become accustomed to demand of art in general a similar effect to that produced by works of plastic art, namely the stimulation of *pleasure in beautiful* *forms*. Having recognized that tremendous opposition, I felt a strong need to approach the essence of Greek tragedy and in it the most profound revelation of Hellenic genius: for only now did I believe myself in possession of the magic necessary for my soul to envisage vividly the original problem of tragedy, beyond the phraseology of our habitual aesthetic: and in the process I was granted such a disconcertingly peculiar insight into the Hellenic essence that it necessarily seemed to me as if our classical-Hellenic science which conducts itself with such pride has so far done little more than revel in shadow games and superficialities.

We might perhaps touch on this original problem by way of the following question: what aesthetic effect is produced when those intrinsically separate artistic powers of the Apollonian and the Dionysian come together actively? Or to put it more succinctly: how is music related to image and concept?—Schopenhauer, whom Richard Wagner praised for his unsurpassable clarity and transparency of exposition on precisely this point, expresses himself most exhaustively on this matter in the following passage which I shall reproduce here in full. *The World as Will and Representation*, I:* 'As a result of all this, we can regard the phenomenal world, or nature, and music as two different expressions of the same thing, which is therefore itself the sole mediating element in the analogy between the two, and knowledge of which is required in order to see the analogy. Music is accordingly, when viewed as the expression of the world, a universal language to the highest degree, which even has roughly the same relationship to the universality of concepts as concepts have to individual things. Its universality is, however, far removed from that empty universality of abstraction, and of a completely different kind, linked with a clear and thorough definition. In this respect, it resembles the geometric figures and numbers which as the universal forms of all possible objects of experience may be applied to all a priori,* and yet are not abstract but visible and thoroughly defined. All possible strivings, impulses, and expressions of the will, all those processes which take place within the heart of man, which reason comprehends under the broad negative concept of feeling, are to be expressed through the infinite number of possible melodies, but always in the universality of mere form, without content, always only according to the in-itself, not according to the phenomenon, but according to its innermost soul as it were, without the body. This intimate relationship between music and the true essence of all things can also explain how when appropriate music accompanies any scene, action, event, or surroundings, it seems to reveal to us its most secret meaning and emerges as the most accurate and clearest commentary upon it: to such an extent that he who devotes himself entirely to the impression of a symphony feels as if he is watching within himself all the possible events of life and the world move past in procession: and yet he cannot, when he stops to reflect, demonstrate any similarity between that play of melody and the things which hovered before him. For music, as we have said, differs from all the other arts in that it is not a copy of the phenomenon or, more accurately, of the adequate objectivity of the will, but an unmediated copy of the will itself and so represents the metaphysical in relation to the whole physical world and the thing in itself in relation to the whole phenomenal world. Accordingly, one could just as well call the world embodied music as embodied will: so, on this basis, it is possible to explain why music allows every picture, indeed every scene of real life and the world to stand out with greater meaning; all the more so, admittedly, the more analogous its melody is to the inner spirit of the given phenomenon. This is why it is possible to subordinate to music a poem as song, a visual representation as pantomime, or both as opera. Such individual images of human life, subordinated to the universal language of music, are never bound to it nor do they correspond to it with complete necessity; rather they stand in relation to it as a random example to an universal concept: they represent in the certainty of reality that which music expresses in the universality of pure form. For the melodies are, as it were, like all universal concepts, an *abstractum** of reality. This reality, then, the world of individual things, supplies the visible, the particular and individual, the individual case, both to the universality of concepts and to the universality of melodies, these two universalities being united but also in a certain respect opposed; while the concepts contain only the forms which are abstracted in the first place from the visible world, the outer shell of things as it were once it has been removed, and so are completely genuine *abstracta*,* music on the other hand gives the innermost core which preceded all assumption of form, or the heart of things. This relationship may be perfectly well expressed in the language of the Scholastics by saying that: the concepts are the *universalia post rem*, but music gives the *universalia ante rem*, and the real world the *universalia in re*.*—But that a relationship between a composition and a visible representation is at all possible rests, as we have said, on the fact that both are no more than different, albeit completely different, expressions of the same inner essence of the world. When now in a particular case such a relationship really exists, when the composer has been able to express the impulses of the will which constitute the core of an event in the universal language of music, then the melody of the song, the music of the opera becomes expressive. The analogy between these two found by the composer must have proceeded from the unmediated knowledge of the essence of the world, without the conscious intervention of reason, and must not be a conscious and deliberate imitation mediated by concepts, otherwise music does not express the inner essence, the will itself, but only offers an unsatisfactory imitation of its phenomenal appearance, like all truly imitative music.'

So, following Schopenhauer's doctrine, we understand music as the unmediated language of will and feel our imagination stimulated to give shape to that invisible and yet so vivid world of spirits which speaks to us, and to embody it in an analogous example. On the other hand, under the influence of a music which provides a true correspondence, image and concept reach a heightened significance. So Dionysian art usually exercises two types of influence on the Apollonian capacity for art: music stimulates the *allegorical contemplation* of Dionysian universality, and music allows the emergence of the allegorical image in its *most significant form*. From these facts, intelligible in themselves and accessible to any more perceptive observer, I deduce the capacity of music to give birth to *myth*, which is the most significant example, and precisely the *tragic* myth: the myth which speaks of

Dionysian knowledge in allegories. With respect to the phenomenon of the lyric poet, I have shown how in the lyric poet music
struggles to reveal its essence in Apollonian images: if we now
imagine that music in its most heightened form must also seek to
reach its greatest transformation into images, then we must consider it capable of finding symbolic expression for its real Dionysian wisdom; and where else should we look for this expression if
not in tragedy and above all in the concept of the *tragic*?

The tragic cannot be honestly deduced from the essence of art
as it is commonly understood in terms of the single category of
appearance and beauty; it is only on the basis of the spirit of
music that we can understand the joy experienced in the annihilation of the individual. For it is only in the individual examples of
such an annihilation that the eternal phenomenon of Dionysian
art is made clear to us, the Dionysian art which gives expression
to the will in its omnipotence as it were behind the *principium
individuationis*, the eternal life beyond all phenomena and in spite
of all annihilation. The metaphysical joy in the tragic is a translation of the instinctively unconscious Dionysian wisdom into the
language of images: the hero, the greatest phenomenon of the
will, is negated for our pleasure, because he remains only phenomenon and the eternal life of the will remains untouched by his
annihilation. 'We believe in eternal life', such is the cry of tragedy; while music is the unmediated idea of this life. The art of
the sculptor has a completely different goal: here Apollo overcomes the suffering of the individual through radiant glorification of the *eternity of the phenomenon*, here beauty triumphs over
the suffering which is inherent to life, pain is in a certain sense
effaced from the features of nature by a lie. In Dionysian art and
in its tragic symbolism, this same nature speaks to us in its true
undistorted voice: 'Be as I am! Beneath the incessantly changing
phenomena, I am the eternally creative original mother, eternally
compelling people to exist, eternally finding satisfaction in this
changing world of phenomena!'

17

Dionysian art too wants to convince us of the eternal joy of existence: only we should seek this joy not in phenomena but behind phenomena. We should recognize how everything which comes into being must be prepared for a painful demise, we are forced to peer into the terrors of individual existence—without turning to stone: a metaphysical consolation tears us momentarily out of the bustle of changing shapes. For a few short moments we really are the original essence itself and feel its unbridled craving for existence and joy in existence; the struggle, the agony, the annihilation of phenomena now seem necessary to us, in the context of the excess of countless forms of existence which crowd and push their way into life, of the overwhelming fertility of the world-will; we are pierced by the raging thorn of these agonies in the same moment as we have become one as it were with the immeasurable original joy in existence and as we sense the indestructibility and eternity of this pleasure in Dionysian rapture. In spite of fear and compassion, we are the fortunate living beings, not as individuals, but as a *single* living being, with whose joy in creation we are fused.

The story of the emergence of Greek tragedy now tells us with luminous certainty how the tragic work of art of the Greeks was really born out of the spirit of music: as a result, we believe that for the first time justice has been done to the original and so astonishing significance of the chorus. At the same time, we must however admit that the meaning of the tragic myth as presented above never became transparent in conceptually clear terms to the Greek poets, let alone the Greek philosophers; the actions of their heroes as it were speak more profoundly than their words; the spoken word fails absolutely to offer myth adequate objectivation. The structure of scenes and the visual images reveal a more profound wisdom than the poet himself can grasp in words and concepts: the same process can be observed also in Shakespeare's Hamlet for example, whose actions likewise speak more profoundly than his words, so that the lesson of *Hamlet* mentioned earlier is not to be derived from the words but from the contemplative immersion in and overview of the whole. With respect to Greek tragedy, which, admittedly, we only encounter as verbal drama, I have even signalled that this lack of congruence between myth and word could easily lead us astray into thinking it shallower and less significant than it is, and accordingly into presupposing that it has a more superficial effect than it must have had according to the testimony of the ancients. For how easily one forgets that what the poet failed to achieve in words, namely the highest spiritualization and ideality of myth, he might at every moment succeed in achieving as creative musician! We admittedly must reconstruct for ourselves in an almost scholarly manner the superior power of musical effect, in order to receive something of that incomparable consolation, which must have been the property of true tragedy. But we would have experienced even this superior musical power only if we were Greeks, while in the whole development of Greek music—compared with the infinitely richer music which we know and are familar with—we believe that we hear only the opening notes of the youthful song of musical genius intoned with a timid sense of power. The Greeks are, as the Egyptian priests say, the eternal children,* even in tragic art they remain mere children unaware of the sublime plaything which has emerged in their hands and which those same hands—smash to pieces.

That struggle of the spirit of music for revelation in image and myth, which builds in intensity from the beginnings of lyric poetry to the Attic tragedy, suddenly breaks off just after achieving a sumptuous development and disappears as it were from the surface of Hellenic art, while the Dionysian world-view born from this struggle lives on in the mysteries and through the most miraculous transformations and degenerations continues to attract more serious natures. Will it not rise once again from its mystical depths as art?

We are concerned here with the question of whether the power on whose opposing influence tragedy foundered has sufficient strength to prevent for all time the artistic re-awakening of tragedy and of the tragic world-view. If ancient tragedy was forced off the rails by the dialectical drive to knowledge and scientific optimism, then we might deduce from this the existence of an eternal struggle between the *theoretical* and the *tragic world-view*, and only after the spirit of science has been pushed to its limits and its claim to universal validity annihilated through the demonstration of these limits might it be possible to hope for a rebirth of tragedy: a form of culture for which we would have to establish the symbol of *Socrates the maker of music*, in the sense discussed earlier. In this opposition, I understand by the spirit of science the belief in the fathomability of nature and in the universal healing power of knowledge which first came to light in the person of Socrates.

Anyone who remembers the most immediate consequences of this restlessly advancing spirit of science will see at once how it annihilated *myth* and how through this annihilation poetry was driven from its natural ideal soil and from that point on made homeless. If we have correctly ascribed to music the power to give birth once again to myth, then we will also have to seek the spirit of science in the place where it engages in hostile confrontation with this myth-creating power of music. This takes place in the development of the *New Attic Dithyramb*,* whose music no longer expressed the inner essence, the will itself, but only reproduced the phenomenon in an unsatisfactory way, in an imitation mediated through concepts, and from whose intrinsically degenerate music the truly musical natures turned away with the same repugnance which they felt towards the Socratic tendency with its lethal consequences for art. The sure and acute instinct of Aristophanes* was undoubtedly right in directing the same feeling of hatred towards Socrates, Euripidean tragedy, and the music of the New Dithyramb and in sensing in all three phenomena the characteristic signs of a degenerate culture. Through this New Dithyramb, music has been sacrilegiously reduced to the counterfeit imitation of the phenomenon, for example a battle or a sea-storm, and has of course in the process been robbed of its myth-creating power. For if music seeks to stimulate our delight by forcing us to seek external analogies between a life or natural event and certain rhythmic figures and characteristic sounds, if our understanding is to be satisfied with the knowledge of these analogies, then we are reduced to a mood in which any reception of the mythical is impossible, for myth wants to be experienced vividly as an individual example of universality and truth staring into the infinite. We encounter truly Dionysian music as such a universal mirror of the world-will: the vivid event refracted in this mirror immediately expands emotionally for us to become the copy of an eternal truth. Conversely, such a vivid event is immediately stripped of any mythic character by the tone paint-ing* of the New Dithyramb; music has now become the wretched copy of the phenomenon and so infinitely poorer than the phenomenon itself. And this impoverishment has reduced the emotional value of the phenomenon for us, so that now for example a musical imitation of a battle exhausts itself in the noise of marching and the sound of signals, and retains our imagination precisely at the level of these superficialities. Tone painting is therefore in every respect the reverse of the myth-creating power of true music: through it the phenomenon is made more impover-ished than it already is, while Dionysian music enriches the indi-vidual phenomenon and expands it into an image of the world. The estrangement of music from itself and its enslavement to the phenomenon in the development of the New Dithyramb was a mighty triumph for the un-Dionysian spirit. Euripides, who must be described in a higher sense as a thoroughly unmusical nature, is for precisely this reason a passionate supporter of the new dithyrambic music and squanders all its effects and mannerisms with the liberality of a robber.

We see the power of this un-Dionysian and anti-mythical spirit in operation from another angle, if we turn our gaze to the ram-pant development of the *representation of character* and of psycho-logical refinement in tragedy from Sophocles on. The character is no longer intended to expand to become the eternal type, but rather to make such an individual impression through artificial secondary traits and shadings, through the finest clarity of its lines, that the spectator no longer feels the myth at all but rather the powerful natural truth and imitative power of the artist. Here too we perceive the triumph of the phenomenon over the universal and the delight in the individual anatomical specimen as it were, here we are already breathing the air of a theoretical world, in which scientific knowledge is more highly regarded than the artistic reflection of a world principle. The movement towards the characteristic accelerates still further: while Sophocles still paints whole characters and subordinates myth to their refined development, Euripides already paints only conspicuous individual character traits which can be expressed in intense passions; in the New Attic Comedy, all the masks wear a *single* expression, producing an unending procession of doddering old men, matchmakers who get their come-uppance, and mischievous slaves. Where has the myth-forming spirit of music gone? What remains of music is designed to elicit either excitement or nostalgia, music has become either a stimulant for dulled and exhausted nerves or tone painting. As far as the former is concerned, the text scarcely matters any more: already in Euripides, when his heroic choruses first intone their song, things proceed in a very slovenly manner; what point might it have reached in his impudent successors?

But the new un-Dionysian spirit reveals itself most clearly in the *conclusions* of the new drama. In the earlier tragedy one could feel the metaphysical consolation which can alone explain pleasure in tragedy; perhaps it is in *Oedipus at Colonus** that the reconciling sound from another world rings out in its purest form. Now that the genius of music has fled from tragedy, tragedy is strictly speaking dead: from what source should that metaphysical consolation be derived now? So a worldly solution to the tragic dissonance* was sought; the hero, after undergoing sufficient torture at the hands of fate, harvested his well-deserved reward in a stately marriage, in divine attestations of honour. The hero had become a much-wounded gladiator who occasionally received his freedom after putting up an effective fight. The *deus ex machina* took the place of metaphysical consolation. I do not mean to say that everywhere the tragic world-view was completely destroyed by the intrusion of the un-Dionysian spirit: we know only that it was forced to flee from art into the underworld, as it were, degenerating into a secret cult. But over the widest expanse of the Hellenic character raged the consuming breath of

the spirit which announced itself in the form of 'Greek serenity',
the spirit which we discussed earlier as a senile and unproductive
pleasure in existence; this serenity is a counterpart to the magnificent 'naïveté' of the earlier Greeks, as, according to the characteristics outlined previously, it is to be understood as the flower
of Apollonian culture springing forth from a gloomy abyss, as the
Hellenic will's triumph over suffering and the wisdom of suffering through its mirroring of beauty. The noblest form of that
other form of 'Greek serenity', the Alexandrian,* is the serenity of
the *theoretical man*: it shows the same characteristic signs which I
have just deduced from the un-Dionysian spirit—it combats
Dionysian wisdom and art, it seeks to dissolve myth, it replaces
metaphysical consolation with a worldly consonance,* even with
its own *deus ex machina*—namely the god of machines and
melting-pots,* that is, the powers of the natural spirits which are
known and used in the service of higher egoism—it believes that
the world is to be corrected through knowledge, that life can be
guided by science, and indeed it is actually capable of casting a
spell on the individual, confining him to a very narrow enchanted
circle of soluble tasks, within which he says serenely to life: 'I
want you: you are worth knowing.'

18

It is an eternal phenomenon: the craving will always find a way
to maintain its creatures in life and to compel them to live on by
spreading an illusion over things. One man is held fast by the
Socratic delight in knowledge and the delusion that it can help
him to heal the eternal wound of life, another is entangled in the
seductive veil of artistic beauty which hovers before his eyes, yet
another enthralled by the metaphysical consolation that under
the whirl of phenomena eternal life flows on indestructible, not to
mention the more common and almost more powerful illusions
which the will holds ready at any moment. Those three stages of
illusion are reserved exclusively for the more nobly constituted
natures who feel the burden and weight of existence with pro-

found displeasure and who must be deluded into forgetting this displeasure through a selection of stimulants. From these stimulants arises everything which we call culture: according to the proportions of the mixture we have a predominantly *Socratic* or *artistic* or *tragic* culture; or if I may avail myself of historical examples: either an Alexandrian or a Hellenic or an Indian (Brahmanic) culture.*

The whole of our modern world is caught in the net of Alexandrian culture and takes as its ideal the *theoretical man* who is equipped with the highest powers of knowledge, works in the service of science, and whose archetype and progenitor is Socrates. All our means of education have originally had this ideal in view, every other form of existence has to struggle laboriously upwards alongside it, as tolerated but not intended forms of existence. In an almost terrifying sense the educated man has long been found here only in the form of the scholar; even our poetic arts have had to develop from scholarly imitations and in the main effect of rhyme we recognize still the emergence of our poetic forms out of artificial experiments with a non-indigenous, genuinely scholarly language. How unintelligible must *Faust*,* the in himself intelligible modern man of culture, have appeared to a true Greek, the Faust who storms dissatisfied through all faculties, who is devoted to magic and the Devil because of his drive for knowledge, the Faust whom we have only to compare with Socrates to recognize that the modern man begins to sense the limits of that Socratic delight in knowledge and in the middle of that wide and desolate expanse of the sea of knowledge longs for land. When Goethe said to Eckermann with reference to Napoleon: 'Yes, my good man, there is such a thing as a productiveness of deeds',* he reminds us in a gracefully naïve way that the non-theoretical man is for the modern man something incredible and astonishing, so that the wisdom of a Goethe is required to find such a disturbing form of existence intelligible and even pardonable.

And at this point we should not conceal from ourselves what lies hidden in the womb of this Socratic culture! An optimism which deludedly believes itself without limits! Now we should not be afraid if the fruits of this optimism ripen, if the society which is steeped in such a culture down to its lowest depths gradually starts to tremble with the surge of rampant desires, if the belief in the happiness on earth for all, if the belief in the possibility of such a universal culture of knowledge, gradually turns into the threatening demand for such an Alexandrian happiness on earth, in the conjuring up of a Euripidean *deus ex machina*! Let us take note: Alexandrian culture needs a slave-class in order to be able to sustain its existence over any length of time, but in its optimistic view of existence, it denies the necessity of such a class and therefore, when the effect of its beautiful words of seduction and reassurance about the 'dignity of man' and the 'dignity of labour' is exhausted, it gradually drifts towards its end in horrific annihilation. There is nothing more fearful than a barbaric slave-class which has learnt to regard its existence as an injustice and is preparing to take revenge not just for itself but for all generations.* In the face of such threatening storms, who dares to call calmly on our pale and exhausted religions, whose very foundations have even degenerated into religions for scholars? This is so to such an extent that myth, the necessary presupposition of every religion, is already everywhere paralysed and even this religious domain has succumbed to the domination of that optimistic spirit which we have just characterized as the seed of our society's annihilation.

While the disaster slumbering in the womb of theoretical culture gradually begins to frighten modern man, and he searches in agitation among the treasure of his experiences for means to avert the danger without himself really believing in these means, while he therefore begins to sense the consequences of his predicament, great men of versatility have meanwhile been able with incredible level-headedness to use the tools of science itself in order to lay bare the limits and relative nature of knowledge itself and so to deny decisively the claim of science to universal validity and universal goals. In the process, the delusion which presumed to fathom the innermost essence of things with the aid of causality was for the first time recognized for what it was. The great audacity and wisdom of *Kant* and *Schopenhauer* succeeded in winning the most difficult victory, the victory over the optimism which lies hidden in the essence of logic, the optimism which is also the substratum of our culture.* While this optimism, founded firmly on the *aeternae veritates*,* had believed that all the enigmas of the world could be known and fathomed, and had treated space, time, and causality as utterly absolute laws of the most universal validity, Kant revealed how all these only really served to elevate the mere phenomenon, the work of Maya,* to the status of the single and highest reality and to put it in the place of the innermost and true essence of things, thereby making real knowledge of the latter impossible, that is, according to an expression of Schopenhauer's, lulling the dreamer into a deeper sleep (*The World as Will and Representation*, I*). With this knowledge a culture is introduced which I dare to describe as tragic, a culture whose most important characteristic is that wisdom replaces science as the highest goal, wisdom which, undeceived by the seductive distractions of the sciences, turns a calm gaze towards the whole image of the world and seeks to grasp as its own the eternal suffering found there with a sympathetic feeling of love. Let us imagine a future generation with this fearless gaze, with this heroic predisposition towards the tremendous, let us imagine the bold stride of these dragon-slayers, the proud audacity with which they turn their back on all the weakling doctrines of optimism, in order to 'live resolutely'* as completely as possible: would it not be necessary for the tragic man of this culture in the process of his self-education in seriousness and terror to desire a new art, the art of metaphysical consolation, to desire tragedy as his own Helen and to cry out with Faust:

> And should I not, most yearning power,
> Bring this most unique form to life?*

But now that Socratic culture only manages to hold on to the sceptre of its infallibility with trembling hands, having been shaken from two sides—once out of fear of its own consequences, which it at last begins to sense, and then again as it begins to doubt its former naïve trust in and conviction of the eternal validity of its foundations—it is a sad spectacle to behold as the dance of its thought continually plunges longingly towards new forms in order to embrace them, only then suddenly to recoil with a shudder, like Mephistopheles with the seductive Lamiae.* This is indeed the characteristic sign of that 'break' of which everyone customarily speaks as constituting the original suffering of modern culture, that the theoretical man, horrified and dissatisfied by the consequences of his predicament, no longer dares to entrust himself to the fearful icy current of existence, but instead runs anxiously up and down the river bank. He no longer wants anything whole, with its share of the natural horror of things. To such an extent has he been softened by the optimistic view of things. Moreover, he feels how a culture which is constructed on the principle of science must meet its end when it begins to become *illogical*, that is to flee from its own consequences. Our art reveals this universal distress: it is in vain that one relies on all the great productive periods and natures for models to imitate, it is in vain that one assembles the whole of 'world literature'* around modern man in order to console him and surrounds him with the artistic styles and artists of all times, so that he might, like Adam with the animals, give them a name:* he still remains eternally hungry, the weak and joyless 'critic', the Alexandrian man, who is basically a wretched librarian and proofreader blinded by book dust and printer's errors.

19

There is no clearer way to describe the innermost content of this Socratic culture than to call it the *culture of opera*:* for in that domain this culture has expressed its will and knowledge with its own particular naïveté, to our astonishment, when we compare the genesis of opera and the facts of its development with the eternal truths of the Apollonian and the Dionysian. I remind the reader in the first place of the emergence of the *stilo rappresentativo* and of recitative.* Is it credible that this completely externalized opera music, which is incapable of reverence, could be received and cherished with enthusiasm and good will, as the rebirth of all true music as it were, by an age in which none other than the inexpressibly sublime and holy music of Palestrina* had risen up? And on the other hand, who would consider those Florentine circles* with their sumptuous addiction to distraction and the vanity of their dramatic singers solely responsible for such an impetuous spread of delight in opera? That at the same time, indeed in the same people, alongside the vaulted architecture of Palestrina's harmonies in whose construction the whole of mediaeval Christianity had participated, that passion for a half-musical way of speaking awoke, I can only explain to myself by an *extra-artistic tendency* at work in the essence of recitative.

In that half-song, the singer corresponds to the listener who wishes to hear clearly the words beneath the sung music, by speaking rather than singing and heightening the pathos of the verbal expression; through this heightening of pathos, the singer makes the words easier to understand and overcomes the remaining musical half. The real danger which threatens the singer now is that he may give music the upper hand at the wrong moment, thus destroying the pathos and clarity of the words, while on the other hand he always feels the drive to musical discharge and to the virtuoso presentation of his voice. Here the 'poet' comes to his aid, who can offer him enough opportunities for lyrical interjections, repetitions of words and sentences: at which points the singer can now rest in the purely musical element without consideration of the words. This alternation between speech which is emotionally penetrating but only half sung and interjections which are entirely sung, an alternation which is the essence of the *stilo rappresentativo*, this rapidly switching effort, now to work on the concept and the idea, then to work on the musical ground of the listener, is something so completely unnatural and something so intrinsically in contradiction with the artistic drives of both the Dionysian and the Apollonian in equal measure, that one must deduce an origin of recitative which lies outside all the artistic instincts. In terms of this description, the recitative is to be defined as the mixture of epic and lyrical recital, by no means an intrinsically durable mixture, which is impossible in the case of such completely disparate things, but the most superficial mosaic-like conglutination, the like of which is without precedent in nature and experience. *But this opinion was not shared by the inventors of the recitative*: they themselves and their contemporaries believed that the *stilo rappresentativo* had discovered the secret of ancient music, which could alone explain the great effect of an Orpheus, of an Amphion,* indeed even of Greek tragedy. The new style was regarded as the re-awakening of the most effective music, ancient Greek music: indeed, in the general and completely popular view of the Homeric world as the *original world*, one might be entitled to succumb to the dream of having once again descended into the paradisiacal beginnings of humanity, in which music too must necessarily have possessed that unsurpassed purity, power, and innocence described so movingly in the pastoral plays of the poets. Here we may gaze into the innermost development of this really modern artistic genre, the opera: a powerful need wrests from itself an art, but it is a need of an unaesthetic kind: the longing for the idyll, the belief in an original prehistoric existence of the artistic good man. The recitative was considered the rediscovered language of that original primitive;* the opera as the rediscovered land of that idyllic or heroically good essence which simultaneously in all its actions follows a natural artistic drive, which in everything it has to say at least hums some tune or other in order at the slightest emotional stimulation to burst immediately into full-blooded song. It is for us now a matter of indifference that with this newly created image of the paradisiacal artist the humanists of that time* were struggling against the old ecclesiastical notion of man as in himself a corrupt and lost soul: so that opera is to be understood as the opposing dogma of the good man, which at the same time offered consolation for the pessimism induced in the serious men of that time by the horrific uncertainty of all conditions of life. It is enough to have recognized how the real magic and genesis of this new art-form lies in the satisfaction of a completely unaesthetic need, in the optimistic glorification of man himself, in the view of the primitive as the naturally good and artistic man: this operatic principle has gradually transformed itself into a threatening and terrible *demand*, which we with respect to the present socialistic movement* can no longer overlook. The good primitive, the 'noble savage'* demands his rights: what paradisiacal prospects!

I juxtapose to this another equally clear assertion of my opinion that opera is built on the same principles as our Alexandrian culture. Opera is the birth of the theoretical man, of the critical layman, not of the artist: one of the most disturbing facts in the history of all the arts. It was the demand of truly unmusical listeners that the words must be understood above all; so that a rebirth of the art of music is only to be expected through the discovery of a form of singing in which the words of the text dominate the counterpoint like the master the servant. For just as the soul is nobler than the body, the words are nobler than the accompanying harmonic system. It was with the crudeness of these lay, unmusical opinions that the link between music, image, and word was treated in the beginnings of opera; it was in the spirit of this aesthetic that the first experiments took place in the lay circles of the Florentine nobility, through the poets and singers who found patronage there. The artistically impotent man creates for himself a kind of art precisely because he is none other than the essentially unartistic man. Because he has no sense of the Dionysian depth of music, he transforms the enjoyment of music into the intelligible word-and-sound rhetoric of passion in the *stilo rappresentativo* and into the sensuality of the arts of song. Because he is incapable of seeing a vision, he presses the machinist and the decorative artist into his service; because he cannot grasp the true essence of the artist, he conjures up before himself the 'artistic primitive' according to his tastes, that is the man who sings and speaks verse passionately. He dreams himself back into a time when passion was sufficient to produce songs and poetry: as if emotion has ever been in a position to create something artistic. The presupposition of opera is a false belief concerning the artistic process, the idyllic belief that every man with feelings is really an artist. According to this belief, opera becomes the expression of the laity in art, the laity which dictates its laws with the serene optimism of the theoretical man.

Should we wish to unify in a single concept the two ideas just described at work in the emergence of opera, then it would only remain for us to speak of an *idyllic tendency in opera*: in the course of which we need only limit ourselves to Schiller's terminology and explanation.* Either, says Schiller, nature and the ideal are objects of mourning, when the former is represented as lost and the latter as unattained. Or both are objects of joy, in that they are imagined as real. The first instance produces the elegy in a narrow sense, the second the idyll in its widest sense. At this point, the shared characteristic of those two notions in the genesis of opera should be pointed out, namely that in them the ideal is neither felt to be unattained nor nature felt to be lost. This sentiment assumes the existence of an original age of man when he lay at the heart of nature and in this natural state had simultaneously achieved the ideal of humanity, in a paradisiacal goodness and artistry. From this perfect primitive we are all supposed to be descended, indeed all supposed to remain his faithful image: only we would have had to discard certain things in order to recognize ourselves once again as this primitive, through a voluntary renunciation of superfluous scholarliness, of over-rich culture. The Renaissance man of culture allowed himself to be led back through his opera-like imitation of Greek tragedy to such a harmony of nature and ideal, to an idyllic reality, he used this tragedy, as Dante used Virgil, as a guide in order to reach the gates of Paradise:* while he from that point on made his own way, made the transition from an imitation of the highest Greek art-form to a 'restoration of all things', to an imitation of the original artistic world of man. What good-natured confidence there is in these audacious efforts, right in the womb of theoretical culture!—a confidence to be explained only by the consoling faith that 'man in himself'* is the eternally virtuous opera hero, the eternally flute-playing or singing shepherd, who must in the end always rediscover himself as such, should he have ever really lost himself, a confidence to be understood only as the fruit of that optimism, which here rises out of the depths of that Socratic world-view like a sweetly seductive column of vapour.

So the features of opera do not bear the slightest trace of the elegiac pain of an eternal loss, but rather the serenity of eternal rediscovery, of comfortable pleasure in an idyllic reality, which one can at least imagine as real in that moment. But in imagining this, perhaps one day the suspicion might form that this supposed reality is nothing but a fantastically silly flirtation, and then all those capable of measuring it against the fearful seriousness of true nature and of comparing it with the real original scenes of the beginnings of humanity would be obliged to shout out in disgust: Away with this phantom! Nevertheless, one would be deceiving oneself if one believed it possible to frighten off such a flirtatious being as opera with a great shout, as if it were a ghost. He who wishes to annihilate opera must take up the struggle against the Alexandrian serenity which uses it to express its favourite idea with such naïveté, indeed whose real art-form it is. But what is to be expected for art itself from the operation of an art-form whose origins do not lie in the aesthetic domain at all but which has rather stolen over into the field of art from the half moral sphere and is only sporadically capable of deceiving us as to its hybrid origin? On what juices does this parasitic opera-being feed itself, if not on those of true art? Is it not to be suspected that under the influence of its idyllic seductions, of its Alexandrian arts of flattery, the highest task of art, the one which is most truly to be called serious—that of redeeming the eye from gazing into the horror of the night and of rescuing the subject from the convulsive impulses of the will through the healing balsam of appearance—will degenerate into an empty tendency to delightful distraction? What becomes of the eternal truths of the Dionysian and the Apollonian in such a mixture of styles as I have shown to constitute the essence of the *stilo rappresentativo*? where music is regarded as servant and the word as master, where music is compared with the body and the word with the soul? where the highest goal is at best directed towards an approximate tone painting, similar to that seen previously in the New Attic Dithyramb? where music is completely alienated from its true dignity as Dionysian mirror of the world, so that it only remains for it to imitate, as slave to the phenomenon, the latter's formal essence and to stimulate a superficial delight through the play of lines and proportions. On close scrutiny, this disastrous influence of opera on music coincides with the whole development of modern music; the optimism lurking in the genesis of opera and in the essence of the culture it represents has with frightening speed succeeded in stripping music of its Dionysian global purpose and in imprinting on it the character of a pleasurable play with forms: a transformation comparable only to the metamorphosis of the Aeschylean man into the serene Alexandrian.

But if in the exposition just outlined we have been right to relate the disappearance of the Dionysian spirit to the extremely striking but up until now unexplained transformation and degeneration of the Greek man—what hopes must revive in us when the very surest auspices guarantee the *reverse process*, *the gradual awakening of the Dionysian spirit* in our modern world! The divine power of Hercules cannot languish eternally in the luxurious slavery of Omphale.* From the Dionysian ground of the German spirit a power has risen up which has nothing in common with the original conditions of Socratic culture, a power which Socratic culture can neither explain nor excuse, but which it rather senses as something horrifically inexplicable, something overpoweringly hostile: *German music*, as we have to understand it principally in its powerful solar course from Bach* to Beethoven, from Beethoven to Wagner. What, under the most favourable circumstances, can the Socratic system of our time with its lust for knowledge even begin to do with this daemon rising from the unfathomable depths? Neither in the swooping movement and arabesques of operatic melody nor with the aid of the arithmetical abacus of the fugue and of contrapuntal dialectic can the formula be found in whose thrice-powerful light it would be possible to subjugate that daemon and force him to speak. What a spectacle we have before us now as our aestheticians cast the net of a 'beauty' which is peculiar to them, fishing for the genius of music which darts around with incredible vitality, with movements which ask to be judged as little in terms of the eternally beautiful as in terms of the sublime. One has only to take a close look at these suitors of music as they are in the flesh, tirelessly crying out 'Beauty! Beauty!', to judge if they distinguish themselves as the spoilt favourite children of nature, formed in the womb of the beautiful, or if they are not rather in pursuit of a deceitful disguise for their own lack of refinement, an aesthetic pretext for their own sobriety and poverty of feeling: here I am thinking for example of Otto Jahn.* But the liar and hypocrite should beware of German music: for, in the middle of all our culture, it is precisely music which is the sole unadulterated, pure, and purifying fire-spirit, out of which and into which, as in the doctrine of the great Heraclitus of Ephesus,* all things move in a double cycle: everything which we now call culture, education, civilization will at some stage have to appear before the infallible judge, Dionysus.

Let us recall then how Kant and Schopenhauer made it possible for the spirit of *German philosophy*, which flows from the same sources, to annihilate the complacent delight in existence taken by the scientific Socratic system, through the demonstration of the latter's limits, and how this demonstration introduced an infinitely more profound and serious consideration of ethical questions and art, which we might describe as the *Dionysian wisdom* grasped in concepts. In what direction does the *mysterium** of this unity between German music and German philosophy point if not towards a new form of existence, whose content we can only surmise on the basis of Hellenic analogies? For us who stand on the watershed between two different forms of existence, the Hellenic precedent possesses the incalculable value of bearing the stamp of all these transitions and struggles in a classical-didactic form: only we by analogy are living through the great periods of the Hellenic character in *reverse* as it were and now for example appear to be moving backwards from the Alexandrian age into the age of tragedy. In the process we feel as if the birth of a tragic age represents for the German spirit a return to itself, a blissful rediscovery of the self, after a long period during which the previously helpless barbaric form of this spirit had been suppressed by tremendous encroaching powers and forced into a feudal subservience to outside form. Now at last this spirit may, upon its return home to the original source of its character, dare to stride boldly and freely before all peoples, cut loose from the apron strings of a Romanic civilization:* if only that spirit understands how to learn untiringly from a people, the Greeks, whose pupils enjoy high praise and rare distinction merely for their ability to learn from such teachers. And when did we need these very greatest of teachers more than now, as we experience the *rebirth of tragedy* and are in danger of neither knowing where it comes from nor being able to interpret where it is going?

20

The eye of an impartial judge might at some stage decide in what age and in which men the German spirit has so far striven most powerfully to learn from the Greeks; and if we confidently assume that this distinction would have to be conferred exclusively on the noblest cultural struggle undertaken by Goethe, Schiller, and Winckelmann,* then it should in any case be added that since that time and the immediate effects of that struggle the effort to arrive by the same route at culture and the Greeks has grown incomprehensibly and steadily weaker. Should we, in order not to have to despair completely of the German spirit, not conclude that in some essential point or other those participants in the struggle might have failed to penetrate to the core of the Hellenic character and to establish a lasting bond of love between German and Greek culture?—so that perhaps an unconscious recognition of this shortcoming also aroused in more serious natures the despondent doubt as to whether in the foot-steps of such precursors they could advance further than the Greeks on this path of culture and even reach the goal at all. Since that time, therefore, we have seen the most disturbing degeneration in the value ascribed to the Greeks within educa-tion; expressions of compassionate superiority are to be heard in the most diverse camps of the spirit and of the spiritless. On the other hand, an utterly ineffectual smooth-talking rhetoric flirts with the terms 'Greek harmony', 'Greek beauty', 'Greek seren-ity'. And precisely those circles whose dignity might reside in tirelessly irrigating German culture with water from the Greek river-bed, the circles of teachers in the institutions of higher education, have learnt how best to deal swiftly and comfortably with the Greeks, often to the extent of sceptically renouncing the Hellenic ideal and completely perverting the true intention of all studies of the ancient world. And anyone in those circles who has not completely exhausted himself in the effort to become a reliable corrector of ancient texts or a student of language under the microscope in the manner of a natural historian, might also seek perhaps to appropriate the ancient Greek world 'historically', alongside other ancient worlds, but in any case in line with the method and superior expression of our contemporary cultured historiography.* If accordingly the level of real imagination in the higher institutions of learning has probably never been lower and weaker than at present, when the 'journalist', the paper slave of the day, has in all domains of culture triumphed over the higher teacher and left the latter no choice but to undergo the metamorphosis, experienced so many times before, into a serene scholarly butterfly, fluttering in the journalistic idiom with the 'light elegance' of this sphere—in what embarrassing confusion must such cultured men in such a period stare at that phenomenon which can perhaps only be understood analogically on the basis of the deepest principle of the previously uncomprehended Hellenic genius, namely the re-awakening of the Dionysian spirit and the rebirth of tragedy? There is no other artistic period in which so-called culture and genuine art would have confronted each other in such an estranged and hostile way as we see in the present with our own eyes. We can understand why such a weak culture hates true art; for it fears that it will bring about its demise. But has an entire kind of culture, namely the Socratic-Alexandrian, not outlived itself, when it culminates in such a delicate and shameful point as our present culture! If such heroes as Schiller and Goethe failed to break open that enchanted gate which leads into the Hellenic magic mountain, if their most courageous struggle advanced no further than that longing gaze which Goethe's Iphigenia sends back home over the sea from barbaric Tauris,* then what is to be hoped of the epigones of such heroes, unless the gate itself should suddenly swing open of its own accord on a completely different side, ignored by all the striving of culture so far—with the mystical sound of the re-awakened music of tragedy. Let no one seek to stunt our belief in a forthcoming rebirth of the ancient Hellenic world; for in it alone we find our hope for a renewal and purification of the German spirit through the fiery magic of music. What else could we name which might awaken some consoling expectation of the future in the midst of the desolation and exhaustion of contemporary culture? In vain we look around for a single root with powerful branches, for a spot of fertile and healthy soil: everywhere we see dust, sand, languishing paralysis. Here a disconsolate and solitary man might choose no better symbol than the knight accompanied by Death and the Devil, as Dürer* has drawn him, the knight in armour with the gaze of iron, who is able to make his way along the terrifying path undisturbed by his horrific companions and yet bereft of hope, having only horse and hound at his side. Our Schopenhauer was such a Dürer knight; he lacked all hope, but he wanted the truth. There are none like him.—

But how suddenly that wilderness of our tired culture which we described with such gloom a moment ago changes when touched by the Dionysian magic! A storm sweeps up everything which has outlived itself, everything brittle, broken, and withered, veils it in a spiralling cloud of red dust and carries it up into the heights like a vulture. Our confused gaze searches for what has disappeared: for what it sees resembles something which has risen as from a state of deep contemplation into the golden light, so full and green, so lavishly vital, so longingly immeasurable. Tragedy sits in the midst of this excess of pulsating life, pain, and pleasure, in sublime delight, listening to a distant melancholy song—it tells of the Mothers of Being,* whose names are: wild delusion, will, woe.*—Yes, my friends, believe with me in the Dionysian life and in the rebirth of tragedy. The age of the Socratic man is over: garland yourselves with ivy, take the thyrsus in your hands, and show no surprise when the tiger and the panther lie down fawning at your feet.* Only dare to be tragic men: for you are to be redeemed. You are to lead the Dionysian procession from India to Greece! Prepare yourselves for a hard struggle, but believe in the miracle of your god!

Slipping back from these exhortatory tones into the mood which befits the contemplative man, I repeat that only from the Greeks can we learn what such a sudden miracle-like awakening of tragedy means for the innermost foundation of the life of a people. It is the people of the tragic mysteries which fights the battles against the Persians:* and in turn the people which fought these wars needs tragedy as a necessary healing draft. Who would have suspected precisely in this people, after several generations during which its innermost being was stimulated by the strongest convulsions of the Dionysian daemon, that such a regular powerful effusion of the simplest political feeling, of the most natural home-instincts, of the original manly pleasure in struggle should continue to exist? Yet, if on the one hand, in any significant expansion of Dionysian agitation, one can always sense how the Dionysian loosening of the chains of the individual manifests itself first of all in a reduction of the political instincts, to the point of indifference or even hostility, then just as certainly on the other hand Apollo the genius of the *principium individuationis* is also the builder of states, and the affirmation of the individual personality is indispensable to the existence of the state and the sense of home. From the orgy there leads only one path for a people, the path to Indian Buddhism, which, in order for its longing for nothingness to be tolerated, needs those rare ecstatic states with their elevation above space, time, and the individual, as these states in turn require a philosophy which teaches how to overcome the indescribable displeasure of the intervening states through the force of an idea. A people which takes as its point of departure the absolute validity of the political instincts will just as necessarily end up following a path of extreme secularization, whose greatest but also most terrifying expression is the Roman *imperium*.*

Situated between India and Rome and forced to make a seductive choice, the Greeks managed to invent with classical purity an additional third form, admittedly not one they used personally for long, but for that very reason they achieved immortality. For that the favourites of the gods die young holds true in all things, but it is just as certain that they then enjoy eternal life with the gods. One should not ask of the noblest thing of all that it have the toughness and durability of leather; stout perseverance, as is typical for example of the Roman national drive, is in all probablity not one of the necessary predicates of perfection. But when we ask which remedy enabled the Greeks in their period of greatness, at the time of the extraordinary strength of their Dionysian and political drives, to avoid exhausting themselves either in ecstatic brooding or in a consuming pursuit of global power and prestige, and to achieve rather that glorious mixture resembling a noble wine, which both inflames and induces contemplation on the part of the drinker, then we must remember the tremendous power of *tragedy* which stimulates, purifies, and discharges the whole life of the people; whose highest value we only sense when it draws near us, as in the case of the Greeks, as the epitome of all prophylactic healing powers, as the mediator which holds sway over the strongest and in themselves most disastrous characteristics of the people.

Tragedy absorbs the most intense musical orgy into itself, so that it truly brings music to perfection, for the Greeks as for us. But then it juxtaposes to music tragic myth and the tragic hero, who, like a mighty Titan, relieves us of the burden of the whole Dionysian world by taking it on his shoulders. On the other hand, through this same tragic myth, in the person of the tragic hero, tragedy can also offer redemption from the craven impulse for this existence and with an admonishing gesture remind us of another being and of a higher joy, for which with a sense of foreboding the struggling hero prepares himself through his destruction rather than through his triumphs. Tragedy inserts between the universal validity of its music and the listener who is receptive to the Dionysian a sublime allegory, myth, and gives the spectator the impression that music is merely the highest means of representing and bringing to life the plastic world of myth. Trusting to this noble illusion, tragedy may now move its limbs to the dithyrambic dance and surrender itself without a thought to an orgiastic feeling of freedom, in which it is allowed to flourish as music in itself, thanks alone to this illusion. Myth protects us from music, while on the other hand myth alone gives music its highest freedom. For that reason, music in return lends tragic myth a penetrating and persuasive metaphysical significance which word and image could never achieve without that unique help. In particular, it is precisely here that the tragic spectator experiences a certain presentiment of a higher joy, the highest joy* which lies at the end of the path through destruction and negation, so that it appears to him as if the innermost abyss of things speaks to him audibly.

If in these preceding sentences I have been able to give no more than a provisional expression to this difficult idea, one which will be understood by only a few, then especially at this point I must continue to exhort my friends to further effort and ask them to use a single example of our common experience to prepare themselves for a universal principle. In this example, I will refrain from referring to those men who use the images of what takes place on stage, the words and emotions of the characters, to help them to approach the feeling of music; for none of these men speak music as their mother-tongue and in spite of the help they acquire proceed no further than the entrance-hall of the perception of music, without ever being permitted to touch its innermost shrines; some of these men, such as Gervinus,* do not even get as far as the entrance-hall. But I address myself exclusively to those who, directly related to music, born of its maternal womb as it were, relate to things almost exclusively through unconscious musical relations. To these genuine musicians I direct the question of whether they can imagine someone capable of experiencing the third act of *Tristan and Isolde** purely as a vast symphonic movement, with no help from word and image, without expiring under the convulsive beating of the wings of the entire soul? Imagine a man, who as here has laid his ear as it were on the heart chamber of the world-will, who feels the mad desire for existence flow outwards into all the veins of the world in the form of a thundering torrent or of the gentlest spraying brook, should such a man not suddenly shatter into pieces? How could such a man, enclosed in the miserable glass shell of human individuality, endure the echo of countless cries of pleasure and woe from the 'wide space of the night of the worlds',* without inexorably fleeing to his original home in this pastoral roundel of metaphysics? But if such a work could still be perceived as a whole, without negating individual existence, is such a creation possible, without smashing its creator to pieces? Where do we find the solution to such a contradiction?

Here the tragic myth and the tragic hero interpose themselves between our highest musical stimulation and this music, basically as mere allegories of the most universal facts of which music alone can speak directly. If we experienced feelings as pure Dionysian beings, however, myth would now, as allegory, come to a standstill beside us, completely ineffective and ignored, and fail to distract us for a moment from listening to the echo of the *universalia ante rem*.* Yet here the *Apollonian* power breaks out, directed towards the restoration of the almost shattered individual, with the curative balm of a blissful illusion: suddenly we believe that we still see nothing more than Tristan standing motionless, asking himself in muffled tones: 'The old melody; why does it wake me?'* And what appeared to us earlier as a hollow sigh from the centre of being now only wants to say how 'desolate and empty is the sea'.* And where we wrongly imagined our breathless extinction, in the racked convulsions of all our feelings, and imagined ourselves with little to tie us to this existence, we now see and hear the hero, mortally wounded and yet not dying, with his desperate cry: 'Longing! Longing! To die longing and through longing not to die!'* And if earlier, after such an excess and surplus of consuming torments, the jubilation of the horn cuts us to the heart almost as the highest torment, so the exultant Kurwenal* now stands between us and this 'jubilation in itself',* turned towards the ship which carries Isolde. In spite of the violence with which compassion affects us internally, its sympathetic suffering* rescues us in a certain sense from the original suffering* of the world, just as the allegorical image of myth rescues us from the direct contemplation of the highest world idea, just as thought and word rescue us from the unbridled outpouring of the unconscious will. That magnificent Apollonian illusion makes it appear as if even the realm of music confronts us as a plastic world, as if Tristan and Isolde's fate had been formed and moulded in it too, as in the most tender and expressive material.

So the Apollonian tears us away from the Dionysian universality and allows us to delight in individuals; it chains the arousal of our compassion to these individuals, and through them it satisfies the sense of beauty which craves great and sublime forms; it leads a procession of images of life past us and stimulates us to grasp in thought the core of life contained in them. With the tremendous proliferation of the image, the concept, the ethical doctrine, the arousal of sympathy, the Apollonian principle tears man up out of his orgiastic self-annihilation and deceives him about the universality of the Dionysian process by deluding him that he sees one single image of the world, Tristan and Isolde for example, and that, *through music*, he should merely *see* it better and more inwardly. What can the healing magic of Apollo not achieve, when it can even arouse in us the illusion that the Dionysian is really in the service of the Apollonian and that it is really capable of heightening the latter's effects, and indeed even that music is essentially a representational art with an Apollonian content?

In that pre-established harmony* which reigns between the perfect drama and its music, theatre reaches a very high degree of vividness, otherwise unattainable for verbal drama. In the independently moving melodic lines, all the living forms of the stage resolve themselves before us into the simplified clarity of the curved line, and the juxtaposition of these lines rings out to us in the alternation of harmonies which sympathizes in the most delicate way with the movement of the action on stage: through these harmonies, the relations of things become directly available to our senses in a concrete and not at all abstract manner, as we likewise recognize that it is only through these relations that the essence of character and of melodic line reveals itself clearly. And while music thus forces us to see more widely and more inwardly than otherwise and to spread out the action of the stage before us like a delicate web, the world of the stage is for our spiritualized inward-looking eye infinitely expanded and illuminated from within. What could the poet offer by way of comparison, the poet who strives to achieve that inward expansion of the visible world of the stage and its inward illumination with a much less perfect mechanism, by indirect means, through word and concept? Although the musical tragedy itself admittedly includes the word, it can still at the same time juxtapose the underworld and the birth-place of the word and clarify its development for us from the inside.

But one could with equal certainty say of the process just described that it is merely a magnificent appearance, namely that Apollonian *illusion* which was mentioned before, whose effect seeks to unburden us of the Dionysian compulsion and excess. Indeed, at bottom, the relation between music and drama is precisely the opposite: music is the real idea of the world, drama is only the reflection of this idea, its isolated shadow image. That identity between the melodic line and the living form, between harmony and the character relations of that form is true in an opposite sense to that in which it might appear to us as we contemplate musical tragedy. However much we agitate, animate, and illuminate this form from within with the greatest visibility, it still remains a mere phenomenon, from which there is no bridge leading to the true reality, to the heart of the world. But music speaks from this heart; and no matter how many phenomena of that kind may accompany the same music, they would never exhaust its essence, but rather always remain only its externalized copies. With respect to the difficult relation between music and drama, nothing is to be explained and everything to be confused by the popular and completely false opposition between soul and body; but the unphilosophical crudity of that opposition seems to have become precisely for our aestheticians a well-known article of faith—for who knows what reasons—while they have learnt nothing about the opposition between the phenomenon and the thing in itself, or, for likewise unknown reasons, refuse to learn anything about it.

If our analysis has yielded the result that the Apollonian element in tragedy has through its illusion triumphed completely over the original Dionysian element of music and subordinated it to its aims, namely, the highest clarification of the drama, then it would be necessary to add a very important qualification: at the most essential point that Apollonian illusion is broken through and annihilated. Drama, which with the aid of music unfolds before us all its movements and forms in such inwardly illuminated clarity—as if the fabric is being woven on the loom before our very eyes as the shuttle moves back and forth—achieves an over-all effect which lies *beyond all Apollonian artistic effects*. In the overall effect of tragedy, the Dionysian again achieves predomin-ance: tragedy concludes with a sound which could never ring forth from the realm of Apollonian art. And in the process the Apollonian illusion shows itself for what it is, the veiling for the duration of the tragedy of a real Dionysian effect. Yet this Diony-sian effect is so powerful that it ultimately forces the Apollonian drama itself into a sphere where it begins to speak with Dionysian wisdom, negating itself and its Apollonian visibility. So the dif-ficult relation between the Apollonian and the Dionysian in tra-gedy should really be symbolized through a fraternal bond between both deities: Dionysus speaks the language of Apollo, and Apollo finally speaks the language of Dionysus, and so the highest goal of tragedy and of art itself is achieved.

22

On the basis of his own experience, let the attentive friend imagine the effect of a true musical tragedy in a pure and unadulterated form. I think I have described this effect from both sides in such a way that he is now in a position to interpret his own experience for himself. For he will remember how the myth which passed before him made his faculties feel heightened to a kind of omniscience, as if the power of his vision now no longer stopped short at the surface of things, but penetrated to their inside, as if the aid of music enabled him to see before him, made visible to the senses as it were, the surging of the will, the conflict of motives, the rising torrent of the passions, like an abundance of vividly moving lines and figures, and thus allowed him to immerse himself in the most delicate secrets of the unconscious impulses. But while he becomes conscious of such a great heightening of those drives directed towards visibility and transfiguration, he feels just as surely that this long series of Apollonian artistic effects still *fails* to bring about that contented lingering in will-less contemplation produced in him by the works of art of the sculptor and the epic poet, those truly Apollonian artists: that is, the justification of the world of the *individuatio** achieved through such contemplation, which is the pinnacle and epitome of Apollonian art. He sees the transfigured world of the stage and yet negates it. He sees the tragic hero before him in epic clarity and beauty and yet takes pleasure in his annihilation. He comprehends the action on stage to its innermost core yet gladly takes refuge in the incomprehensible. He feels the actions of the hero to be justified and yet is even more edified when these actions annihilate their author. He shudders at the sufferings which the hero will encounter and yet senses in them a higher, far superior pleasure. He sees more widely and more deeply than ever before and yet wishes he were blind. Where must we seek the cause of this miraculous self-division, this breaking of the Apollonian pinnacle, if not in the *Dionysian* magic which, while apparently stimulating the Apollonian impulses to the highest pitch, is still capable of forcing the exuberance of this Apollonian force into its service. The *tragic myth* is to be understood only as a transformation of the wisdom of Dionysus into images through the artistic means of Apollo; the myth pushes the world of phenomena up against its limits where it negates itself and seeks to flee back into the womb of the one true reality, where it then seems to intone its metaphysical swansong with Isolde:

> In the heaving swell
> Of the sea of bliss,
> In the ringing sound
> Of the perfumed waves,
> In the wafting Whole
> Of the world-breath—
> To drown—to sink—
> Unconscious—highest joy!*

In this way, from the experience of the truly aesthetic listener, the tragic artist himself, we imagine as he, like a sumptuous deity of the *individuatio*, creates his forms, a process which means that his work can scarcely be understood as an 'imitation of nature'— as his vast Dionysian drive swallows up this whole phenomenal world in order to suggest behind it and through its annihilation a highest original artistic joy in the womb of the original Unity. Of course, our aestheticians can tell us nothing about this return to the original home, about the fraternal bond between both artistic deities in tragedy, about the stimulation of the listener, which is as Apollonian as it is Dionysian, while they never tire of describing as the real essence of the tragic the hero's struggle with fate, the triumph of the moral world-order or the discharge of emotions brought about by tragedy: such undauntedness makes me think that they are men incapable of aesthetic stimulation, men who, when they listen to a tragedy, are perhaps to be considered as merely moral beings. Since Aristotle, there has been no explanation of the effect of tragedy from which the artistic state, the aesthetic activity of the listener might be deduced. Sometimes the seriousness of the action onstage is supposed to relieve us of our compassion and fear through discharge, sometimes the triumph of good and noble principles or the sacrifice of the hero in the interests of a moral world-view is supposed to edify and enthuse us; and while I am convinced that this and this alone is the effect of tragedy for countless people, it seems equally clear that all these people, together with their aesthetic interpreters, have experienced nothing of tragedy as a supreme *art*. This pathological discharge, Aristotle's catharsis,* which defies the attempts of philologists to classify it as either a medical or moral phenomenon, recalls a remarkable notion of Goethe's: 'Without a lively pathological interest,' he says, 'I have never managed to treat any kind of tragic situation whatsoever, and I have as a result preferred to avoid them rather than to seek them out. Might it have been one of the merits of the ancients that the highest pathos remained for them no more than an aesthetic game, while for us the truth of nature must participate in order to produce such a work?'* We may now in the light of our magnificent experiences answer this last so very profound question in the affirmative, having witnessed with astonishment precisely in the musical tragedy how even the highest pathos can be nothing more than an aesthetic game: this is why we are entitled to believe that it is only now that the original phenomenon of the tragic can be described with any success. Anyone who at this point continues to talk only of those substitute effects from extra-aesthetic spheres and does not feel himself elevated above the pathological-moral process must doubt his aesthetic nature: whereupon we recommend to him as an innocent substitute the interpretation of Shakespeare in the manner of Gervinus* and the diligent detection of 'poetic justice'.

So with the rebirth of tragedy the *aesthetic listener* is also reborn, whose place in the stalls has up until now usually been occupied by a strange *quid pro quo*,* with half moral and half scholarly pretensions, the 'critic'. Everything in his sphere so far has been artificial and no more than thinly coated with an appearance of life. The representational artist was in fact at a loss as to how to deal with such a critically disposed listener and so, together with the dramatist or opera composer who inspired him, he looked around in agitation for the last vestiges of life in this pretentious and desolate being for whom enjoyment was an impossibility. But up to that point the public was comprised of such 'critics': the student, the schoolboy, indeed even the most harmless female creature had, unknown to them, been prepared through education and newspapers for the same perception of a work of art. The nobler natures among the artists counted on the arousal of moral-religious forces in such a public, and the call of the 'moral world-order' stepped in vicariously where a powerful artistic magic should really have delighted the genuine listener. Or the dramatist presented a greater, at least exciting, tendency of the contemporary political and social world in such a clear way that the listener could forget his critical exhaustion and surrender himself to similar emotions to those experienced in moments of patriotism or war, or before the speaker's platform in parliament, or at the judicial sentencing of crime and sin: a kind of estrangement from the real intentions of art which on occasion could only lead directly to a cult of tendentiousness. Yet what happened next is what has always happened to all artificial arts since time began, a searingly swift depravation of that tendentiousness, so that for example the tendency to use the theatre as an institution for the moral education of the people, which was still taken seriously in Schiller's time,* is already counted among the incredible antiques of an obsolete culture. While the critic had come to dominate the theatre and concert, as the journalist had come to dominate the school, and the press had come to dominate society, art degenerated into an entertainment object of the lowest kind, and aesthetic criticism was used as the means of binding together a vain, distracted, selfish and moreover poor and unoriginal sociability, whose character is explained by Schopenhauer's parable of the porcupines;* so that at no time had there been so much chatter about art yet so little value placed upon it. But is it still possible to have anything to do with a man who is capable of holding a conversation about Beethoven and Shakespeare? Let everyone answer this question according to his feelings: he will in any case prove by his answer what he understands by the word 'culture', assuming that he tries to answer the question at all and is not already struck dumb with surprise.

On the other hand, many a man of naturally noble and delicate disposition, regardless of whether he had gradually become a critical barbarian in the way described, might perhaps have a tale to tell of the unexpected and unintelligible effect which a successful production of *Lohengrin** produced in him: except that perhaps at the time he lacked an admonishing hand to interpret the experience for him, so that the unintelligible diversity and thoroughly incomparable nature of the feeling which shook him at that moment was not repeated and, like an enigmatic star, shone only briefly before extinction. But in that moment he had an inkling of what the aesthetic listener is.

23

Anyone who wants to investigate for himself with complete accuracy to what extent he is related to the true aesthetic listener or belongs to the community of Socratic-critical people, has only to ask himself honestly about the feeling with which he accepts the *miracle* represented on stage: whether his historical sense, with its orientation towards strict psychological causality, feels insulted, whether he concedes benevolently as it were that the miracle might be admitted as a phenomenon intelligible to a child but unfamiliar to him, or whether he experiences anything else. For in this way he will be able to measure to what extent he is capable of understanding *myth*, the compressed world-image, which, as abbreviation of the phenomenon, cannot dispense with the miracle. It is probable, however, that almost everyone on strict examination feels so undermined by the critical-historical spirit of our culture that he can make the former existence of myth credible to himself only in a scholarly way, through mediating abstractions. But without myth every culture forfeits its healthy, natural creative force: only a horizon defined by myths completes the unity of a whole cultural movement. Only myth can rescue all the forces of imagination and of the Apollonian dream from their aimless roaming. The images of myth must be the omnipresent but unnoticed daemonic guardians, under whose protection the young soul grows to maturity and whose signs enable the grown man to interpret his life and his struggles: and even the state knows no more powerful unwritten laws than the mythical foundation which guarantees its connection with religion, its growth from the mythical notions.

Now let us juxtapose to this the abstract man bereft of guiding myths, with his abstract education, abstract morals, abstract law, abstract state; let us imagine the roaming of artistic imagination, bereft of rules and no longer held in check by an indigenous myth; let us imagine a culture, which has no fixed and sacred original seat, but is condemned to exhaust all possibilities and to feed wretchedly on all other cultures—that is our present age, the result of that Socratism directed towards the annihilation of myth. And now the man bereft of myth stands eternally starving among all the past ages and digs and rummages in search of roots, even in the most remote of the ancient worlds. What does the tremendous historical need of this dissatisfied modern culture, the collection of countless other cultures, the consuming desire for knowledge point to, if not to the loss of myth, to the loss of the mythic home, of the mythic maternal womb? Let us ask ourselves if the feverish and so uncanny agitation of this culture is anything other than the starving man's craven grasping and snatching after food—and who would want to give something more to such a culture, which remains unsatisfied by all that it devours and whose touch habitually transforms the strongest, healthiest food into 'history and criticism'?

One would have to have painful doubts too about our German character, if it had already become inextricably entwined, indeed become one, with its culture, as we can observe to our horror in civilized France.* And what was for a long time France's great merit and the cause of its vast superiority, precisely that unity of people and culture, might compel us in view of this sight to praise our good fortune that this so questionable culture of ours has so far had nothing in common with the noble core of our character as a people. Rather, all our hopes reach out longingly towards the perception that under the agitated convulsions and spasms of the life of culture and education a magnificent, intrinsically healthy, ancient, and original force lies hidden, which admittedly only stirs itself powerfully at occasional moments of tremendous importance before returning to its dream of a future awakening. The German Reformation* grew forth from this abyss, the Reformation in whose chorales the future melody of German music first rang out. So deep, courageous, soulful and so effusively good and tender, this chorale of Luther's* rings out from the thick undergrowth as the first Dionysian luring call at the approach of spring. It was answered in a competing echo by that solemnly arrogant festival procession of Dionysian enthusiasts, to whom we owe German music—and to whom we shall owe the *rebirth of German myth*!

I know that I must now lead the sympathetic and interested friend to a lofty place of solitary contemplation, where he will have but few companions, and call out to him in encouragement to hold fast to our brilliant guides, the Greeks. So far, for the purification of our aesthetic knowledge, we have borrowed from them those two divine figures, who rule over separate realms of art, and about whose reciprocal contact and intensification Greek tragedy gave us an inkling. It had to appear to us that the demise of Greek tragedy was the result of a remarkable tearing asunder of those two original artistic drives: a process accompanied by a degeneration and transformation of the character of the Greek people, something which requires that we think seriously about how necessarily and inextricably entwined the fundamental connections are between art and people, myth and morality, tragedy and state. This demise of tragedy was at the same time the demise of myth. Up until then the Greeks felt spontaneously compelled to relate all their experiences to their myths, and indeed to understand their experiences only in terms of this relation: as a result, even the most immediate present often had to appear to them *sub specie aeterni** and in a certain sense as timeless. But the state immersed itself as much as art in this current of timelessness, in order to find respite from the burden and craving of the moment. And the value of a people—like that of a man as well—is determined precisely by its ability to impress on its experiences the stamp of the eternal; for it is in the process de-secularized* as it were and reveals its unconscious inner conviction of the relativity of time and of the true, that is, metaphysical, meaning of life. The opposite occurs when a people begins to understand itself historically and to smash to pieces the mythical bulwarks which surround it, a process which is usually accompanied by a decisive secularization,* a break with the unconscious metaphysics of its earlier existence, in all its ethical consequences. Greek art and principally Greek tragedy postponed above all the annihilation of myth: they too had to be annihilated in order to allow life to be lived free from the indigenous soil, without restraint in the wilderness of thought, morality, and the deed. Even now that metaphysical drive still tries to create for itself a form of transfiguration, albeit an attenuated one, in the Socratism of science which compels one to live; but in its less developed forms this same drive led only to a feverish quest, which gradually lost itself in a pandaemonium of myths and superstitions assembled from all over and piled on top of one another: in the midst of which the Hellene sat with a heart still unquenched, until he learnt how to mask that fever with Greek serenity and Greek frivolity, as Graeculus,* or how to anaesthetize himself completely in some Orientally muffled superstition.*

Since the re-awakening of the Alexandrian-Roman ancient world in the fifteenth century, after a long interlude which evades easy description, we have drawn near to this condition in the most striking way. On the heights, we encounter this same lavish pleasure in knowledge, the same unsated delight in discovery, the same tremendous secularization, accompanied by a homeless roaming, a craven imposition on the tables of strangers, a frivolous apotheosis of the present or a dull anaesthetized withdrawal, all *sub specie saeculi*,* viewed from the standpoint of the 'present': these similar symptoms suggest a similar lack at the heart of this culture, the annihilation of myth. It seems scarcely possible to transplant a foreign myth with lasting success, without irreversibly damaging the tree in the process: the occasional tree may perhaps prove sufficiently strong and healthy to excise the foreign element through a fearful struggle, but must more usually consume itself in stunted infirmity or in rampant but sickly growth. We think so highly of the pure and strong core of the German character that we dare to expect it to excise the foreign elements which have been forcibly implanted and consider that the German spirit may well be in the process of returning to itself. Some may think that this spirit must begin its struggle with the excision of everything Romanic:* and for this task they might consider the courageous triumph and bloody glory of the recent war* an external preparation and encouragement, but they must seek the inner necessity in the struggle to remain always worthy of the sublime pioneers on this path, Luther as much as our great artists and poets. But may they never believe themselves capable of waging similar struggles without their household gods, without their mythical home, without a 'restoration' of all things German! And if the German should look around hesitantly for a leader* to bring him back again to the long-lost homeland, whose highways and byways he has almost completely forgotten—let him listen for the blissfully beckoning call of the Dionysian bird, which hovers above him and wants to show him the way.

24

Among the peculiar artistic effects of the musical tragedy we had to emphasize an Apollonian *illusion*, through which we were supposed to be rescued from direct unity with Dionysian music, while our musical agitation could discharge itself in an Apollonian domain and on a visible middle-world interposed between the two. In the process, we thought we had observed how it was precisely through this discharge that the middle-world of stage action, drama itself, became visible and intelligible from the inside out to an extent unattainable in all other Apollonian art: so that here, where Apollonian art was as it were swept up elated into the heights by the spirit of music, we had to recognize the greatest intensification of its powers and thus see in that fraternal bond between Apollo and Dionysus the pinnacle of the Apollonian as well as the Dionysian aims of art.

Admittedly, the Apollonian projected image did not achieve the peculiar effect of the weaker degrees of Apollonian art through inner illumination by means of music; what the epic or the sculpted stone infused with soul can do—force the contemplating eye to that calm delight in the world of the *individuatio*—that could not be achieved here, in spite of a greater infusion of soul and clarity. As we watched the drama, our penetrating gaze entered the turbulent inner world of motives—and yet it seemed to us as if this were only an allegorical image which was passing before us, whose most profound meaning we almost believed we had guessed, and which we wished to pull back like a curtain, in order to catch sight of the original image behind. The most radiant clarity of the image was not enough for us: for this appeared to conceal as much as it revealed; and while its allegorical revelation seemed to invite the tearing of the veil and the disclosure of the secret background, at the same time the total visibility of that radiance held the eye in its spell and prevented it from penetrating more deeply.

Anyone who has not undergone this experience of having to see and at the same time to long for something beyond seeing, will have difficulty imagining how definitely and clearly these two processes are felt to exist in parallel in the contemplation of the tragic myth: while the truly aesthetic spectators will confirm for me that among the peculiar effects of tragedy this existence of two processes in parallel is the most remarkable. If one now translates this phenomenon of the aesthetic spectator into an analogous process in the tragic artist, one will have understood the genesis of the *tragic myth*. The tragic artist shares with the Apollonian sphere of art the full pleasure in appearance and in seeing, and at the same time he negates this pleasure and takes an even higher satisfaction in the annihilation of the visible world of appearance. The content of the tragic myth is in the first place an epic event involving the glorification of the struggling hero: but what explains the in itself enigmatic trait of the hero's fateful suffering, the most painful triumphs, the most tormented conflicts of motive, in brief the illustration of the wisdom of Silenus, or, aesthetically expressed, of ugliness and disharmony, what explains that all this is represented again and again in such countless forms, and with such predilection in precisely the most sumptuous and youthful age of a people, if it is not the source of a very great pleasure?

To say that in life things really do turn out so tragically would be the least satisfactory explanation of the emergence of an art form, if art is not merely an imitation of the reality of nature, but rather a metaphysical supplement to the reality of nature, set alongside it for the purpose of overcoming it. The tragic myth, in so far as it belongs to art at all, also participates fully in art's metaphysical intention to transfigure: but what does it transfigure, when it presents the world of phenomena in the image of the suffering hero? Least of all the 'reality' of this world of phenomena, for it says to us: 'Look here! Take a close look! This is your life! This is the hour hand on the clock of your existence!'

And myth showed us this life in order to transfigure it? But if this is not the case, then wherein lies the aesthetic pleasure, with which we let those images pass before us? I ask about aesthetic pleasure but know very well that many of these images can produce, at the same time moreover, a moral delight, for instance in the form of compassion or of a moral triumph. But as for those who would wish to deduce the effect of the tragic exclusively from these moral sources, as has admittedly for all too long usually been the case in aesthetics, let them at least not believe that they have in the process accomplished something for art: art which above all must demand purity in its domain. To explain the tragic myth, the first requirement is none other than to seek the pleasure peculiar to it in the purely aesthetic sphere, without reaching over into the domain of compassion, fear, of the moral-sublime. How can ugliness and disharmony, the content of the tragic myth, stimulate an aesthetic pleasure?

At this point it now becomes necessary for us to launch ourselves with a bold leap into the metaphysics of art, repeating the earlier principle that existence and the world appear justified only as an aesthetic phenomenon: in this sense the tragic myth has to convince us that even ugliness and disharmony is an artistic game which the will plays with itself in the eternal abundance of its joy. But this original and not easily understood phenomenon of Dionysian art may be grasped in intelligible and unmediated form in the miraculous meaning of *musical dissonance*:* music alone, when placed alongside the world, can give an idea of what is to be understood by the justification of the world as an aesthetic phenomenon. The pleasure produced by the tragic myth shares the same home as the pleasurable sensation of dissonance in music. The Dionysian, with its original joy perceived even in pain, is the shared maternal womb of music and of tragic myth.

Is it not the case that the difficult problem of the tragic effect has not in the mean time been made essentially easier by our enlisting the aid of the musical relation of dissonance? But let us now understand what it means to want to see tragedy and at the same time to long for something beyond seeing: a condition which we would, with respect to the artistic use of dissonance, equally have to characterize as wanting to hear and at the same time longing for something beyond hearing. That striving towards the infinite, the beating of the wings of longing, which accompanies the highest joy* in clearly perceived reality, recall that we must recognize in both states a Dionysian phenomenon, which reveals to us again and again the playful construction and destruction of the individual world as the overflow of an original joy, in a similar way to that in which Heraclitus the Obscure* compares the world-forming force to a child at play, arranging and scattering stones here and there, building and then trampling sand-hills.

So in order to evaluate accurately the Dionysian capacity of a people, we ought to think not only of its music but just as necessarily of its tragic myth as the second witness of that capacity. Similarly, one might now suspect from this most intimate relation between music and myth, that the degeneration and depravation of the one will be linked to the withering of the other: if the weakening of myth really does indicate the failing strength of the Dionysian capacity. But a glance at the development of the German character should leave one in no doubt about either: in opera as in the abstract character of our existence once bereft of myth, in an art immersed in delight as in a life deduced from a concept, that immediately unartistic and as it were life-consuming nature of Socratic optimism reveals itself. For our consolation, however, there were signs that the German spirit might nevertheless remain intact, dreaming peacefully in an inaccessible abyss, in magnificent health, depth, and Dionysian strength, like a knight sunk in sleep: and from this abyss the Dionysian song rises up, telling us that even now this German knight still dreams his ancient and original Dionysian myth in blissful-serious visions. Let no one believe that the German spirit has lost its mythical home for all eternity, when it can still understand so clearly the birdsong which tells it of that home. One day it will awaken in the morning freshness which follows a great sleep: then it will slay dragons, annihilate the spiteful dwarves, and awaken

Brünnhilde—and Wotan's spear* itself will not be able to bar its way!

My friends, you who believe in Dionysian music, you too know what tragedy means to us. There we find tragic myth, reborn from music—and there you may hope for everything and forget what is most painful! But what is most painful for us all is—the protracted disgrace in which the German genius, estranged from house and home, lives in the service of spiteful dwarves. You understand my words—as you will also ultimately understand my hopes.

25

Music and tragic myth are equal expressions of the Dionysian capacity of a people and are inseparable from one another. Both stem originally from an artistic domain which lies beyond the Apollonian; both transfigure a region in whose chords of joy both dissonance and the terrible world-image fade away seductively; both play with the thorn of displeasure, trusting to their extremely powerful magic arts; and through this play, both justify the existence of even the 'worst world'. Here the Dionysian shows itself, in comparison with the Apollonian, as the eternal and original power of art, which calls the whole world of phenomena into existence: in whose midst a new transfiguring appearance becomes necessary in order to keep alive the busy world of individuation. If we could imagine dissonance in human form*—and what is man but that?—then this dissonance, in order to be able to live, would need a magnificent illusion to cast a veil of beauty over its own essence. This is the true artistic intention of Apollo: whose name summarizes all those countless illusions of beautiful appearance, which in each moment make existence worth living and compel us to live on to experience the next moment.

In the process, only precisely as much of that foundation of all existence, of the Dionysian substratum of the world, may enter into the consciousness of the human individual as can be overcome again by the Apollonian power of transfiguration, so that both of these artistic drives are compelled to develop their forces in strict proportion to one another, according to the law of eternal justice. Where the Dionysian powers rise up so impetuously, as we are now experiencing them, there Apollo must already have descended to us veiled in a cloud; Apollo, whose most sumptuous effects of beauty will probably be seen by the next generation.

But that this effect is necessary should be sensed intuitively and most surely by everyone, who has once, even in dream, felt himself transported back into an ancient Hellenic existence: strolling beneath lofty Ionian colonnades, gazing up towards a horizon defined by pure and noble lines, accompanied by reflections of his transfigured form in the shining marble at his side, surrounded by men who move with solemn stride or delicate gait, speaking a language of harmonious sounds and rhythmic gestures—would he not, in the face of this continual stream of beauty, have to raise his hand to Apollo and call out: 'Blessed people of the Hellenes! How great Dionysus must be among you, if the god of Delos* considers such magic necessary to cure you of your dithyrambic madness!'—But a venerable old Athenian, observing him with the sublime eye of Aeschylus, might reply to someone so moved: 'Yet say this too, you miraculous stranger: how much must this people have suffered in order to become so beautiful! But now follow me to the tragedy and let us perform a sacrifice in the temple of both deities!'

EXPLANATORY NOTES

1 *The Birth of Tragedy ... Attempt at a Self-Criticism*: title-page of the second edition of 1886. In the second edition, the title-page of the first edition of 1872 was retained, as here, before the Foreword to Richard Wagner.

3 *'serenity'*: in German: *Heiterkeit*.

Franco-Prussian War of 1870–1 ... battle of Wörth ... Metz ... Versailles: in the summer of 1870, following a dispute over the succession to the Spanish throne, Napoleon III, Emperor of France, declared war on Prussia. After a rapid succession of military defeats and the capture of Napoleon III at Sedan on 2 September 1870, the Second Empire was dissolved and a new French republic declared on 4 September. The new government finally capitulated on 28 January 1871. The battle of Wörth took place on 6 August 1870, the battles of Metz on 14, 16, 18 August, and 31 August to 1 September. As medical orderly, Nietzsche probably participated in the last engagement. The newly unified Germany became an Empire (*Reich*) when King Wilhelm I of Prussia was declared Emperor in Versailles on 18 January 1871. The peace agreement between the Empire and France was negotiated at Versailles on 26 February 1871.

Indians: for Nietzsche, Indian culture represents the triumph of a culture of fatalism and passivity, embodied in Buddhism.

4 *'fear'*: in German: '*das Fürchten*'. Allusion to Wagner's *Siegfried* (1871), where the Wanderer (Wotan) spares the dwarf Mime's life, reserving it as a future forfeit for one '*der das Fürchten nicht gelernt*' ('who has not learnt how to fear') (I. ii). This subsequently turns out to be Siegfried himself.

Socratism: for Nietzsche, Socrates represents the beginning of rationalism and the end of the culture of Greek tragedy based on myth rather than reason.

Epicurean: the Greek philosopher Epicurus (341–270 BC) advocated an attitude of impassivity (*ataraxie*) in the face of mortality and a striving for earthly happiness.

5 *'Storm and Stress'*: in German: *Sturm und Drang*. A literary-historical term for the early German Romanticism of the late eighteenth century, with its strong reaction against the rationalism of the Enlightenment.

Richard Wagner: German composer (1813–83); major early influence on Nietzsche. He sought to achieve a synthesis of music and drama in opera based on the declamatory delivery of text and the repetition of musical leitmotifs, and pioneered the move of modern music away from traditional harmony by experimenting with chromaticism and dissonance.

'best of its time': allusion to the Prologue of Friedrich Schiller's *Wallenstein*, lines 48–9: 'For he who has satisfied the best of his age has lived for all ages' (*'Denn wer den Besten seiner Zeit genug | Getan, der hat gelebt für alle Zeiten'*).

logical hygiene: the language of the 1886 Foreword is characterized by a rhetoric which relies principally on physiological and medical metaphors to criticize perceived cultural decadence. On this aspect of Nietzsche's later work, see the Introduction.

in artibus: Latin: in the arts.

6 *profanum vulgus*: Latin: the profane crowd.

'unknown god': quotation from Acts of the Apostles 17: 23.

Dionysus: the son of Zeus and Semele, daughter of Cadmus, king of Thebes. Induced by Zeus' jealous wife Hera to implore her lover to visit her in divine form, Semele was consumed by the lightning which surrounds the god. Zeus rescued Dionysus from the ashes of his mother and carried him in his own thigh, from which he was later born. Hera continued to pursue him and as an adult he was persecuted by many who refused to recognize his divinity but eventually managed to extend his influence into Asia. Dionysus was traditionally the god of wine and tragedy, and his worship associated with intoxication and loss of identity, sometimes leading to sexual excess and violence. He is frequently represented in animal form, as half-goat. According to myth, only women were permitted to participate in the celebration of secret Dionysian rites. For Nietzsche, Dionysus is, together with Apollo, the Greek god who represents one of the two competing and complementary tendencies within Greek culture. While Apollo embodies the limits and achievements of form and individual identity, Dionysus represents the profound spiritual insights acquired through loss of identity in religious ecstasy.

Maenad: the Maenads were women associated with the ecstatic cult of Dionysus.

it should have sung . . . spoken: paraphrased by Stefan George in his poem 'Nietzsche' collected in *Der siebente Ring* (*The Seventh Ring*) (1907): '*sie hätte singen | Nicht reden sollen diese neue seele!*'

philologist: literally, a lover of words. Classical philology, Nietzsche's academic discipline, is the study of the history of the language and literature of ancient Greece and Rome.

7 *Pericles (or Thucydides)*: Pericles (*c*.495–429 BC) was the most influential Athenian statesman of his age. His career, including his celebrated funeral oration for the Athenian dead of the Peloponnesian War, is related by the Greek historian Thucydides in his *History of the Peloponnesian War*, ii. 35–6.

neuroses: in the late nineteenth century, general term for psychological disturbance; first given a specific psychoanalytic definition (as physical symptoms induced by represssion) by Sigmund Freud and Josef Breuer in their *Studies in Hysteria* (1895).

7 *satyr*: figure from Greek mythology. Half-man, half-goat, the satyr is characterized by a wild sexuality and associated with the celebration of Dionysian cults.

an expression of Plato's: allusion to Plato's *Phaedrus*, 244a.

Hellas: Greek term for Greece.

utilitarianism: a philosophy developed by English thinkers Jeremy Bentham (1748–1832) and J. S. Mill (1806–73), according to which the ultimate criterion for useful and ethical action is the greatest good of the greatest number.

8 *appearance*: in German: *Schein*.

'beyond good and evil': allusion to the title of Nietzsche's book *Beyond Good and Evil* (1886).

'perversity of mind' . . . Schopenhauer: Arthur Schopenhauer, German philosopher (1788–1860), author of *The World as Will and Representation* (1818/1844). Along with Wagner, he was a major influence on early Nietzsche. For Schopenhauer, human life was driven by an ultimately insatiable Will, so the only prospect for happiness lay in the suppression of desire. Although largely in agreement with Schopenhauer about the nature of the Will, the later Nietzsche was to reject Schopenhauer's response as pessimistic, and to affirm the Will in spite of the suffering it causes. Schopenhauer writes of 'perversity of mind' in *Parerga and Paralipomena* (1851), II.5, 69.

world of the phenomenon: in German: *Welt der Erscheinung*. In the *Critique of Pure Reason* (1781), the philosopher Immanuel Kant (1724–1804) distinguishes between the perceptible world of phenomena, or things as they appear to our senses, and the world of things in themselves, as they really are essentially. Schopenhauer inherits and elaborates this distinction between phenomenon (*Erscheinung*) and thing in itself (*Ding an sich*), identifying the latter as Will. The term 'phenomenon' recurs frequently throughout *The Birth of Tragedy*, where it is aligned with terms such as 'appearance' (*Schein*) and 'image' (*Bild*) to denote a realm of superficial sensory experience in contrast to an underlying reality variously described as 'thing in itself' or 'essence' (*Wesen*) or 'original unity' (*das Ur-Eine*). Despite the variation in terminology, the fundamental distinction remains the same.

Terminus technicus: Latin: technical term.

9 *affects*: in German: *Affekte*; a specialist psychological term for the emotions. For Nietzsche, Christianity vitiates emotional and psychological as well as physical life.

uncanny: in German: *unheimlich*.

10 *'What gives tragedy ... resignation'*: quotation with slight omission from *The World as Will and Representation*, II.3, 37.

11 *empire ... mediocrity, democracy, and 'modern ideas'*: Nietzsche's later disillusionment with the political events which seemed to offer such hope in 1872 is evident here. For Nietzsche, the founding of the Empire did not bring a regeneration of the German spirit but a soulless modernization which he equates with decadence.

Romantic ... un-Greek: in this 1886 preface Nietzsche argues from the point of view of an opposition between the Romantic (German) and the Hellenic (Greek). In *The Birth of Tragedy* he had thought it possible to unify these terms, as in the work of Richard Wagner, where the Romantic quest for mythical roots would fuse with the musical spirit of Greek tragedy. However, Nietzsche increasingly came to regard German Romanticism as simply a form of crypto-Christianity and as such utterly incompatible with Greek culture.

contrapuntal: in music, counterpoint is the combination of two parts or voices each of significance in itself and resulting in a coherent whole.

nihilism: literally, the belief in nothing. Term designating radical loss of belief and often implying destructive action as a result. It was first introduced by the Russian writer Turgenev in his novel *Fathers and Sons* (1861) and was strongly associated with late-nineteenth-century discourse on decadence.

dragon-slayer: allusion to Siegfried in the *Nibelungen* cycle of myths which formed the basis of Wagner's *Ring*. Siegfried had to slay the dragon Fafner in order to win the treasure of the Nibelungs.

insidiously like the melody of the Pied Piper: in German: *verfänglich-rattenfängerisch*. Allusion to the legend of the Pied Piper of Bremen. When the townspeople of Bremen refuse to pay the Pied Piper for having saved them from a plague of rats by leading the animals to their death through the power of music, he exacts his revenge by luring all the children of the town into a cave which closes behind them.

true Romantic confession of 1830 ... pessimistic mask of 1850: allusion to the July Revolution in France and its impact on Romantic art, followed by an allusion to the mid-century influence of the philosophy of Schopenhauer. Both allusions refer to the enthusiasms of Wagner.

12 *'live resolutely'*: quotation from Goethe's poem 'General Confession' (*Generalbeichte*) of 1802: 'And may we wish following your indication | To strive continually | To lose the habit of the incomplete | And to live resolutely | In the whole, the good and the beautiful.' In German: '*Wollen wir nach deinem Wink | Unabläßlich streben, | Uns vom Halben zu entwöhnen | Und im Ganzen, Guten, Schönen | Resolut zu leben.*'

Helen ... Faust ... to life?: allusions to Goethe's *Faust* (1808/1832), followed by a quotation from *Faust Part Two*, 7438–9: '*Und sollt'ich nicht, sehnsüchtigster Gewalt,* | *Ins Leben ziehn die einzigste Gestalt?'*. The entire passage in smaller type is a quotation from § 18 of *The Birth of Tragedy*.

12 *it is written*: biblical formula from New Testament. See, for example, Matthew 4: 4.

13 *Thus Spake Zarathustra, Part Four*: quotation from 'On the Higher Man', 17–20. Nietzsche omits certain passages from the original. Some editions carry the additional byline '*Sils-Maria*, Upper Engadine | August 1886'.

15 *The Birth of Tragedy . . . Music*: title-page of 1872 edition.

17 *unbound Prometheus*: figure from Greek mythology. Having defied the authority of Zeus by stealing fire and giving it to man, the Titan Prometheus was punished by being bound to a cliff face where an eagle would daily pick out his liver. He was eventually saved through the self-sacrifice of Chiron, who agreed to give up his immortality in exchange for Prometheus' freedom. The myth fascinated artists by its embodiment of energy and political revolution and recurs frequently in Romantic art and literature. In referring to his name on the title-page as that of an unbound Prometheus, Nietzsche is casting himself in the mythic role of a liberated rather than imprisoned rebel against an unjust order. The implication is that the writing of the book itself is to be construed as a liberating act of rebellion.

commemorative text on Beethoven: allusion to Wagner's essay *Beethoven* (1870), in which he argued for the autonomy of music and for the cultural independence of German art from French models.

the horrific and sublime events of the war: see note above on Franco-Prussian War.

as the point around which they twist and turn: in German: *als Wirbel und Wendepunkt*.

19 *the duality of the Apollonian and the Dionysian*: the two competing and complementary forces at work in Greek culture which Nietzsche associates with the figures of two Greek deities. See the note on Dionysus above and the note on Apollo below, together with the Introduction, for further details.

Apollo: Apollo, god of light, prophecy, and medicine, whose attributes are the lyre and the bow, is associated with the discipline and beauty of form and individual identity. He is traditionally the patron of the art of music, but Nietzsche insists rather on his close links with sculpture and architecture.

the Hellenic 'will': Nietzsche here presupposes the existence of an underlying will which expresses itself through the Apollonian and the Dionysian drives.

Attic tragedy: the Greek tragedy of fifth-century BC Athens, represented by the work of the dramatists Thespis, Aeschylus, Sophocles, and Euripides. Initially, in the work of Thespis, tragedy consisted of a single actor and chorus. With the introduction of a second actor by Aeschylus, and a third by Sophocles, the importance of the chorus diminished. Aeschylus also introduced the wearing of robes and masks by actors, while with Sophocles the painting of the stage became the norm. If in Aeschylus the human world appears as part of a meaningful order determined by the gods, Sophocles shows a world of mortal suffering clearly distinct from the life of the gods, and Euripides a world simply abandoned by the gods. While in Aeschylus the source of dramatic action lies in the clash between humans and the gods, Euripides' plays are driven by psychological conflict. In Euripides, the final traditional reconciliation between gods and humans can only be achieved through the artificial and more or less unprepared intervention of a deity, a device known as the *deus ex machina* (god from the machine). As will become clear, Nietzsche regards only Aeschylus and Sophocles as true representatives of Attic tragedy.

Lucretius: Latin poet (*c*.97–55 BC). The reference is to *De Rerum Natura*, v. 1169–82.

20 *Hans Sachs ... Mastersingers ... My friend ... dream-interpretation*: Quotation from Wagner's opera *The Mastersingers of Nuremberg* (1868), III. ii: '*Mein Freud, das grad' ist Dichters Werk, | dass er sein Träumen deut' und merk'. | Glaubt mir, des Menschen wahrster Wahn | wird ihm im Traume aufgethan: | all' Dichtkunst und Poëterei | ist nichts als Wahrtraum-Deuterei.*'

dream-images: in German: *Traumbilder*.

Schopenhauer ... capacity for philosophy: allusion to *The World as Will and Representation*, I.1, 5.

'divine comedy' ... Inferno: allusion to *The Divine Comedy* (*La Divina Commedia*) of Dante Alighieri (1265–1321), with its three-part depiction of the after-life: Inferno, Purgatorio, and Paradiso.

21 *the 'one who appears shining'*: in German: *der 'Scheinende'*.

His eye must 'shine like the sun': in German: *Sein Auge muß 'sonnenhaft' sein*. Allusion to Goethe's poem *Tame Xenia* (*Zahme Xenien*), III: 'If the eye were not sunlike, it could never gaze on the sun' ('*Wär nicht das Auge sonnenhaft, | Die Sonne könnt es nie erblicken*'). The *xenion* or short satirical poem was an ancient Greek literary form revived by Goethe and Schiller.

the veil of Maya: term from ancient Indian philosophy appropriated by Schopenhauer. The veil of Maya is the deceptive world of human perception, whose relationship to any underlying reality is uncertain. See *The World as Will and Representation*, I:1, 3.

'As a sailor sits ... principium individuationis': quotation from Schopenhauer, *The World as Will and Representation*, I:4, 63. *principium individuationis*: Latin for principle of individuation; for Schopenhauer, the principle which accounts for the existence of individual phenomena in their multiplicity. Conversely, the realm of the Will is characterized by an

original unity which pre-exists individuation. See *The World as Will and Representation*, 1:2, 23. In *The Birth of Tragedy*, Nietzsche relies frequently on this model to distinguish between the Apollonian world of individuation and the original unity of the Dionysian experience.

22 *the principle of reason*: in German: *der Satz vom Grunde*. Reference to Schopenhauer's dissertation *On the Fourfold Root of the Principle of Sufficient Reason* (1813). First established by the philosopher Gottfried Wilhelm Leibniz (1646–1716) in his *Monadology* (1714), the principle of sufficient reason states that for every fact there is a reason why it is so and not otherwise. In his dissertation, Schopenhauer proposed a Kantian distinction between valid and invalid reasons in such an argument.

St John's and St Vitus's dancers: both St John and St Vitus were associated as patrons with conditions such as epilepsy, hysteria, and possession. In the fourteenth and fifteenth centuries large groups of St John's dancers moved through parts of Germany and the Netherlands.

Bacchic choruses . . . Sacaea: the Bacchic choruses were worshippers of Dionysus (also known as Bacchus). The Sacaea were originally a Babylonian festival where the transgression of social and sexual boundaries was permitted. From Babylon, the Sacaea spread throughout Asia Minor.

folk diseases: in German: *Volkskrankheiten*.

prodigal son: reference to the New Testament parable: see Luke 15: 11–32.

flowers and wreaths . . . the panther and the tiger: attributes of Dionysus.

Beethoven's 'Hymn to Joy': reference to the fourth movement of Beethoven's Ninth Symphony (1824), whose choral conclusion takes a re-worked version of Schiller's 'Ode to Joy' (*An die Freude*) (1786/1803) as its text. Beethoven uses the first three verses and the first, third, and fourth choruses of the 1803 version of the poem, reordering the sequence of the choruses.

multitudes kneel down awestruck in the dust: allusion to Schiller's 'Ode to Joy', the lines quoted at the end of this section.

23 *impudent fashion*: in German: *freche Mode*; a quotation from Beethoven's reworking of Schiller's 'Ode to Joy'. At one point in the manuscript, Beethoven replaced Schiller's *Deine Zauber bindet wieder,* | *Was die Mode streng geteilt* (Your magic reunites | What fashion strictly separated) with *Deine Zauber bindet wieder,* | *Was die Mode frech geteilt* (Your magic reunites | What fashion impudently separated). Wagner comments on this alteration in his essay *Beethoven* (1870), where fashion (*Mode*) is associated with superficial French civilization.

original Unity: in German: *das Ur-Eine*.

milk and honey: biblical formulation; see e.g. Exodus 3: 8.

Eleusinian Mysteries: the secret religious rites celebrated by initiates at Eleusis in honour of Demeter, goddess of corn. Elements of the rites were associated with the worship of Dionysus.

'Do you fall to your knees . . . creator?': quotation from Schiller's 'Ode to Joy'.

24 *in an allegorical dream-image*: in German: *in einem gleichnisartigen Traumbilde*.

archetypes: in German: *Urbilder*.

the Aristotelian term, 'the imitation of nature': reference to Aristotle's *Poetics* and the notion of *mimesis* or imitation which provides its point of departure.

Homer: Greek epic poet of the eighth century BC, author of *The Iliad* and *The Odyssey*. He was for Nietzsche one of the most important representatives of Greek culture.

Shakespeare: English dramatist (1564–1616). For Nietzsche, he was one of the most important representatives of modern (i.e. non-classical) culture.

the bearded satyr: see above note to p. 7.

25 *'witches' brew'*: allusion to Goethe's *Faust Part One*, the 'Witches Kitchen' scene.

the Medusa's head: the Medusa was one of the three Gorgons, monstrous women with snakes for hair. Her gaze had the power to turn to stone. Perseus slew the Medusa by approaching her using the reflective surface of his shield as a mirror and then cutting off her head. Freud was later to interpret the myth as an allegory of male fear of castration in 'The Medusa's Head' (*Das Medusenhaupt*) (1922/1940).

Doric art: the Dorians were a tribe which settled in northern Greece in the thirteenth and twelfth centuries BC, establishing political and cultural centres in Argos, Corinth and Sparta. Their politics were based on an aggressive independence founded in a military caste, while their art was characterized by clarity and simplicity. Doric architecture in particular inspired the Romantic Classicism of German architects such as Karl Friedrich Schinkel. Such emulation formed part of a more widespread nineteenth-century tendency to assert ethnic and political parallels between the Dorians and the Prussians, as twin representatives of a pure and warlike Aryan race. The beginnings of this process can be traced in the classicist Karl Otfried Müller's *The Dorians* (1824). The more sinister outcome may be seen in exemplary form in Gottfried Benn's essay *Dorian World: An Investigation of the Relationship between Art and Power* (1934) and in the monumental classicism of much National Socialist architecture.

Delphic god: epithet for Apollo, the god of prophecy and thus the patron of the oracle at Delphi.

sentimental: Nietzsche is referring here, as in the following discussion, to Schiller's distinction between 'naïve' (ancient and spontaneous) and 'sentimental' (modern and self-conscious) cultures as developed in his essay

On Naïve and Sentimental Poetry (*Über naïve und sentimentalische Dichtung*) (1795).

26 *Doric architecture rendered in sound*: allusion to Goethe's description of architecture as 'frozen music' (*erstarrte Musik*) in the *Conversations with Eckermann*, 23 March 1829. See above, note to p. 25.

cithara: ancient Greek stringed instrument.

Dionysian dithyramb: the dithyramb was the ancient Greek hymn to Dionysus, whose use was extended to other gods from the sixth century BC. Towards the end of the fifth century BC the new dithyramb appeared, characterized by a looser structure and more independent musical accompaniment. Goethe, Schiller, Hölderlin, and Nietzsche (*Dionysus Dithyrambs*) all imitated the form.

27 *the Olympian pantheon*: according to Greek myth, Mount Olympus was the seat of the twelve gods Zeus, Hera, Poseidon, Demeter, Apollo, Artemis, Ares, Aphrodite, Hermes, Athene, Hephaestus, and Hestia. The Olympians were the third generation of gods to have emerged from the original chaos and were presided over by Zeus whose power rested on having overturned the rule of his father, the Titan Chronos. See note on Titans below.

magic potion . . . Helen . . . 'hovering . . . sensuality': allusion to Goethe's *Faust Part One*, 2603–4: 'Having taken this potion, | You will soon see Helen in every woman' (*Du siehst, mit diesem Trank im Leibe, | Bald Helenen in jedem Weibe*).

King Midas . . . Silenus: when King Midas of Phrygia returned the satyr Silenus to his master Dionysus, the god offered him a wish in return. The notoriously greedy Midas wished that all he touched might turn to gold, but he needed to be saved from the consequences of his avarice by Dionysus when he found himself unable to consume the food and drink with which he came into contact.

28 *the Olympian magic mountain*: in German: *der olympische Zauberberg*. Source for the title of Thomas Mann's novel *The Magic Mountain* (*Der Zauberberg*) (1924).

Titanic powers of nature: according to Hesiod, the Titans were the second generation of gods who emerged from the original chaos. The first generation, Uranus and Gaia, gave birth to six sons and six daughters. This second generation of Titans, under the leadership of the youngest son, Chronos, overthrew their parents, only to be overthrown in turn by the third generation of Olympians led by Chronos' son Zeus.

Moira: in Greek mythology, the three Fates (Clotho, Lachesis, and Atropos) who determine the duration and happiness of human life. While Clotho spins the thread of life, Lachesis draws it off the spindle and Atropos cuts it.

vulture . . . Prometheus: on Prometheus, see above, note to p. 16. The myth was the subject of Aeschylus' tragedy *Prometheus Bound*.

Oedipus: allusion to the myth of Oedipus, the king of Thebes who inadvertently killed his father Laius and married his mother Jocasta. His story formed the basis of a cycle of tragedies by Sophocles.

house of the Atrides . . . Orestes: allusion to the myth of the Atrides. After murdering their step-brother Chrysippos, the brothers Atreus and Thyestes were exiled and cursed by their father King Pelops of Mycenae. Following Pelops' death, Atreus acceded to the throne in spite of his brother's equal claim, whereupon Thyestes seduced Atreus' wife and with her help stole the Golden Ram, the symbol of regal power. In retaliation, Atreus killed his wife and Thyestes' children, whom he served to him on a plate. Thyestes cursed Atreus' descendants (the Atrides) and was eventually avenged by his son Aegisthus, who killed Atreus, enabling Thyestes to become king. After Thyestes' death, the throne passed to Agamemnon, son of Atreus. While Agamemnon was absent fighting the Trojan War, Aegisthus seduced his wife Clytemnestra and together they murdered Agamemnon on his return. The cycle of violence closed when Agamemnon's son Orestes avenged his father by murdering his mother and her lover before fleeing the kingdom. Aeschylus based his Oresteian trilogy of tragedies (*Agamemnon*, *The Libation-Bearers*, *The Eumenides*) on the myth.

the forest god: Dionysus.

the Etruscans: ancient inhabitants of Etruria in western Italy.

theodicy: a defence of God from the reproach that he is reponsible for the evil of the world; practised by the Stoics in the ancient world. The best-known modern version is Leibniz's *Theodicy* (1710).

Achilles: Greek hero of Homer's *Iliad*, son of Peleus and Thetis, killed by Paris during the Trojan War.

29 *day labourer*: allusion to Homer's *Odyssey*, xi. 489–91.

'naïve' . . . Schiller: see above, note to p. 25.

Rousseau's Émile: Jean-Jacques Rousseau (1712–78), Swiss musicologist, novelist, educationalist, cultural critic was a major influence on Romantic thought. The educational treatise in novel form *Émile, or On Education* (1762) proposes a form of natural education designed to forestall the corrupting effects of civilization and to preserve Émile as a child of nature.

30 *that which truly exists and the original Unity*: in German: *das Wahrhaft-Seiende und das Ur-Eine*.

that which does not truly exist: in German: *das Wahrhaft-Nichtseiende*. Nietzsche here is using the traditional distinction in Greek philosophy between Being (the underlying unchanging reality) and Becoming (the ever-changing surface of life). In Kantian terms, the realm of Being is associated with the thing in itself, that of Becoming is assimilated to the phenomenon.

30 *empirical reality*: technical term from Kantian philosophy. In the *Critique of Pure Reason* (1781), Kant describes the world of phenomena available to human perception as 'empirical reality', as distinct from the essential reality of the things in themselves.

   the appearance of appearance: in German: *der Schein des Scheins*.

31 *Raphael*: Italian painter and architect (1483–1520).

   Transfiguration: Raphael's last painting, now in the Vatican museum.

   ambrosia: the food of the gods.

   '*know thyself*': inscription on the Temple of Apollo at Delphi.

   '*nothing to excess*': maxim variously ascribed to the Spartan politician Chilon (*c.*550 BC), the Athenian statesman Solon (640–560 BC), and the philosophers Socrates (470–399 BC) and Pythagoras (570–480 BC).

32 *the riddle of the Sphinx*: the Sphinx, a winged lioness with human head, persecuted the people of Thebes on behalf of the goddess Hera by killing anyone who could not solve her riddle. The riddle asked for the name of the being which first walks on four, then on two and finally on three legs. The answer—human beings, who first crawl on all fours as babies, then walk upright as adults, then walk with the aid of a stick in old age—was provided by Oedipus, who, having rid Thebes of the Sphinx, returned to the city in triumph, inadvertently to marry his mother Jocasta, the widowed queen.

   cancelled, absorbed, and annihilated: in German: *aufgehoben und vernichtet*. *Aufheben* is ambiguous, meaning both to cancel and to preserve.

33 *the 'bronze' age*: the Greek poet Hesiod (*c.*700 BC), author of the *Theogony*, distinguishes between three periods of history in declining order—the Golden, the Silver, and the Bronze.

   four great artistic periods: Nietzsche distinguishes here between four periods of Greek art characterized by myth ('Bronze' or 'Titanic'), epic ('Homeric'), lyric poetry ('Dionysian'), and sculpture ('Doric') respectively.

   Attic tragedy and the dramatic dithyramb: according to Aristotle, tragedy grew out of the dithyramb (*Poetics*, 1449ᵃ).

   Antigone and Cassandra: Antigone was the daughter of Oedipus and Jocasta. After Oedipus' death, his brother Creon became king of Thebes. The city was then attacked by Antigone's brother Polynices, who was killed in the fighting. When, against the express orders of Creon, Antigone insisted on burying her brother according to religious custom, Creon ordered that she should be walled up in a cave, where she hanged herself. Aeschylus, Sophocles, and Euripides all based tragedies on the story. Cassandra was a Trojan prophetess, doomed never to be believed. Cassandra's gift of prophecy was cursed by Apollo when she refused his sexual advances. During the Trojan War, Cassandra was raped by Ajax and enslaved by Agamemnon. Upon her arrival in Greece, she was murdered by Agamemnon's wife, Clytemnestra. For Nietzsche, Antigone's sense of religious ritual associates her with the Apollonian, while Cassandra's refusal of Apollo's advances and her foresight of disaster ally her with the Dionysian.

Archilochus: Greek lyric poet (*c.*680–640 BC), author of short poems characterized by the relation of personal experience and expression of intense feeling.

34 *modern aesthetics*: allusion to *Aesthetics* (1818/1831) by the German philosopher G. W. F. Hegel (1770–1831). Hegel distinguishes between the objective art of the epic poet and the subjective art of the lyric poet.

disinterested contemplation: allusion to Kant and Schopenhauer. According to Kant's *Critique of Judgement* (1790), aesthetic experience is characterized by disinterestedness (Paragraph 2). For Schopenhauer, the value of the aesthetic lies in its ability to suppress the will through disinterested contemplation. See *The World as Will and Representation*, I:3, 34.

chromatic scale: traditional tonal music is based on the diatonic scale, a regular pattern of intervals structured around a tonal centre which gives its name to a particular key. The development of a piece of tonal music in a particular key will tend to gravitate around and ultimately return to this key. The chromatic scale gives increased importance to half-tones which are not part of the diatonic scale proper, and so considerably weakens the sense of a home key to which a particular piece of music belongs. Chromaticism is a feature of some ancient Greek music, but it is more likely that Nietzsche is alluding here to Wagner, who was one of the most celebrated contemporary exponents of chromaticism, as for example in the Prelude to *Tristan and Isolde* (1865). In terms of the history of music, Wagnerian chromaticism opened the way for further development away from traditional tonality in the atonal and twelve-tone innovations of twentieth-century music.

'In my case . . . only follows subsequently': letter from Schiller to Goethe, 18 March 1796.

35 *the headless image of a god*: the likely source for Rainer Maria Rilke's poem 'Archaic Torso of Apollo' (*Archaïscher Torso Apollos*) in *New Poems* (*Neue Gedichte*) (1907/8).

copy: in German: *das Abbild*.

daughters of Lycambes: when Lycambes reneged on his promise to give his daughter Neobule in marriage to Archilochus, the poet avenged himself by writing defamatory verses about Neobule and her sisters, who all committed suicide as a result.

Euripides . . . Bacchae: reference to Euripides' play *The Bacchae*, part of a trilogy comprising also *Alcmaeon in Corinth* and *Iphigenia at Aulis*. *The Bacchae* relates the conflict between Dionysus and Pentheus, king of Thebes. In retaliation for the refusal of the people of Thebes to recognize him as a god, Dionysus drives the women of the city mad and forces them to celebrate his rites on Mount Cithaeron. Against the advice of his grandfather Cadmus and the seer Tiresias, Pentheus rejects the new religion and imprisons Dionysus who then destroys the king's palace by causing an earthquake. Under the influence of Dionysus, Pentheus disguises himself as a woman to observe the rites but is discovered and torn apart by the celebrants, with his mother Agave bearing his severed head into the city. The play ends with the banishment of the family of Cadmus from Thebes. The myth and the play were to provide the source for Heinrich von Kleist's drama *Penthesilea* (1808).

35 *Apollo . . . laurel*: laurel is an attribute of Apollo, who carries a laurel branch in memory of the nymph Daphne, whom he transformed into a laurel tree when she refused his advances.

36 *objectivations*: in German: *Objectivationen*.

'self': in German: *'Ichheit'*; the term first appears in the *Theologia deutsch* of the mystic philosopher Johannes de Francfordia (1380–1440).

37 *'It is the subject . . . emotional state'*: Schopenhauer, *The World as Will and Representation*, I.3, 51.

38 *folk song*: in German: *Volkslied*; term coined by the theologian and cultural philosopher Johann Gottfried Herder (1744–1803). For Herder, the folk song, a simple rhymed song transmitted orally from generation to generation, represented the authentic organic culture (*Kultur*) of Germany, as opposed to the alien impositions of Enlightenment civilization (*Civilisation*). For the Romantics, there was a strong parallel between the oral traditions of Homeric epic and indigenous German folk song. Herder was a major influence on German Romantic thought, whose ideas on culture, through Wagner, exercised a significant influence on Nietzsche's early work.

39 *perpetuum vestigium*: Latin: permanent vestige.

Des Knaben Wunderhorn: in English: *The Youth's Magic Horn*; a major collection of folk songs assembled by the Romantic writers Achim von Arnim and Clemens von Brentano and published between 1805 and 1808. An important source and inspiration for German Romantic writers and composers.

rhapsodes: professional peripatetic reciters, whose material was mostly drawn from Homeric epic.

Terpander: Greek musician of the seventh century BC, who began to sing rather than recite Homer.

40 *Pindar*: Greek lyric poet of the fifth century BC. Only his hymns of praise to victorious athletes have survived intact. In a richly metaphorical style, they seek to celebrate and preserve the virtuous ideals embodied in their subject. A major influence on Hölderlin, who translated a number of his odes.

Olympus: according to legend, a Phrygian flautist who first established the rules for playing the flute.

Beethoven symphony . . . pastoral . . . 'Scene by a Brook' . . . 'Merry Gathering of Rustics': allusions to Beethoven's Sixth Symphony (1807–8), also known as the Pastoral Symphony, whose second and third movements are respectively entitled 'Scene by a Brook' and 'Merry Gathering of Rustics'.

41 *lightning burst*: in German: *Effulguration*.

essence . . . phenomenon: in German: *Wesen . . . Erscheinung*. The distinction between essence and phenomenon is the same as that between thing in itself and phenomenon. See above, note to p. 8.

allegories: in German: *Gleichnissen*.

images: in German: *Bilder*.

42 *all phenomena are merely allegories*: in German: *ist jede Erscheinung nur Gleichnis*; allusion to the conclusion of Goethe's *Faust Part Two*, 12104–5: 'All that passes | Is merely an allegory' (*Alles Vergängliche | Ist nur ein Gleichnis*).

this tradition: allusion to Aristotle's *Poetics*, iv, 1449ᵃ. Aristotle maintains that tragedy grew out of the dithyramb.

a word of Aristotle's: *Politics*, iii. 8. 6, 1284ᵇ. Aristotle compares the practice of ostracism in Athenian society to the constitution of the tragic chorus.

43 *in praxi*: Greek: in practice.

A. W. Schlegel's thought . . . 'ideal spectator': August Wilhelm Schlegel (1767–1845), German poet, translator, critic, literary historian, Orientalist. Along with his brother Friedrich, a central figure in the Jena circle of Romantic writers and thinkers. One of the major translators of Shakespeare into German. In the fifth of his lectures *On Dramatic Art and Literature* (*Über dramatische Kunst und Literatur*)(1808), he describes the chorus as an 'idealized spectator'.

chorus of Oceanides . . . Titan Prometheus: allusion to Aeschylus' tragedy *Prometheus Bound* (c.458 BC), where the chorus consists of Oceanides, the daughters of the Titan Oceanus who come to console and comfort Prometheus during his punishment for stealing fire from the gods and giving it to humans.

44 *foreword to The Bride of Messina*: reference to Schiller's text *On the Use of the Chorus in Tragedy* (*Über den Gebrauch des Chors in der Tragödie*), published as the foreword to his play *The Bride of Messina* (*Die Braut von Messina*) (1803).

'pseudo-idealism': polemical term criticizing an art which seeks to embody timeless ideals in the manner of Goethe and Schiller during their Weimar period. It implies a position in favour of realist and naturalistic art, based on the imitation of contemporary reality.

45 *cancelled and absorbed by music as lamplight is by daylight*: in German: *von der Musik aufgehoben werde wie der Lampenschein vom Tagelicht*. Quotation from Richard Wagner's essay *Beethoven* (1870). On *aufheben*, see above, note to p. 32.

46 *a Buddhist negation of the will*: Buddhism is an Eastern religion dating from the sixth century BC. Its central teachings argue that the suffering of the world results from individual existence and its will. Through meditation and discipline, the individual will can be suppressed and a state of desirelessness (*nirvana*) reached. Schopenhauer's philosophy was greatly influenced by his reading of Eastern thought and religion.

Hamlet: reference to Shakespeare's tragedy *Hamlet, Prince of Denmark*. Though made aware that his father the king has been murdered by his uncle Claudius, who has inherited the throne and married his mother Gertrude, Hamlet fails to act on this knowledge.

world which is out of joint: *Hamlet*, I. v. 188.

Hans the Dreamer: double allusion. First to Hamlet's soliloquy in II. ii. 563–6: 'Yet I, | A dull and muddy-mettled rascal, peak | Like John-a-dreams, unpregnant of my cause, | And can say nothing', where *John-a-dreams* is rendered as *Hans der Traümer* in the standard German translation (Schlegel–Tieck). Secondly, to the monologue of Hans Sachs in Wagner's *The Mastersingers of Nuremberg*, III. i.

the absurd aspects of existence: in German: *das Absurde des Daseins*. This discussion is one of the sources for the philosophy of the absurd developed by the French writer Albert Camus (1913–60) in *The Myth of Sisyphus* (1942).

Ophelia's fate: in Shakespeare's *Hamlet*, Ophelia, daughter of Polonius, goes insane and drowns herself when Hamlet rejects her and kills her father.

the sublime . . . the comic: an opposition developed by Romantic aesthetics. See, for example, Jean Paul's *Preschool of Aesthetics* (*Vorschule der Ästhetik*)(1804). In France, Victor Hugo was to propose a related distinction between the sublime and the grotesque in his *Preface to Cromwell* (1827). Such developments superseded the eighteenth-century opposition between the beautiful and the sublime proposed by the Irish politician and philosopher Edmund Burke (1729–97) in his *A Philosophical Enquiry into the Origin of our Ideas of the Sublime and the Beautiful* (1756) and elaborated by Immanuel Kant in his *Critique of Judgement* (1790), where the finite and reassuring category of the beautiful (*das Schöne*) is contrasted with the infinite and the terrifying sublime (*das Erhabene*). Nietzsche's distinction between the Apollonian and the Dionysian, as applied to aesthetics, is clearly derived in part from these categories.

47 *the idyllic shepherd*: reference to the long tradition of pastoral poetry taking the life of shepherds as its subject, a genre invented by the Greek poet Theocritus in the third century BC. Revived during the Italian

Renaissance, pastoral poetry did not appear in Germany until the seventeenth century, but subsequently became one of the dominant forms of Rococo poetry in the eighteenth century. Such poetry typically praises the joys of a simple life, close to nature.

the ape: allusion to the work of Charles Darwin (1809–82), English naturalist, author of *The Origin of Species* (1859) and *The Descent of Man* (1871). According to Darwin, human beings were ultimately descended from higher primates or apes. Nietzsche's attitude to Darwin's theory of evolution was ambivalent, but here Darwin's modern scientific view of nature is rejected in favour of the Greek view.

handwriting of nature: in German: *Schriftzügen der Nature.*

48 *expression*: a key term in eighteenth- and nineteenth-century aesthetics, first introduced in that context by Leibniz and the 3rd Earl of Shaftesbury (1671–1713). The notion of art as expression is contrasted with the definition of art as imitation first proposed by Aristotle in his *Poetics*. For Nietzsche, true art expresses a dimension beyond the empirical world and therefore beyond imitation in a literal sense.

orchestra: the circular space in the Greek amphitheatre reserved for the use of the chorus.

51 *opera chorus*: for Nietzsche, the chorus of modern drama and opera has lost its pre-eminent place and become subservient to the main action of the stage, which it merely accompanies, clarifies, and comments upon.

52 *Admetus . . . Alcestis*: Admetus, mythical king of Pherae, learns on his wedding day that he is fated to die imminently. Apollo intervenes with the Fates on his behalf and he is allowed to live longer on condition that he finds someone to replace him at the appointed time of his death. His new wife Alcestis agrees to sacrifice herself for her husband. On the way to one of his Twelve Labours, Hercules visits Admetus and, learning of his predicament, rescues Alcestis from the clutches of Thanatos (Death) and returns her living to her husband. Euripides used the story as the basis for a burlesque play entitled *Alcestis* (438 BC). The myth also provides the subject of a poem by Rilke—'Alcestis' ('*Alkestis*') in *New Poems* (*Neue Gedichte*) (1907/8).

'an eternal sea . . . a glowing life': quotation from Goethe's *Faust Part One*, 505–7: '*Ein ewiges Meer, | Ein wechselnd Weben, | Ein glühend Leben.*'

53 *a projected image thrown on to a dark wall*: in German: *das auf eine dunkle Wand geworfene Lichtbild*; allusion to Plato's Allegory of the Cave in *Republic*, vii, 514a–517a.

54 *Sophocles . . . Oedipus*: reference to Sophocles' plays about Oedipus—*Oedipus the King* (*c*.430 BC) and *Oedipus at Colonus* (*c*.406 BC). As the hero who solves the riddle of the Sphinx, Oedipus is a wise and insightful man, who uses reason to overcome the difficulties he encounters, but as the figure who unwittingly murders his father and marries his mother, he is a blind and ignorant man at the mercy of forces beyond his control. For

Nietzsche, the Oedipus myth represents the ambiguity of the human condition as both Apollonian quest for knowledge and vulnerability to obscure Dionysian forces.

54 *wonderfully intricate knot*: reference to the imagery of knots and unravelling used by Aristotle in his *Poetics* to describe the plot construction of tragedy (xviii, 1455^b). The metaphor is still current in modern terms such as *dénouement* (French: untying, unlacing, unravelling).

Oedipus at Colonus: reference to Sophocles' tragedy, which describes Oedipus' last days as, blinded and exiled from Thebes, he awaits his death in the Attic town of Colonus.

magus: member of an ancient Persian priestly caste.

55 *'The point . . . crime against nature'*: allusion to Sophocles' *Oedipus the King*, lines 316–17, where the seer Tiresias laments the gift of knowledge.

column of Memnon: according to myth, a colossal statue to the Ethiopian king Memnon (killed by Achilles during the Trojan War) stood before a temple in Egyptian Thebes, and would sing at dawn when struck by the rays of the sun.

the Prometheus of Aeschylus: Aeschylus' play *Prometheus Bound*. See above, note to p. 16.

Here I sit . . . the same as I!: quotation from Goethe's early poem *Prometheus* (1773). In German: '*Hier sitz ich, forme Menschen | Nach meinem Bilde, | Ein Geschlecht, das mir gleich sei, | Zu leiden, zu weinen, | Zu geniessen und zu freuen sich, | Und dein nicht zu achten, | Wie ich!*'

56 *twilight of the gods*: in German: *Götterdämmerung*. In German mythology, the end of the world, the death of gods and men. Wagner was to use the term as the title for the fourth and last part of his *Ring* cycle.

Moira: see above, note to p. 28.

Aryan community of peoples: the ethnic term Aryan originally denoted the peoples of the Indo-Iranian branch of the Indo-Germanic family of languages (Persians and Indians essentially). In the nineteenth century, the sense shifted to include the ancient Greeks and Romans and the modern Germans, as heirs of antiquity. Much nineteenth-century classical scholarship sought to advance the thesis that ancient Greece was an essentially Aryan civilization, free from any significant influences from the Middle East and North Africa. This coincided with a more general tendency to view cultures in terms of ethnic typologies, such as Hebraic versus Hellenic, and also overlaps with the development of political anti-Semitism in Europe which insisted on an absolute distinction between Aryan (understood as European) and Semitic (understood as Jewish) languages and peoples. Nietzsche's remarks carry the resonance of these contexts. The Prometheus myth is viewed positively as an active, masculine, Aryan myth, while the myth of the Fall is viewed negatively as a passive, feminine, Semitic myth.

the myth of the Fall: the story of the expulsion of Adam and Eve from the Garden of Eden, as related in Genesis 2 and 3. Having been tempted by the Devil in the form of a serpent to eat the forbidden fruit of the Tree of Knowledge, Eve urges her husband to do the same. To punish his creatures, God expels them from the perfect garden into a life of hardship and consciousness of sin.

57 *palladium*: originally, a protective image of the goddess Pallas Athene associated with the Trojan War. Later, any talismanic object or charm.

sacrilege . . . sin: in German: *der Frevel* and *die Sünde* respectively.

58 *We do not mind . . . the man gets there*: quotation from Goethe's *Faust Part One*, 3982–5: '*Wir nehmen das nicht so genau: | Mit tausend Schritten macht's die Frau; | Doch wie sie auch sich eilen kann, | Mit einem Sprung macht's der Mann.*'

Egyptian inflexibility and coldness: it was generally held in the nineteenth century that ancient Egyptian art and architecture was characterized by schematic and lifeless forms.

the Titan Atlas: the Titan Atlas was forced to support the earth on his back as punishment for his defiance of the Olympian deities.

That is your world! That is a world indeed!: quotation from Goethe's *Faust Part One*, 409: '*Das ist deine Welt! Das heisst eine Welt!*'

59 *someone or other . . . untragic*: Aristotle, *Poetics*, v, 1448[a].

Platonic distinction . . . 'idea' . . . 'idol': Plato distinguished between the essential realm of ideas beyond this world and the realm of copies (idols) which constitutes human experience in the world. So in the Allegory of the Cave, human perception is limited to the shadows thrown on the wall and does not extend to the ideal forms which throw the shadows (*Republic*, vii, 514a–517b).

allegorical appearance: in German: *gleichnisartige Erscheinung*.

Zagreus: alternative name for Dionysus in the Orphic myths. According to this tradition, Zagreus was the son of Demeter and Zeus. At the instigation of Zeus' wife Hera, the Titans attacked and dismembered the child Zagreus. The goddess Athena rescued his heart, from which Zeus was able to remake Zagreus and implant him in Semele, from whom he was reborn as Dionysus.

earth, wind, fire, and water: according to ancient philosophy, the four elements or basic constituents of which the material world is composed. The doctrine of the four elements was first developed by the pre-Socratic philosopher Empedocles (*c*.500–430 BC).

60 *the epopts*: the highest grade of initiate into the Eleusinian Mysteries. See above, note to p. 23.

Demeter: the mother of Zagreus (Dionysus).

metempsychosis: Greek: transmigration of souls, reincarnation.

60 *Tartarus*: the part of the Underworld reserved for gods who had committed sacrilege.

61 *mythical dream . . . history*: in the fifth and fourth centuries BC, Greek myths began to be reinterpreted in secular terms as versions of historical events.

scornful Lucians: allusion to the sophist Lucian of Samosata (AD 120–180), known for his satirical writing.

masked imitation myth: in German: *einen nachgemachten, maskirten Mythus*.

Hercules' ape: an imitation Hercules. In ancient Greek, a pejorative expression designating an arrogant man.

62 *sophistical dialectic*: in ancient Greece, dialectic was originally the art of learned argument directed towards the truth, while a sophist was simply a man of unusual wisdom. In the fifth century BC the name was applied to itinerant teachers who specialized in rhetoric. Nietzsche uses both terms in a pejorative sense derived from Plato, for whom sophists were men dedicated to advancing their self-interest through verbal persuasion, and dialectic was the rhetorical means of achieving this.

suicide: for Nietzsche, the tragic culture of the Greeks destroys itself from within.

Tiberius: Claudius Nero Tiberius (42 BC–AD 37), Roman Emperor (AD 14–37).

'The great Pan is dead': allusion to Plutarch, 'On the Removal of the Oracle', *Moralia*, 17. According to Plutarch, in the time of Tiberius passengers on a ship sailing along the west coast of Greece heard a voice shouting from the islands of Paxi that Pan, the god of shepherds and flocks, was dead. In the Christian tradition, the legend is associated with the victory of Christianity over pagan religions.

epigones: literally, 'those born after'. In myth, the sons of the seven Greek princes who died in the war against Thebes. By extension, artists who live in the shadow of a previous generation and simply repeat the inherited forms of the past.

Euripides: after Aeschylus and Sophocles, the third major tragedian of fifth-century Athens. Euripides introduced innovations which for Nietzsche ultimately resulted in the death of tragedy by stressing the rational structure and psychological realism of the drama.

63 *New Attic Comedy*: formulaic drama developed in Athens from the fourth century BC. Greatly influenced by Euripides, it established the model for later European comic drama, with its five-act structure, recognizable cast of types, and love-plots.

Philemon's desire . . . Euripides: Philemon the Elder (*c*.365–260 BC), Greek dramatist associated with New Attic Comedy. According to legend, Philemon once expressed the wish to die so that he might communicate with Euripides. Philemon's work frequently parodied that of Euripides.

Menander: Greek dramatist (342–291 BC), the first major exponent of New Attic Comedy, whose work bore the influence of Aristotle's *Nicomachean Ethics* and Theophrastus' *Characters*.

Graeculus: Latin: little Greek.

Aristophanes' The Frogs . . . Aeschylus: in *The Frogs* (405 BC) by the Greek comic dramatist Aristophanes (*c*.445–*c*.385 BC), the dead Aeschylus and Euripides engage in a contest to decide who is the better poet. Euripides claims that he has reduced the pomposity of Greek drama and taught the people how to speak.

64 *that genre of drama which resembles chess*: reference to the formulaic nature of New Attic Comedy.

'*in old age foolish and silly*': quotation from Goethe's poem *Epigrammatic Inscription 2* (*Epigrammatische Grabschrift 2*). In German: '*Als Greis leichtsinnig und grillig!*'

the fifth estate . . . now comes to predominance: Nietzsche was later to develop this historical narrative into his theory of the slave revolt in morals (*Sklavenaufstand der Moral*) in *Beyond Good and Evil* (1886) and *On the Genealogy of Morals* (1887).

65 *Pythagoras and Heraclitus*: Pythagoras (*c*.570–*c*.480 BC), Greek philosopher and mathematician, best known for his doctrine of the transmigration of souls and Pythagoras' Theorem. Heraclitus (*c*.550–480 BC), pre-Socratic philosopher whose work only survives in fragments. A major influence on Nietzsche's thought in his insistence that existence is ultimately characterized by violence and flux. In the fourth *Untimely Meditation*, *Richard Wagner in Bayreuth* (1876), Nietzsche associates Heraclitus' idea of the productivity of antagonism and conflict with the chromaticism and dissonance of Wagner's music.

pandaemonium: a modern coinage based on ancient Greek, perhaps attributable to the English poet John Milton (1608–74), who used the term as the name for the capital of Hell in *Paradise Lost*, Book One. An assembly of evil spirits or, by extension, any disorderly gathering.

66 *Lessing*: Gotthold Ephraim Lessing (1729–81), the most important critic, writer and philosopher of the German Enlightenment. In his *Hamburg Dramaturgy* (*Hamburger Dramaturgie*) (1767–9), he sought to define modern tragedy and comedy in the terms set out by Aristotle in his *Poetics* (fear and pity, catharsis, the three unities).

67 *tropes*: figures of speech.

68 *Pentheus in the Bacchae*: see above, note to p. 35.

Cadmus and Tiresias: see above, note to p. 35.

daemon called Socrates: *daemon* is the Greek term for a divine being without a specific form, a protective or persecuting spirit. Allusion to Plato's *Apology*, where Socrates in his defence talks of his daemonium, a spirit which often advised him against, but never in favour of, a specific course of action (31d).

69 *Goethe . . . Nausicaa*: Goethe planned to write a tragedy based on the story of Nausicaa as related in Homer's *Odyssey*. The plot was to turn on the tragic fate of Nausicaa, the daughter of the Phaeacian king Alcinous, who drowns herself after being rejected by Odysseus. Goethe abandoned the project after completing a fragment of the first act in 1787.

young rhapsode . . . 'When I say . . . pounds with fear': Plato, *Ion*, 535c.

70 *naturalistic and unartistic aberration*: while criticizing the greater psychological realism of Euripides' work, Nietzsche is also attacking late-nineteenth-century realism and naturalism in art, with its emphasis on environmental and biological determinism and its exclusion of any dimension beyond the factual and the material.

'Knowledge is virtue': compare Plato's *Protagoras*, 361a–c.

Euripidean prologue: while earlier tragedies began with the entrance of the chorus, Euripides added a prologue delivered by a single actor to explain the plot and characters of the drama to follow.

71 *not plot but pathos*: according to Aristotle's definition, traditional tragedy was driven by action and plot rather than by character and psychology (*Poetics*, vi, 1449^{b})

compassion and fear: in German: *Mitleiden und Mitfürchten*. Allusion to Aristotle's discussion of the function of tragedy as catharsis, a sympathetic discharge of the emotions of fear and pity (*Poetics*, vi, 1449^{b}).

Descartes: René Descartes (1596–1650), French philosopher and mathematician. In the *Méditations* (1641), Descartes argued that the existence of the concept of perfection implies that a perfect being must also exist.

72 *deus ex machina*: see above, note to p. 19.

'In the beginning . . . created order': Anaxagoras (*c*.500–425 BC), pre-Socratic philosopher, exiled from Athens because of his atheism. Nietzsche quotes a saying attributed to Anaxagoras by Diogenes Laertius, *Lives and Opinions of Eminent Philosophers*, ii. 6.

nous: a term used by Anaxagoras in two different senses: first, the human faculty for knowledge of being; and second, the creator of the universe. In the preceding quotation, *nous* is translated as understanding (*Verstand*).

divine Plato . . . interpreter of dreams: Plato, *Ion*, 533e–534d; *Phaedrus*, 244a–245a; *Laws*, 719c.

73 *the new Orpheus*: Orpheus was the son of a Muse and a gifted musician. He was dismembered by Maenads after attempting to displace the cult of Dionysus and his severed head was cast into the river Hebrus, which carried it singing to the island of Lesbos, where it was buried. Nietzsche identifies Socrates with Orpheus as an opponent of Dionysus.

Lycurgus: in the course of an attempt to invade Thrace, Dionysus' army was captured by Lycurgus, king of the Edoni. Dionysus himself escaped by diving into the sea and taking refuge in the cave of the goddess Thetis. In revenge, the Dionysian cults later overran Thrace.

Socrates . . . with his writing: recorded by Diogenes Laertius, *Lives and Opinions of Eminent Philosophers*, ii. 18.

Marathonian efficiency: allusion to the battle of Marathon (490 BC), where the Greeks defeated the invading Persian army of Darius.

Aristophanic comedy: in *The Clouds* (418–416 BC), Aristophanes parodies Socrates' ideas and pedagogy.

sophist: see above, note to p. 62.

Alcibiades: Athenian politician (*c*.450–404 BC), renowned for his skill in sophistical argument and his self-serving unscrupulousness. For a time, he was an enthusiastic pupil of Socrates and he appears as such in Plato's *Symposium* (*c*.384 BC).

74 *Delphic oracle . . . Euripides*: the *Scholia Aristophanica* relating to *The Clouds*, section 144, relates how the Delphic oracle declared to Charephon that Sophocles was wise, Euripides wiser, but Socrates the wisest of men.

'Exclusively from instinct': reference to Plato's *Apology*, 22b.

Phidias: Athenian sculptor (*c*.490–430 BC), the best-known artist of the ancient world, who directed the Athenian building programme under Pericles and was in charge of the decoration of the Parthenon.

Pythia: the priestess of the Delphic oracle.

75 *'Woe! Woe! . . . it falls apart!'*: from Goethe's *Faust Part One*, 1607–11: '*Weh! Weh! | Du hast sie zerstört, | Die schöne Welt, | Mit mächtiger Faust; | Sie stürzt, sie zerfällt!*'

'daemonium of Socrates': see above, note to p. 68.

per defectum: Latin: from weakness, infirmity.

defectus: Latin: weakness, infirmity.

uncontrolled growth: in German: *Superfötation*.

76 *Plato's account . . . symposium*: Plato, *Symposium*, 223c–d.

the true eroticist: in German: *dem wahrhaften Erotiker*. In Plato's *Symposium*, Alcibiades discusses the link between Socrates' sexuality and the seductiveness of his ideas (215a–222b).

Cyclops's eye: the Cyclops were a race of one-eyed giants. The reference here is towards the limited perspective of Socrates.

'sublime and much praised' . . . Plato: Plato, *Gorgias*, 502b.

Aesopian fable: Aesop was the most famous composer of Greek fables, short narratives with a moral in which animals play the part of humans. While awaiting execution, Socrates rewrote some of Aesop's fables in verse (Plato, *Phaedo*, 61b).

76 *'You see . . . very bright'*: from *The Bee and the Hen* (*Die Biene und die Henne*) (1744) by Christian Fürchtegott Gellert (1715–69), a German writer specializing in dramatic comedy and verse fables. In German: '*Du siehst an mir, wozu sie nützt,* | *Dem, der nicht viel Verstand besitzt,* | *Die Wahrheit durch ein Bild zu sagen.*'

77 *the pleasing . . . the useful*: allusion to the *Ars Poetica* of the Roman poet Horace (65–8 BC), according to which the dual function of art is to please and to provide useful moral instruction.

the youthful tragic poet Plato: according to Diogenes Laertius, Plato wrote poetry and tragedies before meeting Socrates, but burnt his work when Socrates advised against having it performed in a theatre contest (*Lives and Opinions of Eminent Philosophers*, iii. 5).

Cynics: philosophers who followed the teaching of Diogenes of Sinope (*c*.400–*c*.325 BC), characterized primarily by a rejection of all social convention and a critical and mordant view of those who remain governed by it. The term is derived from the Greek word for dog (*kyon*), which the Greeks considered the most shameless of animals.

78 *ancilla*: Latin: maidservant.

bourgeois drama: a type of eighteenth-century German drama, which enacted social and ideological conflicts between middle class and aristocracy or within the bourgeoisie itself, as represented, for example, by Lessing's *Emilia Galotti* (1772) or Schiller's *Kabale und Liebe* (1783).

'poetic justice': the causal relationship between guilt and punishment which is maintained within literary texts. One of the functions of the *deus ex machina* was to ensure just retribution at the end of the tragedy.

79 *Aristotle . . . chorus*: in the *Poetics* Aristotle states that the chorus should be integrated into the action of the stage (xviii, 1455$^\text{b}$).

Agathon: Athenian dramatist (*c*.448–*c*.405 BC), who began to invent his own characters and plots rather than rely on myth. He replaced the songs of the chorus with simple intermissions, thus preparing the way for New Comedy. For Nietzsche, Agathon represents another step in the decline of Greek tragedy.

syllogisms: in logic, a syllogism is a deductive argument usually involving three terms, each of which appears twice. For example: 'All men are mortal, and no gods are mortal, therefore no men are gods.'

80 *'Socrates, make music'*: Plato, *Phaedo*, 60e.

proemium: in rhetoric, the introduction to the subject of a speech. In poetry, introductions which preceded recitals by rhapsodes.

81 *cup of hemlock*: allusion to the execution of Socrates by poison.

a leap of Achilles: allusion to Achilles' renowned ability to leap across great distances; see, for example, Homer, *Iliad*, xxi. 303–5.

eyes of Lynceus: Lynceus, one of the Argonauts, possessed the gift of seeing great distances and even of seeing through the earth.

82 *that single naked goddess*: literally, truth. An early figurative instance of Nietzsche's later identification of truth with woman. See the Preface to *The Gay Science*, the Preface and § 220 of *Beyond Good and Evil*, the Third Essay of *On the Genealogy of Morals*, and the Epilogue to *Nietzsche contra Wagner*.

Lessing: reference to Lessing's *Duplik* (1778).

83 *mystagogue*: a priest initiated into the Mysteries.

the single point . . . turns and twists: in German: *den einen Wendepunkt und Wirbel der sogenannten Weltgeschichte*.

evil in itself: in German: *das Uebel an sich*; an allusion to Kant's notion of the thing in itself (*Ding an sich*).

84 *sophrosyne*: Greek term for the virtue of equanimity and self-control.

maieutic: literally, inducing or encouraging childbirth. Socrates used the metaphor of midwifery or maieutics to describe his pedagogical method. See Plato, *Theaetetus*, 149a–151d.

logic . . . bites its own tail: the ancient motif of a serpent biting its own tail, known as Ouroboros, appears on gemstones and in other visual representations. It is often interpreted as representing time or eternity, and although it has no such resonance here, it recurs in *Thus Spake Zarathustra* (1883–5) in the form of Zarathustra's emblematic pair of animals— the eagle with a serpent wrapped around its neck—and also seems implied in some its imagery (Part IV, 'The Drunken Song', 11). Here the image denotes the way in which logic runs up against its own limits, resulting in a closed and frustrating circularity.

85 *must also enter into the fray!*: an earlier and much shorter version of *The Birth of Tragedy* entitled *Socrates and Greek Tragedy* (*Socrates und die griechische Tragödie*) ended at this point. The argument about the birth and death of Greek tragedy is largely complete, and the remaining sections of the book deal with the imminent rebirth of tragedy in the operas of Wagner.

farce and ballet: farce is a type of broad comedy whose humour is directed towards ridiculing human weakness. The genre attained a certain literary status in the work of Johann Nestroy (1801–62). Ballet developed into an independent art-form in the course of the nineteenth century, after serving as a dance interlude in comedies, opera, and operetta. Here Nietzsche is following Wagner's criticism of ballet in his essay *Beethoven* (1870), where dance is viewed as a visual distraction from the more important art of music.

86 *the Mothers of Being*: reference to Goethe, *Faust Part Two*, 6173–306. The essence of existence is here identified with a feminine and maternal principle.

86 *Schopenhauer, The World as Will and Representation, I*: 1.3, 52.

Richard Wagner . . . Beethoven: see above, note to p. 17.

degenerate art: in German: *entartete Kunst*. The phrase was later to become the standard National Socialist term for modern or non-representational art.

87 *The World as Will and Representation, I*: 1.3, 52. Nietzsche omits one sentence from Schopenhauer's text, after '*universalia in re*'.

a priori: Latin: what comes before; technical term in philosophy. An a-priori proposition is one which can be known to be true or false without reference to experience.

88 *abstractum*: Latin: abstract.

89 *abstracta*: plural of *abstractum*.

Scholastics . . . universalia in re: Scholasticism is the term given to the kind of philosophy practised in the schools of the mediaeval universities, which frequently took the form of a fusion of Aristotelian thought and Christian theology. The allusion here is to the controversy over universals, which turned on the relationship between general concepts (*universalia*) and things (*res*). The debate generated three positions: first, the Nominalist position, according to which the general concept was abstracted from the experience of the senses (*universalia post rem*: universals after the thing); secondly, the Realist position, which held that the general concept possessed a real existence independent of and prior to the reality of things (*universalia ante rem*: universals before the thing); and thirdly, a compromise position, which advanced the idea that the content of the concept determined the thing but could not be separated from the existence of the individual thing (*universalia in re*: universals in the thing). Major figures engaged in the debate included William of Ockham (*c.*1285–1349) on the Nominalist side, Duns Scotus (*c.*1266–1308) on the Realist side, and Peter Abelard (1079–1142) and Thomas Aquinas (1225–74), who attempted to reconcile the opposing views.

92 *The Greeks . . . eternal children*: reference to Plato's *Timaeus*, where an Egyptian priest describes the Greeks as children who never age (22b–c).

93 *New Attic Dithyramb*: see above, note to p. 26.

instinct of Aristophanes: in his plays *The Clouds* and *The Frogs* Aristophanes caricatured Socrates and Euripides respectively.

94 *tone painting*: in German: *Tonmalerei*.

95 *Oedipus at Colonus*: see above, note to p. 54.

tragic dissonance: in music, dissonance or discord is the opposite of consonance or concord. While consonance denotes a chord which is harmonically at rest, dissonance is the term used to describe a chord which is harmonically restless and requires to be resolved. Although present in the work of earlier composers, dissonance was more systematically exploited by Wagner in his exploration of chromaticism, and prepared the way for many of the innovations of modern music. In associating tragedy with a musical effect characteristic of the work of Wagner, Nietzsche is thus anticipating the later development of his argument, where the notion of dissonance plays a key role.

96 *Alexandrian*: reference to the Greek city of Alexandria in Egypt, which became the intellectual centre of the Greek world in the third century BC; it was renowned for its library and its scientific and philological scholarship. Nietzsche regards Alexandria as the triumph of the Socratic tendency and of the theoretical man, diametrically opposed to the active cultural achievements of fifth-century Athens as represented by Attic tragedy.

consonance: see above, note to p. 95.

deus ex machina . . . melting-pots: Nietzsche is alluding here to science and technology.

97 *Socratic . . . or a Hellenic or an Indian (Brahmanic) culture*: Nietzsche is here developing a tripartite cultural typology. The artistic culture of fifth-century Athens is contrasted with both the theoretical Socratic culture of Alexandria and the fatalistic 'tragic' culture of Buddhist India, represented by the priestly aristocratic caste of Brahmins. However, the underlying schema remains the binary one of Apollonian and Dionysian—while Socratic Alexandrian culture represents the overwhelming influence of the Apollonian attention to knowledge, form and limits, the tragic Brahmanic culture is the result of a too profound immersion in the Dionysian insight into the meaninglessness of individual existence in the face of the ongoing creation and destruction of life. Only the artistic culture of Greece succeeds in effecting a workable compromise between the two forces, avoiding both the empty quest for rational knowledge and the passivity of fatalism in its fusion of the formal discipline and beauty of the Apollonian with the the terrifying metaphysical insights of the Dionysian. It should be noted that Nietzsche's use of the term 'tragic' to describe Indian culture is potentially misleading here, since it is used elsewhere in the book to refer to the culture of fifth-century Athens.

For 'Indian (Brahmanic) culture', the editions published by Nietzsche have 'Buddhist culture'. The variation 'Indian (Brahmanic) culture' is based on a correction in Nietzsche's handwriting in his copy of the second edition of 1874/78. The Colli–Montinari text gives the version translated here in the main text.

Faust: the protagonist of Goethe's major tragic drama (1808/1832), who, frustrated by the limits of human knowledge, makes a pact with the Devil in order to relinquish thought for action. For Nietzsche, Faust represents the culmination of the theoretical optimism which begins with Socrates and which must end in frustration because of its failure to recognize its own limits.

97 Goethe . . . 'Yes . . . productiveness of deeds': quotation from *Conversations with Eckermann*, 11 March 1828.

98 *barbaric slave-class . . . for all generations*: see above, note to p. 64.

99 *Kant and Schopenhauer . . . culture*: reference to the 'Transcendental Dialectic' section of Kant's *Critique of Pure Reason*, where Kant criticizes the optimism of philosophy which seeks purely logical and rational knowledge of things. Schopenhauer developed Kant's critique in the first book of *The World as Will and Representation*.

aeternae veritates: Latin: eternal truths.

the work of Maya: see above, note to p. 21.

The World as Will and Representation, I: Appendix: Critique of the Kantian Philosophy, 2.

'live resolutely': quotation from Goethe's poem 'General Confession' (*Generalbeichte*) of 1802: 'And may we wish following your indication | To strive continually | To lose the habit of the incomplete | And to live resolutely | In the whole, the good and the beautiful.' In German: '*Wollen wir nach deinem Wink | Unabläßlich streben, | Uns vom Halben zu entwöhnen| Und im Ganzen, Guten, Schönen| Resolut zu leben.*'

And should I not . . . to life?: quotation from *Faust Part Two*, 7438–9: '*Und sollt'ich nicht, sehnsüchtigster Gewalt, | Ins Leben ziehn die einzigste Gestalt?*' The preceding passage is quoted above in the 1886 Preface, 'Attempt at a Self-Criticism', § 7.

100 *Lamiae*: allusion to Goethe *Faust Part Two*, 7697–810. The Lamiae are vampire-like women.

'world literature': term coined by Goethe in his *Conversations with Eckermann*, 31 January 1827, where he declares that national literatures have been superseded by a world literature.

Adam . . . name: Genesis 2: 20.

the culture of opera: Nietzsche views opera as the modern form of Socratic theoretical culture. Opera emerged in Florence in the late sixteenth century, where a circle of poets, musicians and scholars known as the Camerata attempted to revive ancient drama through a combination of choral and orchestral music with pastoral drama. The first major baroque opera is often considered to be Claudio Monteverdi's *Orfeo* (1607), while the first commercial opera house was opened in Venice in 1637.

stilo rappresentativo . . . recitative: *stilo rappresentativo* is Italian for the 'representational style', a term used by early opera composers to describe the style of presenting character dramatically through recitative. Recitative is a form of declamatory speech-like singing, used for dialogue or narrative, and alternating with the more static and reflective aria.

101 *Palestrina*: Giovanni Pierluigi da Palestrina (1525–94), Italian composer of church music. Often considered the first major composer of classical music.

Florentine circles: allusion to the Camerata. See above, note to p. 100.

102 *Amphion*: the son of Zeus and Antiope. He and his twin brother, Zethus, were rulers of Thebes and built the city walls. The stones were drawn into place by the music which Amphion played on the lyre which he either received from Hermes or invented himself. He is considered the inventor of music.

original primitive: in German: *Urmensch*. *Urmensch* is hereafter translated simply as 'primitive'.

the humanists of that time: allusion to the Renaissance humanism which flourished in Florence and other Italian city-states from the fourteenth century, taking classical civilization as its model for the perfection of humanity.

103 *the present socialistic movement*: European socialism began to organize effectively in the late nineteenth century, making its demands for improved workers' rights, pay, and conditions increasingly powerful. The General German Workers' Union (*Allgemeine Deutsche Arbeiterverein*) was founded by Ferdinand Lassalle in 1863 and the Social Democratic Workers' Party (*Sozialdemokratische Arbeiterpartei*) was founded by August Bebel and Wilhelm Liebknecht and others in 1869.

the good primitive, the 'noble savage': in German: *der 'gute Urmensch'*. This is the standard German translation of the English 'noble savage', the representative of an ideal primitive state first posited by Rousseau in his *Discourse on the Sciences and the Arts* (*Discours sur les sciences et les arts*) (1750).

104 *Schiller's terminology and explanation*: reference to Schiller's *On Naïve and Sentimental Poetry* (1795).

Dante . . . gates of Paradise: in Dante's *Divine Comedy* the Roman poet Virgil (70–19 BC) acts as a guide to Dante, until he reaches the gates of Paradise, where he is met by his beloved Beatrice.

'man in himself': in German: *'der Mensch an sich'*; allusion to Kant's notion of the thing in itself (*Ding an sich*).

106 *Omphale*: the Queen of Lydia, whom Hercules was forced to serve for a year as punishment for killing Iphitus.

Bach: Johann Sebastian Bach (1685–1750), the most important composer of German baroque and of Protestant religious music.

107 *Otto Jahn*: classical philologist, archaeologist, and musicologist (1813–69). Taught in Greifswald, Leipzig, and Bonn, where he became the opponent of Nietzsche's teacher F. W. Ritschl. As a classicist, Jahn was a representative of the strict philological and historical method of interpreting ancient texts. As a musicologist, he was a critic of Wagner's work.

Heraclitus of Ephesus: Heraclitus (Fragments 30 and 31) believed that fire was the origin and end of all existence, causing its creation and destruction.

107 *mysterium*: Latin: mystery.

Romanic civilization: French civilization. Nietzsche here joins a long-standing post-Enlightenment German polemic against the superficial rationalism of French civilization (*Civilisation*) in the name of a deeply rooted organic German culture (*Kultur*). A more immediate source was Richard Wagner's recent essay, *Beethoven* (1870).

108 *Winckelmann*: Johann Joachim Winckelmann (1717–68), German writer, aesthetician, and art historian; major figure in the revival of interest in classical art and architecture in eighteenth-century Europe and author of *Reflections on the Imitation of Greek Works in Painting and Sculpture* (*Gedanken über die Nachahmung der Griechischen Werke in der Malerie und der Bildhauerkunst*)(1755), where he famously defined Greek art in terms of its 'noble simplicity and quiet grandeur' (*edle Einfalt und stille Größe*).

109 *contemporary cultured historiography*: Nietzsche is attacking the methods of historical research associated with figures such as Leopold Ranke, who sought to provide an objective documented reconstruction of the past 'as it really was' (*wie es gewesen ist*).

Goethe's Iphigenia . . . Tauris: allusion to Goethe's play *Iphigenia on Tauris* (*Iphigenie auf Tauris*) (1787).

110 *Dürer*: Albrecht Dürer (1471–1528), German Renaissance artist. The allusion is to his engraving *Knight, Death, and the Devil* (1513).

Mothers of Being: see above, note to p. 86.

wild delusion, will, woe: in German: *Wahn, Wille, Wehe*.

tiger . . . fawning at your feet: see above, note to p. 22.

111 *battles against the Persians*: the wars between the Persians and the Greeks in 492–479 BC and 478–449 BC.

imperium: Latin: empire.

113 *highest joy*: in German: *höchste Lust*. Allusion to the closing lines of Wagner's *Tristan and Isolde* (1865), which are quoted in their entirety in § 22.

Gervinus: Georg Gottfried Gervinus (1805–71), German literary historian and author of a two-volume study of Shakespeare (1850).

Tristan and Isolde: opera by Richard Wagner, first performed in 1865. Wagner derived the plot from Celtic mythology and the mediaeval German version of the legend attributed to Gottfried von Strassburg. King Mark of Cornwall sends his trusted nephew Tristan, a Breton nobleman, to Ireland to woo the Irish princess Isolde on his behalf. In Act One, set on the ship to Cornwall, Isolde tries to poison herself and Tristan in revenge for Tristan's murder of her Irish suitor Morold, but her maid has substituted a love potion for the poison and the couple fall in love instead. In Act Two, the illicit lovers are discovered by King Mark and

Tristan tries to kill himself by falling on a sword. In Act Three, Tristan's servant Kurwenal has brought his mortally wounded master to his home at Kareol in Brittany and sends for Isolde. When Isolde arrives, Tristan dies in her arms and uttering a final lament she sinks lifeless on to his body (the so-called *Liebestod*). The opera's themes of death and the renunciation of desire reflected Wagner's interest in the philosophy of Schopenhauer, while the music represented his most radical experimentation yet with chromaticism and dissonance, and the opera is generally seen as a turning-point in the development of modern music.

114 *'wide space of the night of the worlds'*: in German: *weitem Raum der Weltennacht.* Slightly altered quotation from Wagner's *Tristan and Isolde* III. i: *'im weiten Reich | der Weltennacht'* ('in the wide realm of the night of the worlds').

universalia ante rem: see above, note to p. 89.

'The old melody; why does it wake me?': quotation from Wagner's *Tristan and Isolde* III. i: *'Die alte Weise— | Was weckt sie mich?'*

desolate and empty is the sea: *Tristan and Isolde* III. i: *'Öd und leer das Meer.'*

'Longing! . . . not to die!': *Tristan and Isolde* III. i: *'Sehnen! Sehnen! | Im Sterben mich zu sehnen, | vor Sehnsucht nicht zu sterben!'*

Kurwenal: character in *Tristan and Isolde*; see above, note to p. 113.

'jubilation in itself': in German: *'Jubel an sich'.* Allusion to Kant's notion of the thing in itself (*Ding an sich*).

sympathetic suffering: in German: *Mitleiden.*

original suffering: in German: *Urleiden.*

115 *pre-established harmony*: key concept in the philosophy of Leibniz, according to which God has created all substances in such a way that if each independently follows the law of its own inner development, it will find itself in harmony with all the others. See his *New System of the Nature and Communication of Substances, as well as of the Union existing between the Soul and the Body* (1695).

118 *individuatio*: Latin: individuation. See above, note to p. 21.

In the heaving swell . . . the highest joy: from Wagner's *Tristan and Isolde* III. iii (Isolde's *Liebestod*): *'In des Wonnemeeres | wogendem Schwall, | in der Duft-Wellen | tönendem Schall, | in des Weltathems | wehendem All- | ertrinken—versinken— | unbewusst—höchste Lust!'*

119 *Aristotle's catharsis*: see above, note to p. 71.

'Without . . . such a work?': quotation from a letter from Goethe to Schiller, 9 December 1797.

120 *interpretation of Shakespeare in the manner of Gervinus*: see above, note to p. 113.

quid pro quo: Latin: substitute.

121 *moral education . . . in Schiller's time*: allusion to Schiller's essay *The*

Stage Considered as a Moral Institution (Die Schaubühne als moralische Anstalt betrachtet) (1802).

121 *Schopenhauer's parable of the porcupines*: allusion to Schopenhauer, *Parerga and Paralipomena*, II.31, 396. Schopenhauer's porcupines try to huddle together for warmth but are repelled by each other's quills until they find a optimal distance for congregating together.

Lohengrin: opera by Richard Wagner, first performed in 1850.

123 *civilized France*: see above, note to p. 107.

German Reformation: religious movement begun by Martin Luther (1483–1546), which initially sought to reform the Catholic church threatened by secularization and political crises but then developed into the separate religion of Protestantism. The Reformation began in 1517 with the publication of Luther's Wittenberg Theses and led in 1530 to the religious and political division of the German Empire between Protestant Reformers and traditional Catholics. In 1555 the Emperor allowed local princes freedom of choice between the religions.

chorale of Luther's: originally the unaccompanied song of the Catholic liturgy, the chorale was adapted by Luther into the Protestant hymn, sung either by a single voice or by a choir, which became a central feature of the act of worship. Nietzsche regarded Luther's development of the chorale as a revival of indigenous folk traditions and as the beginning of the musical history which would produce Bach, the first major German composer.

124 *sub specie aeterni*: Latin: from the point of view of the eternal.

de-secularized: in German: *entweltlicht*.

secularization: in German: *Verweltlichung*.

125 *Graeculus*: see above, note to p. 63.

Orientally muffled superstition: allusion to the various Eastern cults and religions which flowed into Greece following the expansionist campaigns of Alexander the Great (356–323 BC) and which eventually led to the almost complete erosion of the indigenous religions.

sub specie saeculi: Latin: from the point of view of the age.

everything Romanic: everything French. see above, note to p. 107.

the recent war: the Franco–Prussian war of 1870–1. See above, note to p. 3.

126 *leader*: Nietzsche is implying that Richard Wagner should fulfil this role, although in the light of twentieth-century German history the passage has a more sinister resonance.

128 *musical dissonance*: for Nietzsche, dissonance gives a pleasurable Dionysian insight into the underlying pain and suffering of existence.

129 *highest joy*: in German: *höchste Lust*. Allusion to Wagner's *Tristan and Isolde*, see above, note to p. 118.

Heraclitus the Obscure: allusion to Heraclitus' Fragment 52.

130 *dragons . . . Wotan's spear*: allusions to the German cycle of *Nibelungen* myths, the basis of Wagner's *Ring* tetralogy. In the third opera of the cycle, *Siegfried* (completed 1871, performed 1876), the eponymous hero slays the dragon Fafner (II. ii) and the dwarf Mime (II. iii) in order to win the treasure of the Nibelungen, and breaks Wotan's spear (III. ii) in order to conquer Brünnhilde (III. iii).

dissonance in human form: to a certain extent, Nietzsche here rejoins and radicalizes the Romantic view of human existence as *Zerissenheit* or divided consciousness. The Dionysian state is one of dissonance which is overlaid and concealed by the harmony of the Apollonian.

131 *the god of Delos*: Apollo; the Aegean island of Delos was according to myth the birthplace of Apollo.

INDEX

The Oxford World's Classics Website

www.worldsclassics.co.uk

- Information about new titles
- Explore the full range of Oxford World's Classics
- Links to other literary sites and the main OUP webpage
- Imaginative competitions, with bookish prizes
- Peruse *Compass*, the Oxford World's Classics magazine
- Articles by editors
- Extracts from Introductions
- A forum for discussion and feedback on the series
- Special information for teachers and lecturers

www.worldsclassics.co.uk

American Literature

British and Irish Literature

Children's Literature

Classics and Ancient Literature

Colonial Literature

Eastern Literature

European Literature

History

Medieval Literature

Oxford English Drama

Poetry

Philosophy

Politics

Religion

The Oxford Shakespeare

A complete list of Oxford Paperbacks, including Oxford World's Classics, OPUS, Past Masters, Oxford Authors, Oxford Shakespeare, Oxford Drama, and Oxford Paperback Reference, is available in the UK from the Academic Division Publicity Department, Oxford University Press, Great Clarendon Street, Oxford OX2 6DP.

In the USA, complete lists are available from the Paperbacks Marketing Manager, Oxford University Press, 198 Madison Avenue, New York, NY 10016.

Oxford Paperbacks are available from all good bookshops. In case of difficulty, customers in the UK can order direct from Oxford University Press Bookshop, Freepost, 116 High Street, Oxford OX1 4BR, enclosing full payment. Please add 10 per cent of published price for postage and packing.